JEWISH MA
IN THEIR

MW01089091

Jewish Major Leaguers in Their Own Words

Oral Histories of 23 Players

Peter Ephross

with Martin Abramowitz

McFarland & Company, Inc., Publishers

Jefferson, North Carolina, and London

All photographs are from the George Brace Collection unless otherwise noted.

LIBRARY OF CONGRESS CATALOGUING-IN-PUBLICATION DATA

Ephross, Peter.
   Jewish major leaguers in their own words : oral histories of
23 players / Peter Ephross with Martin Abramowitz.
      p.   cm.
   Includes index.

   ISBN 978-0-7864-6507-1
   softcover : acid free paper ∞

   1. Jewish baseball players— United States— Biography.
   2. Jewish baseball players— United States— History.
   3. Baseball — United States— History.   I. Abramowitz, Martin.
   II. Title.
   GV865.A1E57 2012
   796.3570922 — dc23   2012002290
   [B]

BRITISH LIBRARY CATALOGUING DATA ARE AVAILABLE

Front cover: Cleveland Indians' Al Rosen, 1954 (National
Baseball Hall of Fame Library, Cooperstown, New York).

Manufactured in the United States of America

McFarland & Company, Inc., Publishers
   Box 611, Jefferson, North Carolina 28640
      www.mcfarlandpub.com

To four generations of baseball fans:
my Grandpa Al; my parents, Paul and Joan;
my siblings, Sara and David; my wife, Bonnie;
and my two sons, Jacob and Samuel. — P.E.

Table of Contents

Acknowledgments

All books have many parents, and this is especially true of an edited collection like this one. First and foremost, thanks to the players themselves, who shared their life stories and gave permission for these stories to be published. Thanks also go to the many individuals who conducted interviews for the collection, most notably Elli Wohlgelernter, who did several of them.

I also owe immense gratitude to Jewish Major Leaguers, the nonprofit organization that has sparked awareness in Jewish baseball players during the past decade, and the American Jewish Committee, which in the late 1970s and early 1980s sponsored many of the interviews that form the bases for the oral histories in this book. The New York Public Library, where those interviews are stored, helped me to obtain them. Mary Brace provided almost all of the photos in the book from an archive created by her father, George, during his decades as a baseball photographer in Chicago. Without the help of the Brace family, this book would not be as rich.

My wife, Bonnie Kerker, provided valuable comments on the introduction and loved and supported me in innumerable ways while I worked on the book. Yigal Schleifer and Rhoda Schlamm also provided comments that improved the introduction. Jeff Yas and my brother, David, helped with photo scanning. I thank them all. — P.E.

Preface

My connection to this project started in the summer of 2004. Then an editor at JTA, a Jewish news service, I jumped at the opportunity to cover a weekend honoring Jewish Major Leaguers at the National Baseball Hall of Fame in Cooperstown, New York. As a lifetime fan, it was a dream come true, especially since I had never been to Cooperstown. Plus, I was thrilled to turn a lifelong hobby of following Jewish sports into one of my journalistic beats. During the weekend, I met Martin Abramowitz, the founder and president of Jewish Major Leaguers, a nonprofit organization devoted to chronicling the ties between American Jews and baseball. Martin and Jewish Major Leaguers not only organized the event, but JML was in the midst of producing what turned out to be several baseball card sets honoring the Jewish connection to the game.

Martin soon asked me to conduct an interview with Mickey Rutner, who in 1947 played 12 games for the Philadelphia Athletics, for a proposed book of oral histories of Jewish baseball players. In January 2005, I traveled to Texas to interview Rutner. I thoroughly enjoyed my few days hearing his baseball stories, which were the loose basis for a novel, *Man on Spikes*, written by Rutner's good friend Eliot Asinof. A few years later, Martin asked me to take over the editorial reins of the book. Not knowing how much work lay ahead, I said yes—and in the summer of 2008, at a Hall of Fame event honoring the seventy-fifth anniversary of Hank Greenberg's rookie year, Martin gave me a large box containing about twenty-five interviews.

About half of the interviews were commissioned by Jewish Major Leaguers and conducted by journalists, scholars, and other interested parties, mostly between 2005 and 2007. Several of the other interviews were conducted in the late 1970s and early 1980s as part of a larger American Jewish Committee project interviewing well-known American Jews. These interviews, ably conducted by Elli Wohlgelernter, a journalist now living in Israel, give us fascinating recollections from Al Schacht, Andy Cohen,

Hank Greenberg, Goody Rosen, Cal Abrams, and Saul Rogovin, all now deceased. The interview of Al Rosen, the oldest living Jewish Major Leaguer as of the winter of 2012, was conducted by Cliff Chanin, also part of the American Jewish Committee project. All of the American Jewish Committee–commissioned interviews are published courtesy of the American Jewish Committee William E. Wiener Oral History Library and are housed at the New York Public Library. Journalistic prodigy Louis Jacobson conducted the Bob Berman and Cy Block interviews in the late 1980s. Then a teenager and now a political journalist, Jacobson did his work as part of a Confirmation project. Rich Topp interviewed Marv Rotblatt (with questions supplied by Jacobson). The Ron Blomberg chapter is excerpted with permission from his autobiography, *Designated Hebrew: The Ron Blomberg Story*, as told to Dan Schlossberg.

The other interviews were conducted by John Woestendiek (Harry Danning chapter), Joe Eskenazi (Sam Nahem, Ed Mayer), Marc Katz (Lou Limmer, Jose Bautista), Bob Ruxin (Larry and Norm Sherry), Susan E. Cayleff (Mike Epstein), Rebecca Alpert (Elliott Maddox), Howard Goldstein (Jesse Levis) and myself (Adam Greenberg).

As I leafed through the interviews, it became apparent that editing them down would be my largest challenge: Some of them run more than two hundred pages. Balancing the number of baseball tales with the amount of Jewish content was also difficult: Was it more important to showcase a detail about a player's minor league days, his jobs after his playing days were over, or his thoughts, as a Jew, about the state of Israel? I based each of my judgment calls on which experience shed more light on the player's life, as well as on the length of the interview. Most of the interviews came to me in question-and-answer format, which I converted into first-person narratives. I edited the interviews to make them compelling reads, which included reordering some sections to improve narrative flow. At all times, however, I strove to keep the voices of the players intact. I hope that I succeeded in doing so. — P.E.

Introduction

Nearly all fans of baseball history have heard of Hank Greenberg. Most have heard of Al Rosen. But fewer have heard of Cal Abrams, and hardly any, it's safe to say, have heard of Lou Limmer. All four are part of a compelling team — the 165 American Jews who have played Major League Baseball between the 1870s and the end of the 2010 season. They are also among the twenty-three players, from Bob Berman, who played in 1918, to Adam Greenberg, who played in 2005, interviewed in these oral histories of Jewish Major Leaguers.

Why should we care about Jews who played in the Major Leagues? As the interviews in this book demonstrate, baseball helped American Jews feel at home and helped non–Jewish Americans feel comfortable around them. There's the famous Hank Greenberg story, recounted by Greenberg himself in the book, of sitting out a game on Yom Kippur in 1934. As he modestly describes it in the interview:

> Well, to me it was a question of two things. One was Yom Kippur is, you know, the Day of Atonement, and you're supposed to put everything aside and just pray for the sins, atone for the sins of the year, that was one, and the other was respect for my parents. This is what they believed in, so naturally I would, out of respect for them, go along with not playing on Yom Kippur.

As filmmaker Aviva Kempner has shown in her documentary on baseball's first Jewish superstar, *The Life and Times of Hank Greenberg*, Greenberg's actions and his home runs made him a hero to Jews and non–Jews alike.

The decision of whether to play on Yom Kippur, the holiest day on the Jewish calendar, is one that has resurfaced for many players, from Sandy Koufax and his decision not to pitch in the first game of the 1965 World Series to, more recently, outfielder Shawn Green and his seemingly annual conundrum. Every time a star player rests on the High Holidays, it generates national headlines and fosters Jewish pride. Of course, non-stars have to make the same call, and several of the players in the book recount their own decisions of whether or not to play.

But these oral histories go beyond the well-trod turf of the "High Holidays dilemma." Several players recount their stories of rebutting anti–Semitism by fighting hecklers, sometimes on the opposing bench. Al Rosen, who was an amateur boxer before turning professional baseball player, wasn't shy about using his fists if necessary. Saul Rogovin, a more mild-mannered Jewish player, was once on the opposing team when Rosen stood up to some anti–Semitic slurs from one of Rogovin's teammates:

> So Rosen grounded out one night and as he trotted back in front of our dugout somebody yelled, "Well, we got you that time, you 'Jew bastard,'" or something like that, and Al ... Al was a tough guy, you know, Al was a fighter at one time, he was a club fighter, and Al stopped, you know, he stopped in his tracks, he didn't know who it was, and I looked myself because I didn't like it. It embarrassed me. I don't know who it was till this day and I didn't ask, I didn't want... It was so unpleasant I didn't want to bother to ask, you know, I just kept quiet. And Al walked over to our dugout and he said, "That son of a bitch that called me a 'Jew bastard,' would he care to say that again?" you know, and everybody was just sitting there, you know. And I had mixed feelings. I felt very funny because here I am, I'm an opposing player and also I'm a Jew, you know. [laughs] I had mixed feelings over that. I felt good for Al, you know, I really ... oh, thatta boy, Al, give it to them, you know, and I also felt sort of disloyal, feeling for an opposing player, you know, funny feeling.

By the 1990s, anti–Semitism had taken on a different, more introspective meaning for Adam Greenberg, whose unfortunate claim to fame is being hit in the head in his only (as of the end of the 2011 season) at-bat in the Major Leagues. There weren't "so many misconceptions; it was just more questions, curiosity," among some of his college teammates at North Carolina, Greenberg says. "And I certainly enjoy that because it challenges me to, if I don't know, I better start knowing."

Anti-Semitism is just one of the themes that resonate throughout this collection: Racial awareness is another. Most Jewish players understood some the prejudices that black players faced — and some, like Cal Abrams, felt a special bond with their black teammates: "I associated with them because we had a rapport about being with each other," Abrams says of his black teammates on the Brooklyn Dodgers, including Jackie Robinson. "We kibitzed around with each other, but I didn't go out with them. I mean, I wouldn't go into the end of town to go dancing with the black people, but whenever we could we were together, clowning around and kidding around."

Some Jewish players stood up for their black teammates. Ed Mayer, who pitched for the Chicago Cubs in 1957 and 1958, remembers one of these times when he was in the minor leagues:

> We were traveling from Montgomery through Georgia. And we stopped, and everyone wanted to buy a Coke. The machine was outside of a gas station, and there was a guy on my team from San Diego, a black guy who later became a famous pitcher, Earl Wilson. So, we all get off the bus to buy a Coke and Earl goes to put his nickel in the machine — a nickel, ha! — and the cracker attendant comes out and points a gun at him and says, "No N — is going to buy a Coke out of my machine." I jumped in front of him and pushed him back on the bus and bought him his Coke.

Often, however, players felt powerless to change status quo, as Al Rosen explains:

> The black players on the team were treated shabbily. Particularly at spring training time when we traveled through the South on trains, and we played in some of these southern towns and sometimes we spent the night and they weren't allowed to stay in the hotels, they weren't allowed to ride in the taxi cabs — and it was a horrendous experience for them. And I always felt very badly about it and you might say, "Well, what did you do about it?" Well, there's very little that can be done in a situation like that. Sociological changes hadn't taken place in the South as yet, and therefore they were treated differently. They were revered on the ballfield for their exploits by the whites. But they were not treated as equals any other place.

Jewish pride is another recurrent trope. As Ron Blomberg makes clear, he made many New York Yankees ushers happy when he debuted for the team in 1967.

> Most of them were Jewish, with names like Hymowitz or Lichstein, and three or four of them told me they never thought they would ever see a Jew play baseball in Yankee Stadium. They had tears in the eyes and said to me, "You little Yid, you're someone I can look up to now."

Like Blomberg, most Jewish Major Leaguers were aware that they embodied Jewish pride. Several of them discuss connections they made with Jewish communities in places they played, particularly in the smaller Southern cities that housed minor league teams.

Pride in being Jewish is one thing, but being actively Jewish is another — and most players in the collection, like most American Jews, weren't observant. Many were raised Orthodox — Al Schacht says his mother wanted him to be a cantor — but none seemed to have maintained this level of observance as adults. It makes sense: Eating kosher food and maintaining any sense of Shabbat, which restricts behaviors from sundown Friday through sundown Saturday, would be impossible to do while pursuing a professional baseball career.

Another theme that resonates throughout the collection is personal pride: Understandably, these athletes were simply thrilled at making it to the Major Leagues, even if only for a short while. Mickey Rutner, who hit .250 in twelve games in 1947 for the Philadelphia Athletics, was a New York City native. Almost sixty years after the fact, Rutner remembered his finest Major League moment, a game-winning hit at Yankee Stadium:

> It was in the late innings. We had a man on first and second, and I hit a ball past third base. And [Phil] Rizzuto made a helluva play and he threw to second, but Pete Suder was on first, and he hustled and slid into second and beat the throw. Rizzuto couldn't throw me out and it was a base hit, and the run scored from second. That was the biggest thrill of my life.

The collective accomplishments of Jewish Major Leaguers will surprise most people. Jews, who made up about 3 percent of the U.S. population during the twentieth century, made up just 0.8 percent of baseball players from 1871 to 2002, the latest year for which complete figures are available. But Jewish players, on the whole, have fared better than average. They had hit 2,032 homers — 0.9 percent of the Major League total, and a bit higher than would be expected by their percentage of all players. Their .265 batting average is 3 percentage points higher than the overall average. Jewish pitchers are twenty games over .500, with six of baseball's first 230 no-hitters (four by Sandy Koufax, including a perfect game, and two by Ken Holtzman). The group ERA is 3.66, a bit lower than the 3.77 racked up by all Major Leaguer hurlers. With the recent influx of top-flight Jewish Major Leaguers — Kevin Youkilis, Ryan Braun, Ian Kinsler come to mind — these statistics might even have improved since 2002.

The one stat in which Jews have fallen short is stolen bases, with a total of 995 through 2002 — many fewer than Rickey Henderson stole all by himself. Apparently, Jewish players have observed the Eighth Commandment: "Thou shalt not steal." (The credit for most of these statistics goes to researcher Sean Forman.)

Of the 141 Jewish Major Leaguers as of 2002, 122 were born into families in which both parents were Jewish and thirteen had one Jewish parent (seven with a Jewish father and six with a Jewish mother). Six players — including one featured in this book, African-American Elliott Maddox — converted to Judaism. Sixty-eight players hailed from New York or California, and the rest were born in twenty-one other states, as well as

Russia, France, Canada, and the Dominican Republic. Ten players changed their last names, all but one of them before Hank Greenberg played.

The collection offers many countless little-known stories that paint a vivid picture of what it was like to be a Jewish Major Leaguer. It cannot feature all Jewish players who made the Major Leagues, with the famously reclusive Sandy Koufax being the most noteworthy example. This omission does not diminish the book's value and uniqueness. In only a few books—most notably, Lawrence Ritter's pathbreaking *The Glory of Their Times: The Story of Baseball Told by the Men Who Played It*—have Major Leaguers, Jewish or not, told their stories in their own words.

In editing these oral histories, I found the stories to be both entertaining and moving: Andy Cohen admits to being something of a ladies' man, Saul Rogovin discusses how his undiagnosed narcolepsy affected his career, and Goody Rosen describes his wintertime trip to spring training in an open-air car. I hope you will be entertained and touched by the players' own words as well. Lou Limmer, by the way, was a slugger who played for the Philadelphia Athletics in 1951 and 1954.—P.E.

BOB BERMAN
Washington Senators, 1918
(1899–1988)

I wanted to become a boxer and I wanted to become a ballplayer.
It came in handy, let me tell you. And nobody would call me—
it was a very famous expression— a "Jew this" or a "Jew
that."— Bob Berman, interviewed in June 1987

I used to go to synagogue regularly. I was an honest-to-goodness Jewish youngster growing up in the Lower East Side. Then we moved to the Bronx. We had our tough times. There were three of us: myself and two sisters. We were the children. And I grew up among a lot of youngsters who liked to play ball. And believe it or not, we lived on Fulton Avenue and right across the street there was Crotona Park. So that meant there were no houses there at all. All clear. Lovely! And we're in a series of apartment houses owned by a Jewish man by the name of Greenberg. There were Irish, there were Jews, every race you could think of were living in those five apartment houses. Now I'll say this: I was a tough kid, and no question about it. Nobody was ever going to call me "Jew-this" or "Jew-that" and get away with it. He had to put up his hands.

I grew up there, and all we could do was play ball. And we managed. And being an aggressive youngster, I made progress. I played wherever I could play. The high school team was called Townsend-Harris Hall. It's a three-year school for City College of New York. On the same street as City College. And you had to be a good student to get in. This is Manhattan; I'm living in the Bronx. Now this is the school that I was supposed to go to, because my cousin went there and graduated. It was one of those real high-class schools. Well, I wasn't a very, very fine student; I was a good student. If I liked the subject, I studied for it, and so on. I went there; naturally, I played baseball. I did all right there for a while. And then I decided, "Gee, I'm not getting anywhere." I wanted to be on the teams, and so on. I wanted to get into [baseball], and here I was getting torn apart by too much studying. You had to make a certain average, and you had to work hard. And I couldn't see myself doing that.

So I spent a couple of years at the school — I was about to graduate. I got into a jam with one of the teachers there. I left there. I only had another year to go. I left there before, I think, the third year was up to go to Evander Childs. I went there — I think they needed a catcher. That's what started it all. And I was becoming a fair catcher: aggressive, and I loved the game. So I went there, and did all right. Well, now the question comes up, "What am I going to do? Am I going to continue to play ball, and so on?" Here I am, a kid, about fifteen years of age. I'm a senior in high school. Nobody to guide me. Pop? You can forget about him. Mother and I were really the only two who had a good relationship. Well, I still wanted to play ball — I had the determination to do it. And eventually it worked out.

My mother died at a young age. I had a lovely, lovely mother. I lived with my father. I had two sisters younger than me. My dad was a tough guy. Let's put it that way. He drank too much. He smoked too much. He was a marble polisher. He was a tough man.

I never drank in my life — never drank liquor. Never touched liquor in my life. My mother, when I was getting out of public school, she said, "Bobby, do me a favor." I had a father, may the good Lord rest his soul, he was a tough guy. Five-feet-eleven, weighed about 180, 190 pounds. With a temper that went with it. And he drank all the time. So she said to me, "I want you to promise me one thing. Don't *ever* take a drink." I said, "Mother, I understand. I shall never drink in my life." And you want to know something? I never have.

I got down to Washington Senators spring training. Here I am, the only Jewish kid in the crowd. And I made up my mind I'm not taking any malarkey from anybody. I'm ready to grapple with them. This one fellow, I forget his name now, he was a pitcher. A farm boy, about 6-foot-2 or -3. Something like that. Probably about 190 pounds. Big kid. And this is his first season with the ballclub, too. He's trying to make the ballclub, just like I'm trying to make it. And we're in an intrasquad game. And he got pummeled one inning. And he's coming back to the bench.

The guys started to kid him, which is normal. He turns around and he says, "What do you expect when you have this Jew," with an epithet attached to it, "behind the plate. This catcher, he doesn't know how to call 'em [pitches] or anything like that." I didn't say anything. I put my glove down, took my mask off, my chest protector off, took my shin guards off and I said, "Pardon me? What did you say? I didn't hear you." And he repeated it again. And "Bing!" I hit him. Down he goes. Can't get up. The fellows are getting all excited. He says, "I didn't mean it." I said, "No, he's gonna apologize. Otherwise, I'm going to beat the living life outta him. Nobody can do what he did to me. I don't care who he is." And he was made to apologize. And Walter Johnson was the one who interfered, nicely. He said, "Thatattaboy." And from then on, the word went out, "Leave that kid alone. He's got the guts to fight, and he'll fight." And I made the ballclub. But it was tough going. Let me tell you.

It was tough all the time. There were very few Jewish kids in baseball at the time. I think I was numbered as the first kid with the Senators, and that was really something. And to make matters more interesting, naturally you're always bound to get a hold of some jerk who wants to show you up or something, So you had to show him you could also fight. And between the — I was a pretty fair boxer — I had two choices. I could call it. I wanted to become a boxer, and I wanted to become a ballplayer. It came I handy, let me tell you something. And nobody would call me — it was a very famous expression — a "Jew-this" or a "Jew-that" and so on. But that's the way they carry on.

The thing is with me — it got around very quickly: "don't fool around with Berman." He's a fine kid, leave him alone. That's all. They saw that I'm ready to scrap, and I could handle myself. That helped a lot.

One year in the American League, with Washington. Practically one year. I was in the Major Leagues and *nobody* can take that away from me. And the fact that I made it, I was walking on the clouds. I was getting $150 a month. And — listen to this — I would have played for *nothing*. Just to be playing ball there. Here I am, a young Jewish kid from the Lower East Side, and suddenly I'm thrust into baseball — Walter Johnson, Nick Altrock, that bunch. I was in seventh heaven.

They sent me to Jersey City. I was in the International League for a couple of seasons. I was with the Philadelphia Hebrews. I was a star then, in those days. The South Philadelphia Hebrews — we were, next to pro, the finest semipro you could find anywhere. We traveled, barnstorming. I don't know how the hell we went, but we traveled. Listen, we're talking about 1918, 1919, things were pretty tough. Money was scarce, and here you are, a Jewish ball team, strictly Jewish. Mama mia! I played for House

"It was tough all the time," Bob Berman recalled of his time with the Washington Senators in 1918 (T. Scott Brandon Collection).

of David [another semipro team that, despite its name, wasn't Jewish], too. I joined these clubs as a catcher.

I became a Health Ed. teacher. That was my regular work, then, after I was through with professional ball. I saw that I couldn't stay up there and play it. I wanted to do something with my love for playing ball, and I decided to become a baseball coach. So I went back, I finished my schooling, became a coach, and in 1925 I took my exams and became a coach in New York City. I was a coach from 1925 to 1968. It was a long time.

I exercise every day, despite my condition. I used to teach ballroom dancing. I developed a bad case of osteoarthritis in my left hip — two hip replacements. It's tough, but it's up to the individual, that's all. And the good thing that helped me was that I loved to dance. I was teaching at Franklin K. Lane High School. One day a week, I used to teach them dancing. And then the thought came to me, "Why can't I have the girls dance too?" So I became interested in it. And then I'd have the girls and the boys come in on Friday, and have, say class, at seven o'clock or eight o'clock. That's the first time that ever happened in the school system. I enjoyed it. I loved it. I knew how important it was, especially as you grew up a little bit. I was pretty good at it. I taught it at Arthur Murray's. And to me, ballroom dancing is a must among kids.

AL SCHACHT

Washington Senators, 1919–1921

(1892–1984)

Al Schacht played parts of three seasons in the Major Leagues and coached for 13 more. He was at the 1932 World Series and says he saw Babe Ruth call his famous home run in Game 3, even though many believe that call didn't happen. But Schacht, interviewed in June 1980, is more famous for what he did after his formal baseball career was over. He made his name as the "Clown Prince of Baseball," entertaining millions of people, including U.S. servicemen during World War II, with his baseball pantomimes. After the war ended, Schacht became a successful restaurant owner: the menus at the Manhattan eatery bearing his name looked like oversized baseballs and featured dishes named after old-time players.

My parents were both born in Russia. I had five siblings, four boys and a girl. I'm the second oldest. My father was in structural ironworks. He did some work for Teddy Roosevelt in the White House. I played baseball at the High School of Commerce in New York City. My brother Larry later played on a team there with Lou Gehrig. I quit school after that and I started playing semipro baseball. I joined the Cincinnati club. Clark Griffith then was the manager of Cincinnati, and I was too young. I only weighed a hundred and thirty-seven pounds when I was pitching, so I was too.... Anyway, so I quit high school to play semi-pro ball and I played this little town, Walton, New York. I got $4 a week and board. I could have made more money catching runaway horses on Park Avenue. That's a gag I used to use, just a gag.

We lived in New York City, up in the Bronx, right opposite a park, and there used to be a lot of kids from downtown go up and play amateur baseball and they'd always wind up in fights. My mother'd look out the window, "That's what you'll be, one of those bums," see. My mother was very much against it. My mother had a wonderful sense of humor. Well, I sang in a Jewish choir three different seasons when I was a kid, see. She wanted me to be a cantor.

I had a pretty good voice as a kid. I used to go to synagogue, of course, Yom Kippur and Rosh Hashanah, those holidays, and my mother always bringing a rabbi in the house to go over the history and the ... you know, teach me, Jewish history, see. I wanted to play ball. I still go to, say, different holidays I always attend. Comes the holidays, I went, no matter what city I was in, I'd go. If I was out of town, I'd just go. I didn't appear in the World Series on the holidays, on Yom Kippur. Rosh Hashanah I did, but not Yom Kippur. That must have been in Boston. 1935.

I went with Joe Cronin when he was manager of the Washington club and he was traded to Boston. He wanted me to come as his assistant, as I was in Washington. So in Boston during the holiday, I went to the synagogue, which was on Yom Kippur. I did appear one year on Rosh Hashanah; I think that was in 1927, '26 or '27. The first World Series I worked in was in 1920, that's the Yankees and the Giants, and then my last one was in 1946 in Boston.

I appeared in twenty-five different World Series and fifteen All-Star Games, and old-timers' games, different ballparks, 50, 60,000 people, and every day in the American League averaging about 30,000 people, over 160 ballgames. You add that up and it's millions and millions over any other entertainer who appeared in person. I'm not talking about television. I'm not talking about radio. Talking about in person. I made many appearances as an entertainer when I quit the American League in 1937 and that's when I went out and appeared in a hundred and ... I averaged 128 towns in 130 days. I made it in an automobile. I would average about 240 miles a day.

It's hard to explain the acts. What I would do, I impersonated different events that happened, like the swell-headed pitcher, but everything was pantomime. Nobody taught me anything, I never rehearsed anything. Never! Cause the kind of work I did, there's no rehearsal. When I came to a ballpark, going to do a show, I can't have a rehearsal with any ballplayer. Once in a while, they'd help me, for a minute do something, I'd ask them, see. But I'd say most of the gags I did were things that happened. Like the Dempsey-Tunney long count, I did a burlesque on that, and I did a swell-headed pitcher, imaginary outfield and infield. I worked alone. I'm the only one that that ever walked out on a ballpark alone and did a show without anybody helping me.

15

As an example, at the All-Star Game at the Polo Grounds it rained and they had to stop the game. I wouldn't remember what date it was. Anyhow, here comes a terrific shower, see, and the game is stopped, and that was at the Polo Grounds, that's years ago. And so I had an idea how to kill time: I'd entertain the fans. So I went out with two bats, they were my oars. I did a gag and I had a mouthful of water and I'm swimming the Channel, the English Channel, and I'm doing this and I'm throwing the water out of my mouth and I keep swimming and I took up about ... oh, about seven minutes, see, while the people were waiting for the rain to stop. I was out behind second base doing this show, see. But I never rehearsed it; I never rehearsed a thing I did. You can't rehearse it.

I had a partner once, Nick Altrock, and toward the end of our being together, I didn't speak to him, see, we.... Anyhow, we did burlesque, we went in vaudeville, we headlined in vaudeville. We played a Chicago theater, the State Lake theater in Chicago, we were headliners, during 1927 this was. This was the burlesque on the Dempsey-Tunney long count. And you know who was on the bill and was getting $300 for the act? There were three of us. The Rhythm Boys. Bing Crosby. We were getting $12.50 and he was getting $300. This is 1927. I got to know Bing very well later. Later years I says, "You got much more money than I have now. Boy, there was a time when I had much more money than you did." [laughs]

I never told the story of why Nick Altrock [another former Major Leaguer and Schacht's entertainment partner for several years] and I broke up. I never will tell the story. I'll tell you one thing. It isn't what I did. It's what he did. That's as far as I'll go on why we split. I can't say it because if I can't say anything good about a person, I don't want to say anything, see. That's it. The last two years we worked together I never spoke to him.

I was going to show you something that's the biggest thrill I ever had in baseball as a player, coach or entertainer. On July 4, 1920, I was a pitcher on the Washington ballclub, and the greatest pitcher that ever lived was my roommate for a while, Walter Johnson, that was the greatest that ever lived and he come within pitching ... within one hit of a no-hitter. So in Boston he pitched his first no-hit game, that was in 1920 against the Red Sox. At that time, the only time Washington would ever have a good crowd was when they announced Walter Johnson's going to pitch. He was the drawing card.

So Clark Griffith, a wonderful man, he was the owner of the club and the manager of the club. We were to appear on the following Sunday, four days later in Washington, so Clark Griffith took advantage of those days

Al Schacht, who played for the Washington Senators from 1919 to 1921, later became famous as the Clown Prince of Baseball, entertaining millions of fans with his on-field antics.

and advertised that Johnson, the big hero, pitched a no-hit game, is going to pitch against the Yankees. So the day of the game they had the biggest crowd that ever saw a ballgame in Washington. Even on the ballfield on the sidelines, there were people sitting there, see, so they all came out to see Johnson.

During batting practice I was in the outfield shagging fly balls, and we're called into the clubhouse, the whole team, and Clark Griffith had a meeting, he says, "Fellows, I've been in baseball many years and I've had tough times and sometimes good times. Today I'm in a terrible spot because years ago when I first started managing the Washington Senators, we advertised Johnson to pitch and he hurt his knee and he couldn't pitch and the people want their money back. They crowded the gates and they want their money back, and the same thing is happening today," see. "Now whoever pitches against this ballclub today, whoever I chose for you, whoever comes through, I want them to know that if they win this ballgame for me, as long as I got anything of this ballclub, they got a job with me." He was then president and manager. "Well, he come in the clubhouse and we're in the clubhouse, he says, "Now, fellows," he says. "Erikson, Courtney, Shaw, or Schacht, who wants to pitch it?"

I said, "Grif, I'll pitch it," and only four days before I got beat 2–1 by the Red Sox. And he put his arm around me he says, "If you win this ballgame today — and by the way, you're not going to get a very good reception out there and neither am I — I don't care if we never win another game, you got a job on this club as long as I have anything to do with this ballclub." So I said, "All right, Grif." I went out there and I started warming up. Now, the crowd is overcrowded, as I mentioned, they're sitting along the side.

The ballpark would seat around 30,000 then. It's the old Griffith Stadium I'm talking about. You had to warm up in front of the grandstand in those days, the pitcher, see. Now they're way out, you can't even recognize them, but you had to be in, right there in front of them. So they thought I was clowning. I had a reputation of clowning then, so they start ... you know. But it got a little serious, now it's about 10 minutes before the game or so and I'm still warming up, and they start and you could hear a little boo, boo, boo, boo. Then they said, "We want Johnson! We want Johnson!" and in a few minutes it was all over, "We want Johnson!" Now Johnson was home in Maryland. He hurt his knee or something, I don't remember what it was, but he couldn't come to the ballpark. He called up and said he couldn't get out of bed. Well, in those days the announcer — they had a megaphone and they come out in the pitcher's box — announce the batteries. So he announced, "the batteries for today: For New York," and he mentioned the pitcher and catcher, and then he announces, "For Washington, Schacht," you know, "Schacht." He never got to the catcher. Out comes the bottles and the cushions all over the ballpark.

Well, they had to finally clear up the field and start the ballgame. In those days, they didn't play "The Star-Spangled Banner" in every ballgame like they do now, and they got to clear the field of the bottles and cushions, everything, you know. Billy Evans was the umpire, and out comes the cushions and bottles again. I finally had to go under the grandstand to warm up again. We waited about fifteen minutes and cleared the field. Well, finally we get the ballgame and I struck out Ruth with the bases loaded in the third or fourth ... third inning or so, and for the first time I heard. [claps] Must have been cousins of mine. [laughs] To make it short, I did win the ballgame and this is the box score of the game.

The great finale of the story is this: After I hurt my arm, I couldn't pitch anymore, and a few years after, when I pitched in the minor leagues and I couldn't even be a good pitcher in the minor leagues, Clark Griffith brought me back, made me the third-base coach for the Washington ballclub. That was the promise he made. That was Clark Griffith. I was there thirteen years.

I always say I'm Jewish, I know I'm Jewish, but I never let it ... it never kept me from doing what I wanted to do. I never felt that I was handicapped, I never thought that way. I was proud to be a Jew, I never denied it. In the business I was in, there were very few Jews and I never denied any part of it. I never was asked, I never remembered anybody asking me when I was a ballplayer.

My mother was very strict, very, very strict, very, and she always had her Jewish book on her, especially when she got very old. The last couple of years, three years of her life, she was blind. But she was a wonderful woman. I lost my dad in 1913, and I was getting $300 a month. No, $150 a month. They didn't pay much money in those days. And I'd spend 10 cents for lunch. I was pitching for Newark in the International League. That's the first year I was with Newark, 1913. In 1914, I pitched the first game against Ruth that he played in professional ball, 1914. He was then with the Baltimore club and he pitched and played the outfield.

There wasn't a lot of anti–Semitism in baseball. There was only one fellow who called me a "Sheeny." There weren't many Jews in baseball; there weren't many Italians in baseball. It was all mostly Southern boys and Irish boys. There were more South-and-North arguments, much more of them. Ty Cobb was a Southerner. A lot of the Southerners and Northerners never got along too well. I think I was very popular when I was in the International League and later in the Big Leagues. I never had any problems. You know something, maybe they hollered at me from the bench, I wouldn't hear them.

There's one guy who followed me years later. He did little dances and something. They call him Patkin, Max Patkin. He makes faces.... That's crap. That's nothing. Let's say there's nobody on the field and somebody says, "All right, Al, let's go. You're on." You walk out on that field and the first thing you do, they understand what the hell you're doing that leads up to the climax. 'Cause you go out there, you don't get no laugh for the first minute or two, you're having a hell of a time getting going, see. I've never been booed, I've never.... You know, when these owners hire you to walk in a ballpark, pay a thousand dollars to go in there and do your show, they've got to like it, too.

You know, in 1920 or '21, the first thing I did was a pantomime pitcher. I played a whole game by myself, see. See what I'd do, the swell-headed pitcher I called it. I called the imaginary catcher, do all the signs at him, and then I wind up and I throw the ball and I duck, ball goes in center field. Now I get the ball back. Then a bunt, do this, and I do different gags. I also did a near-sighted pitcher.

I was in a lot of places during the war. I was in North Africa, Sicily, New Guinea, Dutch East Indies, Philippines, Japan three times, Korea twice, Austria, France, Germany, Trieste, Iceland, Greenland, Alaska, entertaining troops. I only did one baseball game. That was in New Guinea, I did a baseball thing. That was an outfit.... I had my baseball outfit, a high hat, tuxedo coat, and I did a show for a lot of soldiers, see. But I never had.... I worked alone, see. You know, Bob Hope did a great job. You know, he had about 10 people with him. I worked alone everyplace. I used to do four shows a day. Not every place, but I done four when.... My first plane jump was North Africa and then I was in New Guinea. Forty-three I was in North Africa, '44 I was in New Guinea. I flew into the Philippines two days after the war was over, see the occupation troops were there in the Philippines. Then I went into Japan. I was in Japan three different times. When I went to Korea twice, '52 and '55, I also went into Japan. I did a ball game in Japan, I did a clowning act. Fifty-five thousand people, and the next day a guy is impersonating me in a high hat, tuxedo coat, a Japanese. I did a stage show because I didn't do ballgames there.

I went to Dachau after World War II and I was shown the gas chambers. Before that I knew all about Hitler. During the war, I didn't know it was bad as it was, as it turned out to be, but it was known ... the hanging tree we saw. I had the pictures. I don't know what happened to them. Showed the pictures of the hanging tree and the furniture and the caves of ... you know ... the graves, open graves, they were all thrown in, the bodies. Terrible sight, although they cleaned it up quite a bit.

I entertained the British Eighth Army in Catania, on Sept. 2, 1941.

No, '43. '43 or '44. Dates go by me, I've been so many places. I entertained the British Eighth Army and part of Patton's Seventh Army in Catania, Sicily, and that was on the second of September. The reason I remember this date is because it had something to do with what happened the next day, Sept. 3. And I go in this opera house, Catania opera house. At that time, they took an awful beating, you know, in Sicily, you know, before the boys came in. So Col. Smith, he's going to introduce me. He says, "Al, by the way, [British Army Gen. Bernard] Montgomery's up there in the balcony with his boys." So now I'm introduced, and there's Patton's gang, Seventh Army, not all, but part of it, they're down in the orchestra, and the British Eighth Army, they got their tanks outside, and I recognize Montgomery, he had a ... by his beret, see, and I said, "Fellows, we have a gentleman here, a great soldier, and I know you American boys would love to meet this great general. Gen. Montgomery, will you please take a bow," and we applaud. He took a bow and he sat down. "Just a minute, general, we didn't all see you. Take another bow, but don't get your bowels in an uproar." [laughs]

When we got through, see, after I got through working, see, I went up next day, Sept. 3, see, that night, Sept. 3, and I got up around Messina Straits just about, 18 miles after I left Catania, Sicily, these are the straits, and I hear a lot of rumbling, five o'clock in the morning, and that is Montgomery, the same gang that I was entertaining the day before, made an invasion of Italy, the boot of Italy. Sept. 3, 1934, I was there.

"Cannonball" Reading of the Lincoln Giants struck out twenty-four men and beat me 1–0. The game was played in Olympic Field on 137th Street. The famous Lincoln Giant baseball team. They were a great Negro team. Most of the Negro teams would be traveling all the time, play these smaller towns. That's when they didn't allow the Negro to go into big-time baseball, but they had some great ballplayers, great ones. I played against Josh Gibson as a gag, clowning, pitching, in Mexico where the famous Pittsburgh Giants, Negro team, played our white team, which was Jimmie Foxx, Simmons, left field. We had an All-Star team. Foxx broke up a fifteen-inning ballgame. I haven't seen the ball yet. He hit it so damned far. I mean it went out of sight. In Mexico City. That's when we had an All-Star American League team traveling through Mexico. This was 1937, '35. Went by train.

Babe Ruth was a nice guy. He was a little on the distant side. He'd rather be around women than men. He was a great guy, did a lot for the kids. He did an awful lot for kids because kids were crazy about him and he went out of his way. I tell a story about the Babe. I saw the Babe hit, I think, the longest ball ever was hit. We were fighting the Yankees for the pennant, 1924 — Washington club. Bucky Harris was the manager. They had in Washington the Polish legation, and the Polish ambassador was a great baseball fan, and Ruth, Ruth was a big man, see, and Joe Dugan, third baseman for the Yankees in those days, and Goslin on our club, Goose Goslin.

So Bucky Harris said, "Al, I want you to do me a favor. I want you and Goslin to go out there with the Babe and stay right with him, see that he gets plenty of drinks." I said, "Bucky, he don't need me to be cockeyed." He said, "Well, I want you to go out there anyhow." So Goose and I go out there and Joe Dugan, is with ... he's on the Yankee ball club, third baseman, and the Babe is there, and Waite Hoyt, who was a pitcher then for the Yankees. So the Babe is going like anything, he's really going to town. Now it gets about a quarter to twelve and Dugan says, "Jeez, I got to go back to the hotel."

They were staying at the same hotel I stayed in Washington, Logan Park Hotel. So Dugan leaves, Waite Hoyt leaves; they had to be in the hotel by twelve o'clock. So now the only ones left were Babe and I, and Babe is really going. Now it's 12:30; I got to pitch.... Those days I pitched batting practice, see. I was the coach of the club. I said, "Come on, Babe, you and I got an appointment in the Walter Reed Hospital in the morning. Let's go and get some sleep. We got to be there by ten o'clock." I says, "They're going to call for us at ten o'clock. Got to be ready for them." He says, "Go on down to the hotel, sissy." He's got a gal, see. When I left him, he was feeling pretty good. So the next day I get to the ballpark, I says to Bucky Harris, "Bucky," I says, "we got him." 'We got who?" I said, "The Babe. He was cockeyed last night." He says, "You got him?" I said, "Yeah," and I tell him what happened.

His first time up, Babe.... They have a fence that's about ... oh, about three stories high, way in deep centerfield. That way if anybody can hit a home run inside the park to this fence, they can make an inside-the-park home run. And above this high fence in centerfield was a tree overlooking the fence, see, and over the tree there was the American flag, a pole with the American flag. And the Babe hits one over the fence, over the tree and over the flagpole for, naturally, a home run. When he come in to home plate he said to the batboy — then there was a hunchback batboy, I forget his name — "Gee, I'd like to get ahold of that one," like it was just a pop fly to him, see. [laughs] So when the game was over — he beat us that game — Harris says to me, "Jesus, we got him, haven't we? We got him."

I was in Chicago; I worked in that Series in '32 when he [Babe Ruth] pointed that.... I saw it, he did that. He stepped out of the box. I used to do an impersonation of that on the ballfield. I did it for years and nobody questioned me because I was there. If they asked me, I was there. 1932 in Wrigley Field.... And the Babe came up. I don't know what was said from the bench, the Chicago bench, but after he had two strikes on him he suddenly stopped and he put his hand up. Then he walked back there and with his bat and he said something to them. I didn't hear what was said, of course, but I know he pointed. I saw him point toward the center-field bleachers. On the next pitched ball, he hit it right where he pointed. Fantastic. I saw it. He wasn't laughing until he reached third base. Then he laughed a little bit and looked at the bench, the Chicago bench.

The closest anybody came to Cobb — not as a hitter, I'm talking about all-around ballplayer, was Mays. That was the closest. That was the closest because Mays could steal bases, he could hit, he could run, he was a great fielder. He was a better fielder than Cobb, better fielder, but Cobb could do more things. But it's hard to describe Cobb, to appreciate when you talk about him because you'd have to see the guy to appreciate him, you know. They say, "So-and-so hit .340." So I come right back and I say, "Look, that guy hit .367. All these great hitters didn't even come close to him."

ANDY COHEN
New York Giants, 1926, 1928–1929
(1904–1988)

In the 1920s, Andy Cohen was the "Great Jewish Hope" for the New York Giants. Indeed, legendary Giants manager John McGraw called Cohen up to the Major Leagues in 1926 in part because McGraw thought having a Jewish player would boost his team's ticket sales. Cohen, interviewed in September 1981, didn't play poorly, but he only was with the Giants for a few years. After that, he enjoyed a lengthy minor league and coaching career. Cohen's brother Syd also played three years in the majors, with the Washington Senators in the mid–'30s.

The Jewish newspaper, the Forverts, is that still there? They started printing the baseball box scores on the front page when I broke in and then got off to such a great start, and so one day when we had an off-day and didn't play, they came out on the front page and said, "Well, no game today. Andy must be sick," see. That's a true story. And then fans would come to the ballpark and the ticket taker would say, "Now, where do you want to sit? Do you want a box seat behind third or first? "I want it behind second," see. They wanted to be near Andy Cohen, you see? [laughs]

McGraw made a big fuss about that [Cohen being a Jewish ballplayer], you know, to the delight of the Jewish fans there, you know. But don't forget that McGraw, he was interested in getting any kind of a good ballplayer, didn't care what he was, and the fact that I was a Jew made the icing even sweeter, you see. See, McGraw was always a bit of a showman, too, and he thought that was part of the game, to have a Jewish player out there, that he was the guy that brought him there, see, and while he wasn't the president or anything like that, he still had to say who to bring there. He was more or less the master there, you see.

I guess from the time I was seven or eight years old I used to throw a ball. My father was a man who would get out and play catch with me. He'd throw high flies to me and I'd get under, and he'd throw them damn near out of sight, where I managed to catch them. My brother and I both played when we were very young kids, and then I went on and played in grade school, at a local El Paso high school, then from there to the University of Alabama, where I played on the team.

I was born in Baltimore and we moved to Virginia for a few years, Norfolk, Virginia, then we came out here when I was about seven or eight years old, so I've lived here practically all my life. Many of the local people here think I was born here, and I let them keep thinking that. I don't bother to correct them because I don't mind having the reputation of being born in El Paso. I have a lot of friends here. This is my hometown.

My father in Baltimore was a cigarmaker. A lot of people don't know it, but he tried out with the Baltimore Orioles when he was a youngster, many years ago. When McGraw and Willie Keeler and Dan Brouthers, they were with the old Orioles, he tried out with them and he couldn't quite make it. He was just a little fellow. They said he was too small. Later he and my mother, after they got to Virginia, opened up a store, a grocery store, and then my mother's health was getting a little bad, so she moved out here [El Paso]. There was a separation there between father and mother. I guess I was about twelve or thirteen.

My father came over from Lithuania and my mother Russia, from Kiev. They observed the Jewish holidays, I guess. Rosh Hashanah and Yom Kippur, you know, if you can call that being religious. When I was a real small child, why, I used to go to what they call cheder, you know. In Virginia. Of course, I married a non-Jewish girl from Elmira, New York. At first, my mother took it pretty hard, you know, marrying out of the faith, but she became adjusted all right, especially after our kids started arriving.

It had never occurred to me to be anything else but a professional ballplayer. And when I was in high school here playing, a couple of people scouting for Texas League clubs came to see me and talk to me, and actually I signed a contract with Galveston of the Texas League while I was still in high school, so that when I decided to go to college the Galveston club wrote me a letter that said, "Well, you go to college, son. When you're through, you can report to us." In the meantime, I went to the University of Alabama, and Galveston sold their franchise to Waco of the Texas

Manager John McGraw called up Andy Cohen, above, to the New York Giants in 1926 in part because he thought having a Jewish player would boost ticket sales.

League for $25,000, so when I was ready to report I was told to report to Waco, and then by the time the season was just about over I was sold to the New York Giants for twenty-five thousand.

In my day with the Giants, I broke in at five thousand a season [laughs] and I thought that was pretty good money. Then I got raised up to seventy-five hundred and the most I ever made there was eleven-thousand-five. I guess I was about 5-8½, close to 5-9, weighed about 160 at my best weight.

The time I got hit in the head by a pitch from a fellow named "Fiddlin' Phil" Collins, I was scared because I saw one great big star. [laughs] That was many years ago. And we didn't wear any other protective gear. In fact, anybody that wanted to wear anything protective, you were called chicken. So none of us wanted to be called chicken, so we'd wear no liners or anything like that.

I remember one time I was playing a game in Louisville, Kentucky, when I was playing with the Minneapolis Millers of the American Association, and there was one fan there in Louisville that night who was really letting me have it, about Christ-killer and all that kind of stuff, and he kept it up for me the whole game. Finally, in the eighth inning, I kind of lost my temper, which I shouldn't have done because when you turn around to argue, you only invite disaster. So anyway, he kept up that Christ-killing stuff, and so I grabbed a bat and ran up in the stands and I said, "Yes, and I'll kill you, too," see. Well, the fans were all sympathizing with me for a while, but when I went up in the stands after this guy with a bat in my hand they started booing me, so I knew I had made a mistake. And players on the other team, they didn't really mean to be nasty, but they said it to try to get my goat, get my mind off the games.

The whole Chicago Cub bunch used to give me a fit when I'd come to bat. They'd ride me so hard that the umpire, "Beans"... Do you remember "Beans" Reardon? He was a great umpire and a hell of a fine fellow. He said, "Look, I wouldn't let a dog take this stuff." He went over to their bench and he said, "The next one of you guys who opens your mouth to this kid, you're out of the game," see. So when I came to bat the next time everything was quiet. So then I asked for it. I said, "What's the matter with you so-and-so over there, you losing your guts?" "Beans" said, "Well, kid, you asked for it."

Also, there was one fan in New York. I don't know who he was; he never signed his name. But when I first was there, you know, I got off to a great start and the papers were making a big fuss about me, see, so I used to get a weekly letter from some guy there, kept up for about three months, and he'd start off each letter with something like, "You cocky kike." The next one said, "You showy sheeny," the next one would say, "You stupid hebe." Stuff like that, see. I tried every way in the world to trace it back and had no luck. I've even still got some of those letters put away in my little storage room back in my driveway. This was nothing but a prejudiced guy, and if I did good, it really burned him up, see. The best way to stop that kind of stuff is to go out and try to do something good. Try to get a hit when you need it or make a great play when you need it, something like that, see.

The one tough thing about being a Jewish ballplayer was they were painting me up as a great ballplayer, as a great man and all that stuff, and I was trying too hard to live up to that reputation that they painted for me, see. Consequently, I had some bad memories on the field by trying too hard, you know?

I first came up in '26 at the end of my Texas League season. Well, I was a little nervous, you know. Those days, we didn't wear zippered coats, we had big thick mackinaws with big buttons, and I couldn't get a button undone, see? So I finally got there in front of where McGraw's sitting. I opened it up and there were buttons flying everywhere. McGraw says, "What does he care for expenses?" So when I went up to pinch-hit for Frankie Frisch.... We had the game won by a score of 8–1. This was in the eighth inning, so I guess he wanted to put me in to see what I'd do. So I grabbed my bat, went up to the plate and swung at the first pitch, hit a line-drive single to center field and I scored a couple of minutes later. When I got in, Mr. McGraw said, "Congratulations, young man, today you are leading the National League in hitting."

The Giants called me back up for '28. They traded Rogers Hornsby to the Boston Braves for Jimmy Walsh and "Shanty" Hogan. So when the season was over, Hornsby led the league in hitting; hit .387, I think I hit .275. So my argument was that he not only beat me, he beat everybody else in the league in hitting, see?

On Opening Day in 1928 at the Polo Grounds, it seemed like everything I did was right; I couldn't do anything wrong. We won 5–3 and I either drove them all in or scored them. Boy when that game was over, I never saw such a mad scramble to get out on the field. They picked me up and carried me off the field. [New York City Mayor] Jimmy Walker came over to pat me on the back, Jack Dempsey, some of the big guys. I've got a picture of that in my scrapbook.

We were playing Cincinnati one day, and they had a fellow named Sammy Bohne. His real name was Cohen. Not many people knew it, but.... And when we played in Cincinnati, Sammy sent me a note over from his bench, "Welcome to the big leagues, kid." I'll never forget that.

I hit .294 in 1929, and I was only twenty-five or twenty-six, but McGraw thought I was slowing up. It's a funny thing; I came up with a sore leg there one day and I didn't want to tell McGraw because I knew he'd put somebody else in, and in those days you hated to get out because somebody might come in and take over the damn job regularly. So that day we were playing in Cincinnati and I hit a sort of a soft line drive, what we call a semi, you know, just over second base, and to me it looked like it was going directly out to center field. In the meantime, Huey Kreitz, playing second for Cincinnati, ran over and made a marvelous backhand stop, flipped the ball on one hop to first base, and threw me out because I kind of automatically slowed down going to first when I thought the ball was a clean hit to center, see. So when that happened, McGraw said, "Well, it looks like young Cohen has football legs, slowing up," so that's why he sent me away at the end of the year. He traded me to Newark for a left-handed pitcher named "Doc" Pruitt, screwball pitcher. It was a hard blow to take after breaking in the way I did and then two years later, why, I'm gone.

In 1931, I had a good year at the bat and in the field. In fact, I set an International League record for consecutive chances without an error, and so McGraw sent one of his scouts over to look me over to see if I was really improving, had big-league potential. The guy reported good, Art Devlin, he's an old-timer, and so McGraw himself came over to watch me play in Newark toward the end of the season.

I was having a pretty good day, when all of a sudden one of the fellows hit a drive through the box, started toward second, and I blew for second base to try to make a backhand stop. Meantime, it bounced off the glove of the pitcher, and I had to stop all of a sudden to come back and go after the ball, and as I did something popped, and I went in and picked up the ball barehanded and leaped up and threw the guy out, but I couldn't walk anymore. They had to carry me off the field. Meantime, McGraw was about to go up and sign the papers to come back to New York, see, but when this happened I couldn't move anymore and that killed the deal. And then Bill Terry became the manager [of the Giants] and I wrote him letters about ... when I was at Minneapolis because right at the end of that year Newark, who was then working for the Yankees, brought in Jack Saltzgaver, who was one of their future stars. So when they got Saltzgaver they traded me over to Minneapolis, where I stayed for many years.

During that time, I was going pretty good and Bill Terry was having a rough time at second base, see, between Ott and Andy Reese, and so I wrote Bill a letter. I wrote him a couple of them. Never answered me. OK, showed that he wasn't interested, see. So I didn't get back to the big leagues.

A lot of people have asked me, especially when I've spoken to Jewish groups, "Andy, why aren't there more Jews in baseball?" So my answer is.... This is before all these big bonuses were coming out. I said, "The thing is, the parents of the Jewish boys would like their kids to get into something more substantial, that baseball is uncertain, you never know where you're going to be or when or how much you're going to make or what. So even if you've got a job from year to year, the uncertainty of it makes it insecure and they want their kids to get into something with more security, more potential and all that, see, and that's the reason I think more Jewish boys don't get into the business.

In the '39 season, Larry MacPhail called up Mike Kelley, who owned the Minneapolis team, says, "Mike, I need a playing manager to send to Pine Bluff, in the old Cotton States League. How about Cohen? He's been with you a long time; he's ready to come down, isn't he?" so Mike called me in there and told me that MacPhail wanted me to go to Pine Bluff to be a playing manager. "OK, Mike, if that's the way it is. All right."

I went over during the invasion. North Africa, 1942. Landed in Casablanca. Our hearts were in our throats most of the time. We were at a staging area at Fort.... What was that fort's name? In New Jersey. Anyway, we were told to get ready to Staten Island, we were going to board a ship, take us overseas. We got on board the ship and when we woke up in the morning we were put in the middle of the Atlantic, and the general comes up to us and says, "Men, our destination North Africa. Mission, to destroy Rommel." That's all he said, see. Then from then on we were on our own. [laughs] Yes.

Then we finally landed there, and we stayed over in Africa about a year and a half and then spent another year and a half in Italy. This is one of those experiences that you wouldn't give a million to do again or take a nickel for what you did, you know, one of those things. But thank God, I came through it all right.

I did get to one town there in North Africa where I saw a lot of people wearing the yellow ribbon around their arms. That signified they were Jews. We were garrisoned at Casablanca for a while, and one of my buddies and I got off for the night and went downtown, and we entered a bar that was run by a Jewish woman. A lot of Jews used to go there to drink beer and have fun, you know, and listen to music. So we went in. By this time, I was a first sergeant, see, had all those stripes up and down. So when they found out that this Yankee is a Jew, they gathered around me, two guys hugged me and gave me big kisses on the cheek, they couldn't get over it, see. I felt so sorry for them I felt like crying because it was tough being a Jew over there.

See, I was a platoon sergeant at first and the first eight guys to lose their lives were in my platoon, and the fellows got to thinking, "Goddamn, we got to get away from Sarge Cohen." First eight guys that lost their lives were in my platoon. But how they lost their lives, two of them from a sickness and four of them from booby traps. See our job was to defuse booby traps and stuff like that, you know. Oh yes, we lost about eight men. By the time of the end of the war I think we had lost a total of twelve, and when I had a chance to go home, boy, I grabbed at it.

After that, I was a baseball coach, mostly at the University of Texas El Paso and in Denver, and working for the Coors Beer people as a sort of PR man and salesman.

John Quinn [of the Phillies] called me up at the end of the 1959 season and he says, "Andy, we'd like for you to be a coach for our team." I reported there as a coach the next year and we didn't have a good team. And so we opened up our season in Cincinnati and played there and got beat. Got on the train and making our way to Philadelphia, and I was sleeping in the hotel room when the phone rings and it was John Quinn. "Come on out to see me, Andy, I got something to talk to you about." He says, "You know, Eddie Sawyer resigned." After the one game.

Well, I spoke to Eddie about it later, I said, "How come you resigned so quick?" and he says, "I want to live a little longer." He knew he had a bad ballclub, see. So anyway, I went right out to see John Quinn. He said, "Andy, I want you to manage the game tonight." Opening night against the Milwaukee Braves, managed by Chuck Dressen. I had worked for Quinn before when he was in the Boston Braves organization, you see, so he knew me, and of course I don't think that sat so well with the other coaches who were there because they had been with the team longer. Well, I understood that, but as it turned out, everything broke in my favor. We beat Milwaukee 5–4 in 10 innings, and I was splashed all over the papers the next day.

I knew that Gene Mauch had the job. As soon as Mauch got there, he let me know not to expect to be back next year, see, not in a nasty way, just to tell me as a matter of fact. He got his own man he wants to bring in, see. The other coaches the same way. So we finished a poor last because we did have a poor team, a bad team, I mean under Mauch yet, see. So they put me down as the winningest manager in Philadelphia history. That was one of the biggest thrills of my entire life, my baseball life, managing a big-league club on the opening night and me winning the game. I'll never forget that game as long as I live.

I was about thirty-eight or thirty-nine when I got married. I met my wife when I was playing in Elmira. I met a lot of nice girls in New York. Some of their fathers used to invite me to their homes and tell me what they would do for me if I'd be interested in his daughter, but I never thought of doing it. I'd say, "I don't expect to get married for a long, long time." My sister thinks I was [a ladies' man]. She used to tell my wife, "Any time you want to find Andy, go walk around the halls. If you see a bunch of girls, Andy'll be right in the middle of them." That's my sister talking, see. [laughs] Oh, I admit I liked the gals and I got along well with them. I'd tell them where I was staying. I said, "If you want to call me, we can talk some more on the phone." That started it. I'm not bragging about that, though. But I had my fun, I'll guarantee you.

HANK GREENBERG
Detroit Tigers, 1930, 1933–1941, 1945–1946; Pittsburgh Pirates, 1947
(1911–1986)

Hank Greenberg, the first national Jewish baseball star, made headlines in 1934 when he sat out a game on Yom Kippur. During the 1930s and 1940s, Greenberg was one of baseball's most feared sluggers. He hit 58 home runs in 1938, narrowly missing Babe Ruth's home run record. Greenberg helped lead the Detroit Tigers to two World Series championships, in 1935 and 1945, the latter coming after he completed his service in World War II. After Greenberg's playing career was over, he became a successful baseball executive and investment banker. Greenberg is a member of the Baseball Hall of Fame, elected in 1956. The following is from a July 1980 interview.

Well, to me it was a question of two things. One was Yom Kippur is, you know, the Day of Atonement, and you're supposed to put everything aside and just pray for the sins, atone for the sins of the year, that was one, and the other was respect for my parents. This is what they believed in, so naturally I would, out of respect for them, go along with not playing on Yom Kippur.

But evidently it made a very big.... You see, the press are always looking for unusual news, so they made a big thing out of it. Where it all came about, I don't know if you're familiar with it, but, you see, we were in the pennant race in '34 and Detroit hadn't won a pennant in twenty-five years, so it was very novel, and in '34 the City of Detroit was just coming out of the Depression. They were really hard hit because the automotive industry was down and ... so the question came up of whether I could play on Rosh Hashanah and they took it to the rabbi, high rabbi, in Detroit. So he said that in the Torah it shows that they played ball on Rosh Hashanah. Well, Rosh Hashanah is the New Year, so evidently it's a happy occasion and full of celebrating.

So his interpretation was you could play ball on Rosh Hashanah in those days, so you could certainly play baseball today. So he gave his approval. What happened was, the day we played on Rosh Hashanah we played Boston and we beat them 2–1 and I hit both home runs. Well, naturally this was a tremendous story, you know. Here is the chief rabbi giving me permission to play and we win the game 2–1; in the tenth inning I hit the second home run, so it was Greenberg 2, Boston 1. Naturally it made a big story. Well now, when that came up, then the newspapers followed it up on Yom Kippur: Was I going to play or wasn't I, and when I didn't play, they made a big thing of it.

I guess I was one of the taller basketball players in the City of New York when I was going to school in the mid-twenties. We won the city championships in soccer and in basketball, and we never won in baseball. We lost in the finals in baseball. My main assets or attributes was my size, for one thing, and my enthusiasm and the fact that I enjoyed sports, and it was sort of an outlet for me because I was overgrown, you know, I was so much taller [6–3] than the other kids in school that I was almost a freak. And so, in order to avoid all that awkwardness off the athletic field, I spent most of my time playing sports.

All my money that I ever got as an allowance went for taping the balls. You know, you got the ball, knock the cover off it, then you take the white adhesive tape and tape it up, and when the cover would tear off, it would take some yarn with it, then you'd tape it again. Pretty soon, it got pretty small, you'd have to go out and get another ball. But all my money went for that, and since I was paying for the tape and taping the ball, I would do the batting and everybody else would do the fielding. This was all through my high school career. There's guys that still talk about shagging for me. You know, it's a common thing: everybody claims that they shagged balls for me in the Bronx. I've had a thousand guys come to me and say, "I used to shag balls for you in the Bronx," even guys that were twenty years younger.

I was probably better known as a basketball player than I was as a baseball player in my high school days, strangely enough. But of course basketball was not a sport you could pursue. Baseball was the only sport that you could take advantage of if you wanted to become a professional, so naturally I gravitated toward baseball.

Future Hall of Famer Hank Greenberg's decision not to play a game for his Detroit Tigers on Yom Kippur in 1934 made him a hero to Jewish and non–Jewish fans alike.

I went into baseball because it was an escape from being in the Bronx and being in a small, little neighborhood environment. You know, in those days, people didn't move around like they do today. You know, there were many of my classmates that went to high school with me in the Bronx that had never been downtown, never been to Manhattan. It's hard to believe, isn't it, but they hadn't been two or three miles away from their own neighborhood. Going out of the state was almost unheard of. You know, if you talked about going to Washington, D.C., it was like going to Spain or London today in people's imagination, and also we didn't have the means to travel very far.

My family was moderately well off. We never had any problem as far as worrying about finances. We always had a nice home and my father was a good provider and we had a happy family life. My two brothers and my sister all graduated from college. In fact, I was the only one that only attended college for a year and then dropped out.

My parents were immigrants from a small town in Romania. They met downtown, on the Lower East Side. They were Orthodox. I received the usual training that most Jewish boys at the time received. We went to Hebrew school and we were Bar Mitzvahed and we'd observe the holidays. My mother kept a kosher home during my youth.

I was scouted by the Yankees in 1929. Paul Krichell was a Yankee scout. He found me in high school; he was the first one. They gave me free passes to Yankee Stadium so I went to Yankee Stadium a few times. But I didn't sign with the Yankees when I got those passes from Ed Barrow to go and watch the games. You know, they used to have a pad on which they signed the name and it said, "Admit two to a ballgame," so he gave me about three of them, see? And when I went to watch them play I saw Lou Gehrig out there, and I was in high school and looking at Lou Gehrig, who was a mature man, you know, his shoulders were like this, you know? He looked so powerful, and I decided that I'd never be able to take his place and that was one of the deterrents that kept me from going to New York. And then Detroit came along.

My parents didn't object to me going into baseball; they didn't object at all, and, of course, what changed their minds greatly is when Detroit offered me nine thousand to sign. That was a lot of money in those days for a high school kid and they realized that, you know, I must have some talent or they wouldn't be giving me $9,000. From then on, they were all for it.

They used to come to the games; they got to be pretty good fans. Loved to come to the game. They traveled wherever I went to. Minor leagues, they always showed up once and, you know, spent a week or two and then got on back to New York. Oh yes, they were very proud of me. They got all of kinds of pictures. They were at the World Series and all that sort of thing.

Nineteen thirty-eight, when I had fifty-eight home runs, was not my best year by a long shot. My best year was in 1937. I drove in 183 runs, I hit about .340, and I had fifty-six or fifty-eight doubles and I had forty home runs. But history, it's interesting. During my whole career, my goal was driving in runs. If you're a ballplayer, that's what counts, driving in runs. My average for driving in runs was 150; when I went in the Army, I was just a few short. But after I come back, of course, then my average went way down, but even then I would say, if you took a 154-game schedule and you worked it out on runs batted in, you know, per game, I think that I'd have an average of 135, average. As I say, my goal was to get 154 a season, wind up my career with that, runs batted in per game. That was my goal and that's what everybody's goal is in baseball, that's with the ballplayers. Now, the dramatic part is hitting a home run, see, that's exciting, you know, Babe Ruth. So here my whole goal and my achievement in baseball was driving in runs, and then one year I happened to have fifty-eight home runs and that's all I'm remembered for.

To me, it's always amusing to me, because, you know, that year I had the 183, I drove in one run the last day of the season, which was a 1–0 ballgame, and the day before I had the chance with the bases full, I hit a flyball to right field, fell foul about this far. I would have driven in three more runs, would have had the all-time record. There was never one line in the paper about that.

The toughest for me, of course was Bob Feller. He was tough for everybody; he was a great pitcher. And ["Lefty"] Grove was awfully tough, for a left-hander. Those were the two toughest pitchers in baseball.

I served in the Pacific. I was in China and India, so we were more conscious of the Japanese, you know, the atrocities that they had so-called committed and Pearl Harbor and all that sort of thing. But everybody knew [about the concentration camps], you know. I'm fascinated by World War II, having been a participant, and I read everything I can on Nazi Germany and everything that's ever written about it, I must read it, you know?

Well, you know, the fans would call you "sheeny" or "Jew" or "kike" or whatever. That was part of the psychological warfare and, of course, the fans would ride you, as they do today. Today they throw things at the ballplayers, but even then. Today, you know, they yell down from the stands. There's always a certain number of people who get their frustration or their whatever, anxieties, or whatever it is that makes them feel macho or strong because they can yell at some ballplayer down on the field, and we had it the same way then. I was also big and strong, so that even, you know, made me a bigger target.

Hearing it from the other team's bench was part of the game. I'm sure there were some anti–Semitic, you know, ballplayers. I think in those days a lot of them didn't know what a Jew was. A lot of them came from the rural South and, hell, they didn't know what a Jew was. I know my roommate, Jo-Jo White, who came from Atlanta, I remember him telling me, he said, "Hell," he says, "I thought all those Jews had horns." So he didn't know what a Jew was. He just had heard the word and knew there were people like that, but as far as he was concerned, I could have been Frankenstein, I mean that's what a Jew was supposed to look like. I don't know. I was in baseball for thirty-five years, so I'm sure there's a lot of prejudice that existed on the field, off the field, and exists today, too.

You're going to have a lot of bigoted people in this world and it's not going to change, but I like to feel that being Jewish and being the object of a lot of derogatory remarks kept me on my toes all the time. I could never relax and be one of the boys, so to speak. So I think it helped me in my career because it always made me aware of the fact that I had a little extra burden to bear and it made me a better ballplayer.

I've been in a number of fights on ballfields. I don't know the number, of course. The first thing they do is they call you names. They get on you; that's the first thing they do. Sure. Particularly when you're doing well, they want to upset you. I was in a fight in Dallas, Texas. We had a riot on the field, you know, fistfight with both teams, you know, on the field. They had a big article in the Dallas newspapers. The whole ballpark was jammed the next day with people, and everything was focused on that dirty Jew on the field, you know? This was in 1932.

In 1931 there was a riot in a playoff game in Decatur, Ill. I still have that paper home, the headline, "Fans Charge Fighting Ballplayer." One of the little guys, the third baseman on the other team, just got on me, you know? I'd had a good day and he just kept riding me all the time and the fans picked it up, and hell, they had to get the police to get me out of the ballpark.

So when you ask me how was I conscious of being Jewish, I mean you're never unconscious of this thing happening all the time, you know, fans yelling at you. Every ballpark I went to there'd be somebody in the stands who spent the whole afternoon just calling me, you know, names. If you're having a good day, you don't give a damn, but if you're having a bad, why, pretty soon, it gets you hot under the collar, if you're sensitive a little. And it's hard not to be sensitive.

You respond when, you know, you reach a boiling point. You know, you accept it up to a certain degree and then there's always the straw that breaks the camel's back. I got it even as the general manager in Cleveland all the time, the getting on me. I've had guys yell at me a whole game until I finally just couldn't stand it anymore; I had to go up and punch the guy in the jaw, and he was drunk and he even started to apologize, you know?

Naturally the, you know, Jewish people were proud, you know, everybody would, you know, point to the fact that ... they used me as an example, you know, "If Hank Greenberg can become a ballplayer, so can you," and, of course, there aren't that many Jewish ballplayers. But in every town, of course, I suppose, just as we today, hear of some athlete or some statesman or some gifted, talented artist, if he's Jewish, you take a certain pride in the fact that one of your own people have made good.

I don't resent what ballplayers are making today. We're living in different times. I think maybe part of that is that I'm fairly well-off, so I suppose that if I was destitute, I'd feel very bitter and acrimonious about it. In my day I remember Honus Wagner telling me, in 1947, he knew I was making $100,000. He thought that was, you know, a fortune, which it probably was, but to him it was the same as making a million dollars today. After Ruth passed out of the picture, I became the highest-paid ballplayer.

I was married to a girl named Caral Gimbel, and she's a daughter of Bernard Gimbel of the Gimbel department store. We were married thirteen years. We have three children, two boys and a girl. They've done very well, Now I've been remarried. I got divorced in 1959, I remarried in 1966 and I'm married to a gal by the name of Mary Jo Tarola. She's not Jewish.

My children were very young when I was divorced. I got custody of my kids when we got divorced. But the boys went off to boarding school, one went to Hotchkiss, one went to Andover, and they went at fourteen, I guess. When the boys went off to boarding school, my daughter was left at home, see and she wanted to go live with her mother, so I let her go live with her mother. Well, in the kind of family life we had, the boys were at prep school for four years. Their mother had visitation rights in the summertime, see? So I didn't get to see much of them.

So you don't have the same kind of influence you would have had if we had had a normal married life without a divorce in the family. I think I would have had a little more control over them. I would have been able to guide them a little better. As it is, they had to guide themselves, you know, and make their own decisions. They didn't have any real Jewish training, and maybe if we had not had a divorce when they were younger, they might have had ... they were never Bar Mitzvahed or anything.

If I'm an example, I only an example of in the way I conduct my life, you know? I want to conduct my life in an exemplary manner, so that if people want to emulate me as an individual they're doing it because of my actions. It's not that I'm a leader of any Jewish group. That's my feeling. Now it's always been that I want to just lead my life and set the example of being a good citizen, live by the Ten Commandments, and if that sets a good example, I think that's fine.

HARRY DANNING
New York Giants, 1933–1942
(1911–2004)

Harry Danning was a four-time All-Star catcher for the New York Giants in the 1930s and early 1940s. During his career with the Giants, Danning played alongside several other Jewish teammates: Phil Weintraub, Harry Feldman, Morrie Arnovich, and Sid Gordon. About three weeks before his ninety-third birthday in August 2004, Danning sat in a room cluttered with the memorabilia of a career in Major League Baseball. Grainy black-and-white photographs from his days on the Giants lined the walls. Old catcher's mitts sat on shelves. There were awards and plaques. At the time of the interview, he had an around-the-clock, live-in caretaker. While still mentally sharp, Danning's poor health limited his travels, and he was unable to attend an upcoming Baseball Hall of Fame event honoring Jewish Major Leaguers.

I wish I could go. I really do. I think it's a good idea. It's good for the young kids because there's been so much talk about discrimination. There's been a lot of that, and a lot of hatred. And I think this is good for the kids, to let them know they can do it, if they want to do it. Today there's not the discrimination like they had years ago. Years ago it was tough. They'd be calling you names.

I got interested in baseball when I was a little kid. I've always been able to hit a baseball. When I was in grammar school, I could hit it. We used to play with a golf ball, because it was the only ball we had. I think we had a bat, or maybe it was just a stick. We didn't have gloves. The golf ball would get run over by streetcars, and we'd put tape around it to hold it together. By about the fourth inning you'd think you were throwing a shot put, it had so much tape around it.

The way I became a catcher? Well, we played on a sandlot. All the kids were older than me, and they had everybody chosen but the catcher. They needed a catcher. So I said, "I'm a catcher." When I was about fourteen years old, I made the team at Los Angeles High School, second string. I only played first string one year, because I graduated when I was 16. We won the city championship. It was a great high school, and the coach was named Herb White. You'd go out and you'd try out in street clothes, and if you got a uniform you made the team, follow me? He was pitching, and I hit the ball three times. He said, "Give that boy a uniform." It was one of the greatest thrills I had in my life.

My father was the greatest fan you ever laid your eyes on. He died young. That's the only regret that I have — that he didn't see me play in the majors. But when he was alive, we used to walk to watch a game. We'd go and see the black players on Sunday.

He loved baseball. When we were kids, he would umpire and pitch softball for us.

He was born in Warsaw, Poland. My mother was born and raised in Latvia. They were both immigrants. My name was changed. It wasn't Danning. To this day, I don't know what my real name is. When my dad first came to the country, he was living with a woman whose name was Denning. She's the one who taught him English. He took her last name, except he put an "a" in there.

My mother and father met in Philadelphia and got married there, but they moved to Los Angeles before I was born. My dad was in the furniture business. He was a salesman and he had a store, a used furniture store, in Los Angeles. That was before the stock market crash and the Depression. I was sixteen when my father died. He took sick when I was thirteen. He had Hodgkin's disease, and in those days you only lived one to three. Now they can arrest it and you can live a long time. We all worked and gave my mother money. If I made five bucks, I would give her $4.75. My sisters worked. That's how we got by. We just gave her money. There were six of us — born boy, girl, boy, girl, boy, girl.

I went house to house selling cakes and cookies. I worked cutting lawns, 25¢ an hour. Then I worked on an ice truck, $5 a day, every Saturday, all summer. My mother had a hard time. She could understand English, but she couldn't write very well. But she understood the price of groceries.

My mother went to shul, but my father didn't. The way I understand it, my father had an argument with somebody in the synagogue and he became soured on it. I don't know the details, but he soured on the syn-agogue and I think the whole religion.

When my father died, my older brother was supposed to go to shul [synagogue], but he was playing ball. So I went. I was thirteen, but I went. It was a real Orthodox shul, in a storefront. I learned a lot about the Jewish religion there. Sometimes I'd go three times a day. In between we would hang out in a sweet shop and shoot craps.

But I learned a lot and all through my career, I never played on the holidays. I'd go to shul on the holidays: The Forty-seventh Street shul [in New York City]. I don't go to synagogue anymore. I always felt that it [spirituality] is within yourself anyway. Now, at night, I say a little prayer, I say goodnight to my wife and pray for my family. But back then, I thought it was an obligation to go. It wasn't because I didn't want to play ball. I did. But it was a High Holiday. Rosh Hashanah and Yom Kippur — all the time I played ball — I never played on those days.

Growing up, we didn't live in a Jewish neighborhood. We lived in a Mexican neighborhood until I was ten, and then we moved to an all-white area. At shul, everything was in Hebrew. I didn't learn Hebrew. I still don't know any. None of us were ever bar mitzvahed.

When I got out of school, I worked for a rug house, a wholesaler of rugs. I didn't sell carpets. I was sweeping the floor. The rugs were hanging up. I hung the rugs, took them down when they were sold, hung the new ones. I sold when they were busy. I got $90 a month for that. That was in 1928–29.

I was playing semipro ball. I played for a Mexican grocery store. It was called El Porvenir. They paid the most for a catcher, $7.50 a game. With my glove and my bat and my shoes over my shoulder, I had to take two streetcars way over to the east side of town to make seven and a half bucks. Most of the players were Mexican, and most of the fans. They were great fans. I think there was one other white player.

I got together with Behr Ironworks, and I was playing for them when I got discovered by George Washington Grant. I'd had offers from different places, but it was always for $75 a month. It was always the low minor leagues. I said the heck with it, I'm making more money here where I am. Grant just asked me, "How would you like to sign with the Giants?" I almost fell to the floor.

The Giants signed me to a Bridgeport contract. Bridgeport was my first minor league team. I got $350 a month the first year I played. I hit .320, so I was about the fifth leading hitter in the league. The second year I was with Bridgeport, the league blew up — it went bankrupt. So they sent me to Winston-Salem. I hit about .320 down there. And then that league blew up. There wasn't any money. I remember games where the visiting team would divvy up $36. Each guy got $3. I remember hitting a home run over the left-field fence in Raleigh, and we had to wait for them to bring the ball back.

We didn't have any money. In Winston-Salem, there was a woman named Mrs. Allen who had a boarding house and a country kitchen. She cooked for us, and we ate three meals a day, family style, for a buck. In those days, if you didn't get paid for five weeks, you could become a free agent. We didn't get paid, so we said we were going to become free agents. The Giants only signed three or four of us from Winston-Salem. But immediately, as soon as we could, we paid Mrs. Allen. She trusted us. Without her, we could have starved to death.

I joined the Giants in June of 1933. That first year, I didn't play much. There were two other catchers. I played in a few games in 1933 and 1934, and not at all in 1935 and 1936. I wasn't happy about it. I wanted to play. I couldn't play in the off-season, either. People playing in the Mexican League were getting barred from the majors for five years. It's because of that reserve clause. I couldn't play for my team, and I couldn't play for anyone else. I know the Pittsburgh Pirates were interested in me. They tried to trade for me for five years. But the Giants wouldn't trade me. I guess they knew I was a pretty good player. Then in 1937, Gus Mancuso got hurt. I took over. I helped the Giants win the pennant in 1937, and after that I was the regular man for six-and-a-half years.

See that team picture on the wall there? That's the 1937 Giants. We went to the World Series and got beat by the Yankees. I'm the only one in that picture that's still alive. They're all gone. People say why don't you go see your friends. Where? The cemetery? That's where they all are. I used to go visit eight men in Palm Springs, but they're all gone.

The Giants had several Jewish players when I played. Myself, Phil Weintraub, Harry Feldman, Morrie Arnovich, and then later Sid Gordon came along too. I don't know if they did that on purpose [signed up Jewish players to appeal to fans] or if they just bought 'em because they could play ball. I don't know. I didn't go into that. I didn't delve into anybody's private life. I was just playing baseball. You follow me?

In all the time I have played baseball, I have been called names, but mostly from the dugout. They used to have bench jockeys and they'd call you all kind of names, but usually not to your face. The Italians were

"Dagos." The Jews were "kikes." In those days, I had a pretty good-sized nose. They used to holler when I was at bat, "Pitch under his nose, he can't see the ball." Or they'd say, "Is that your nose, or is that a banana?" And this last one I liked: "He's the only guy who can smoke a cigar while he's standing in the shower and not get the cigar wet." Ha. You gotta laugh. You know they didn't mean anything by it. That's just what a bench jockey did. They tried to get your goat.

In that photo over there, you can see my proboscis a little bit, can't you — my nose? I did have a pretty good-sized nose. I had to see a doctor for a deviated septum and when he was fixing that I said, "Hey, go ahead and take a little bit off here."

There was some discrimination, not as much as the black players faced, but some. In 1934, at spring training, the team was staying at a hotel right off Biscayne Bay. The hotel people said they would take everybody, except for Phil Weintraub and me, because we were Jewish. Bill Terry said, "No, you'll take them all or you'll take none." I didn't even know about until later. Phil told me about it many years later. Had I known, I probably wouldn't even have wanted to go in there. It was worse in the South. When I first went down there, I saw all this. Black people couldn't sit in the same area at motion pictures, or on the streetcar. They even had black and white fountains. I saw all that stuff. But I never had another player call me anything to my face, never. And God knows I talked to all the players, being a catcher. I've had pitchers cuss me out and call me names for getting a home run. But that's different. They'd call everybody names.

The way I got my nickname, the true story, is there was an old radio announcer, Ted Husing. He was announcing one day and he just called me "Harry the Horse." It came from the original Damon Runyon story, and it stuck to me even to this day. I always tell people I don't know if it was because I work like one or I look like one.

I used to bat behind Mel Ott. Pitchers were allowed to throw at you in those days, and they did it, too. There was no rule against it. Once, after Ott, he hit a home run, I came up after him, and the pitcher for Pittsburgh — I think it was Joe Baldwin — he flattened me. I said, "I didn't do anything. Why didn't you throw it at Ott?" They used to do that. When they got frustrated, they would throw at you. If somebody hit a home run, the next up got it. And remember, in those days we didn't have any helmets, just regular baseball caps.

We didn't have television then, or night games. We didn't have any

Harry Danning was an All-Star catcher who played for the New York Giants from 1933 to 1942.

fancy uniforms. We had wool. That's all we had. And wool is hot. And spikes weren't made out of plastic back then.

In 1939, we were playing Cincinnati. We were one and two in the league. I think they were ahead of us. Harry Craft is hitting. And he hit a ball to left field, onto the lower deck of the Polo Grounds, and it was a foul ball. And the umpire called it a home run. And I opened up my big mouth and I argued with him. Three of us ended getting thrown out of the game by three different umpires. I think that's something of a record. It was Billy Jurges, Jo-Jo Moore, and myself. We were all thrown out. I got a picture of it over there on the wall.

The next day I woke up with a red streak on my leg. Blood poisoning. Apparently somebody jumped on me, but I didn't know it. I don't remember any fight, but there were a lot of people milling about. I guess somebody jumped on my leg, I don't know. I couldn't play and the Giants lost eight straight. I just blew my stack. I called the umpire every name I could think of. I just blew up, which is something I very seldom do. I never really fought with umpires. I would say things. If there was a bad call I would say, "Somebody smells up here, and it isn't the catcher and it isn't me." But I just blew my stack. The umpire said, "Nobody's ever talked to me like that." I said, "Wait a minute and I'll say some more." It was just a bad call. You could see the ball all the way. I saw this one all the way. We knew it was a foul ball. I never cursed a man out in my life like that. So they fined me $350, which in those days was a lot of money. They wanted to suspend me, but Bill Terry talked them into fining me.

Willard Hershberger? I'll tell you about that. In 1940, we were playing Cincinnati, and Willard Hershberger was catching for them. In the ninth inning, I hit a home run and the Reds lost. He grieved about calling the wrong pitch. In those days, the catcher called the pitches for the pitchers. Today they don't. He thought it was his fault and, a couple days later, he killed himself. Some people kidded me about being responsible, because of the home run. But it turned out his father had done the same thing. He had other problems, other things on his mind, and this just made him go over the cliff. I felt that if that was the real cause of him killing himself, I wish I would have struck out. You know what I mean? It wouldn't be worth a life for a lousy home run. I really felt sad and sorry, sure. I thought about it for a while.

The big salaries players make today? They don't bother me any. I'm not bitter about it. It's economics. See, I played in the Depression and made $10,000 and $15,000, and that was a lot of money back then. You could buy a Cadillac for $1,300. I paid $800 for a Buick. You could get a Dodge for $600.

The biggest thrill I ever had in baseball? I don't know. The biggest thrill was being able to step on the field. No, seriously, with all the good players that I played with and against, that's my biggest thrill — to have stepped on a Major League field.

I got five hits in a game once, and I hit for the cycle, which is pretty rare. There are more no-hitters than there are guys hitting for cycle. It's the only time in history that someone has hit for the cycle with a home run hit inside the park. At the Polo Grounds, out in center field, there was a flower bed and some monuments, and the ball got in between there. I'm still the co-holder of the record for a team hitting five home runs in one inning. I don't think that one's ever been beaten, but it's been tied. My record for six-and-a-half years is probably better than ninety-six percent of the catchers in the Hall of Fame, but I do not deserve to be there. I didn't play long enough. If could have played fourteen years, I think maybe I could have been considered for that. You know what I mean?

My draft notice came in 1943, and I got another employer. I wasn't surprised when I got it. I was inducted on April 6 and reported on April 13. They gave you a week. I had to go, you know. I didn't try to get out of it. Especially when you read about all the things that happened in Europe, with the Jewish people, I felt that I really wanted to go. So I didn't try to get out, I just went and did what they told me to.

My daughter was three months old when I left. My wife and I got married in 1940. That's her picture up there. Her name was Diane, but she went by Dee Dee. We'd known each other about two weeks when we got married by a rabbi. He was the rabbi for West Point. Diane died quite a while ago — July 28, 1978. We lost twin boys the first year of the marriage. When I went into the service, I was thirty-one. And, you know, they didn't give me a paper saying I was going to come back. They don't guarantee that.

I spent almost three years in Long Beach, California. I worked in a training squadron. I also managed the baseball team. We also had Charlie "Red' Ruffing, the Hall of Famer, and Max West, who was in the 1940 All-Star Game. I probably would have been sent over to India or China, but they put me out on a medical discharge. My left knee went bad; that's part of my troubles today. A doctor in the army hospital told me that if I would play baseball, my leg would lock and I would be stiff-legged the rest of my life.

Back in Los Angeles I saw my orthopedic doctor. He told me the same thing. I talked to my wife and we figured money isn't worth that, so I never went back. It's all shot, my left knee. I don't really know how I hurt it. I think it was baseball. I'm sure at least part of it is from catching, the up and down and up and down, but I don't really know. For all I know maybe I injured it playing football on the sandlot. My knees always hurt when I was playing baseball. In the service it got worse, got so bad I could hardly walk. When I was playing baseball, I didn't pay any attention to it because I figured that was par for the course. And eventually I paid for it. After baseball, I started a car dealership in Los Angeles. I started with the Kaiser Frazier, then I had a Hudson dealership. I hated it. I couldn't stand it. I saw how they worked, the car dealers, and I don't like it to this day. I don't like it at all.

I did some coaching, but I didn't have the patience. Now I do, but I didn't then. And at the time, there weren't too many Jewish coaches and managers. I coached for a year with the Hollywood Stars, at the home games only. That's how I learned I didn't have the patience for it. I sold the car dealership and went back to New York, where I had a friend at the Daily News, and I learned the newspaper and magazine distributing business, but my friend quit and the distributorship went broke. Then I worked for The Daily Mirror in New York as a road man, visiting the dealers, and it closed down. Then I had a friend in San Francisco who had an insurance agency, so I went there. He went broke.

So I went to work for Metropolitan, the insurance company. I spent a lot of years with them, selling, in management and as an inspector. They were a good company. That's probably the one big mistake I made in my whole life — I didn't plan for after I got through baseball. I should have gone to college. I should have gone to real estate school. I didn't plan for my future.

I'm not a rich man, but I have enough to get by, and I save a few bucks a month right now. I have lived conservatively, and we made a little money in real estate. I never lost a nickel in real estate.

The reserve clause — do you know anything about it?

The reserve clause says basically that the owners own you. You couldn't do anything without permission from the owners. Judge Landis [Landis was then the commissioner of baseball] controlled everything. Five years after I played, I called the manager of the Hollywood team and asked him if I could come to coach. He said he'd like that. Well, he came back later and said, "We can't hire you." I said, "Why not?" He said, "You still belong to the Giants." Keep in mind, they hadn't paid me for five years, but they hadn't released me. I could not get another job in baseball until they released me. Follow me? And they wouldn't release me unless I promised I wouldn't play. Well, I could use the money so I said, "Yeah, I'll promise," and I didn't play. I didn't catch. That was the reserve clause. You had to get permission to do everything. There were so many rules, but they were all to protect baseball after the White Sox scandal [the 1919 Black Sox scandal].

Ike Danning was my older brother. He was a catcher, too. He was born in 1905. I was born in 1911. When he started in the minor leagues— I think it was with Idaho Falls— my father was still alive. Ike played in the International League with Baltimore, and then he went to Richmond. He went to spring training with Pittsburgh one year, but he didn't make the team. In 1928, he got to the majors— he made the St. Louis Browns. That was his dream. That was my dream.

Once you start, you want to get to the majors. What did Willie Sutton say? They asked him why he robbed banks, and he said, "That's where the money is." The majors is where the money is. Ike played in two games— six at-bats, three hits. That's a .500 average. But I guess he just couldn't hit enough and they let him go. He was slight. He wasn't too big. But Ike was a rooster. He liked to fight. I'm more easygoing. In fact, he wanted to be a fighter until my dad took him up to the gym and a guy beat the hell out of him.

Ike's real name was Seymour. But he didn't like it so he changed it to Ike. I don't know where the name Ike came from. Maybe it was from Alibi Ike, the comic strip. He was nicknamed Seymour Isaiah, so maybe out of Isaiah he came up with Ike. How did Eisenhower get the name Ike? I don't know.

Ike is famous for one story. At an exhibition game, Ike was catching and Harry Ruby, the great songwriter, was pitching, and supposedly Ike, instead of hand signals, was just shouting out the signals to the pitcher in Yiddish. Jimmie Reese kept coming up and getting hits. Supposedly, Ike said something like, "I didn't know you were so good," and Reese said, "You didn't know my real name is Hymie Solomon." That's a wonderful story, isn't it?

The best player I ever played with was Mel Ott. He was a great ball player. The best of all time? I say Babe Ruth. I don't think there will ever be another person like Babe Ruth, on and off the field. I think he's the best. The best pitcher? Well, of course I'm prejudiced. Carl Hubbell. I caught him one hundred and fifty games. In the American League, the best pitcher was Bob Feller. The nastiest fans were in Philadelphia, and they still are. The ballpark I most liked to play in was Pittsburgh, Forbes Field. The one I liked the least was Braves Field in Boston. It just wasn't a nice ballpark. All the ballparks I played in are gone, except Wrigley.

I was catching when Joe DiMaggio hit his first World Series home run. Also, I was catching when Lou Gehrig hit his last World Series home run. And I was catching when Ted Williams hit the home run to win the All-Star Game in 1941. In every one of those, I had a good seat. At least I was there, you know what I mean?

GOODY ROSEN
Brooklyn Dodgers, 1937–1939,
1944–1946; New York Giants, 1946
(1912–1994)

Goody Rosen enjoyed telling people that he was the only Canadian Jew to play in the Major Leagues. That was true until a few years ago, when Adam Stern played briefly for the Boston Red Sox and Baltimore Orioles. Rosen's best year came with the Brooklyn Dodgers in 1945, when he batted .325 and finished tenth in voting for the National League MVP. He was interviewed in August 1981.

My mother's maiden name was Rebecca Shimkofsky. And my father was Samuel Rosen. They were both born in Minsk Gubernia [District] in Russia and they came to Canada. They were both here by the year of 1907. My mother had come here two years earlier.

What happened was, at the turn of the century, Japan and Russia went to war. My dad had completed military service, and then the war started, and they wanted him back in the army. All the cavalry was being used for cannon fodder, so anyone that could run, you know, had a chance to run, they all ran. So I guess my dad was one that ran, and through some relatives and influential people, he ended up in London, England, with the end destination being Toronto. My mother, rest her soul, was already here.

They were married in Russia; they already had two children. If all of my brothers and sisters were living now, there would be five boys, three girls. My grandparents stayed. My brother Dave, god rest his soul, he was a pretty good ballplayer. I got him a tryout. I started out with Louisville in the American Association, Double A. I never played any lower baseball. I got my brother a tryout, oh, the second or third year I was with Louisville, and my brother was a star, you know, in sandlot ball around here, but he never made it because he couldn't consistently hit the curveball.

We had two sets of dishes growing up. You can understand, you know, me leaving home at a pretty young age, I got away from all of that. I wasn't Bar Mitzvah, but my son was and my daughter had her Bat Mitzvah. My brothers were Bar Mitzvah, too. I was a little bit of an oddball, I guess. I remember the rabbi used to sneak up behind me, you know, I'd be day-dreaming, thinking about whatever sport was playable at the time. He'd sneak up behind me and pull my hair up. So I think one time I kicked him in the shins. So he wouldn't let me back in cheder [religious school]. I wouldn't play ball on Yom Kippur. I wouldn't do that. There was never a problem with that.

My mother was very religious; she was Orthodox. I can't say the same for me. I guess I was never religious, really. I'm religious to the point that I'm proud of being Jewish. I was never a synagogue-goer.

I was probably as good as, if not better, a hockey player than I was a ballplayer. I loved the game of baseball, and I decided at a very early age that I was going to become a ballplayer. But I only weighed 135 when I started out with Louisville. I was never 5-10. About 5-9, 9½, tops.

In 1930, when I was seventeen, I had a tryout with Rochester in the International League. But you must remember that I was small and light, and after I was with Rochester about three weeks for the tryout, Warren Giles, who later became the president of the National League, said to me, he said, "Look," he said, "you got a lot of ability, but you're too small and you will never become a ballplayer."

I never did graduate high school. In '31, there was another fellow who lived in Toronto, Bobby Mabline, and we both loved baseball and we both were going to be big league ballplayers. We used to do odd jobs, wherever we could make, you know, a dollar and we saved the money. He was the banker. We had heard that there was winter baseball in Florida, so we decided that we were going to take off.

First, we went to Brooklyn by bus. Bobby Mabline had relatives there. Then we went to Washington. And we had met a kid by the name of Lou Langbord and he had relatives in Washington and he said if we ever get to Washington to drop in and say hello to them; they'd probably put us up for the night. So we got to his relatives in Washington and he was there. His father was in business and he stole some money from his father and ran off to Washington. So, gee, the next day.... We didn't have too much money, but it was enough for us to hitchhike to Florida and there was a baseball camp there, or winter baseball. Well, we had, you know enough to maybe get by for a while. So we went down to a police sale. Believe it or not, we bought a Ford touring car. You know, it had slats for side windows? Used to press them in?

Before we got to — I'll never forget — Cartersville, Georgia.... What happened there was, it snowed the night before, so we were wiping the snow off and made a hole in the top. It was a canvas top. The next day we were driving, and all of a sudden the top was flapping, and it was cold, it was in the latter part of December. It was cold in that car, I'll tell you, and the side slats, they weren't fitting. [laughs] I think in all we paid about $50 for the car. All of a sudden, the car developed a leak in the gasoline tank. We finally sold it in Tampa, Fla., for eight bucks [laugh], the car. We needed it; we needed the money to eat. God!

While we were in Tampa, we ended up pushing wheelbarrows and pruning oranges. Twenty-five cents an hour, and the funny thing about it was, it was where Cincinnati trained. Eventually, the three of us got on the road. There was no winter baseball, by the way, in Tampa. But through my brother Jake, *alluva sholem* [May he rest in peace], who got killed in 1935, we had gotten a tryout with Little Rock in the Southern League, Class A. We were in Tampa for six weeks, so it's still winter of '32.

We were going to go up to Little Rock and we had to meet this person who would probably house us till spring training started up for Little Rock. We started out hitchhiking.

The first day we're standing there, we each have a bag and, as I recall, we had our overcoats, too. Nobody would give us a lift. So we said, 'Look, we're not going to do any good this way," so we flipped coins. This is the truth. Odd man would go alone; the other two would go together. So this Langbord was the odd man out. So he's single, got a lift, you know, and he's gone. The two of us stood there. Anyway, we got up the next morning; I forget where we spent the night, and we saw a freight train. You must remember. We had a little piece to go, from Tampa to Little Rock, Arkansas. Decided to ride the freight trains, which we did.

In Decatur, Alabama, something happened there that you wouldn't believe. It was about two or three in the morning and all of a sudden the train stopped; both sides of the car opened. There was about sixty of us in the car. "This is the police! Come out with your hands up!" Railroad detectives. They opened both sides of the car. We came out, but we jumped over their heads and we started to run down the track, and we could run, Bobby and I. They shot us a few times, but they shot over our heads, I

In 1945, Goody Rosen hit .325 for the Brooklyn Dodgers and finished tenth in the MVP voting for the National League.

guess. Anyway, he fell, and I'll always remember, he cut himself, oh, he was bleeding terribly. We ran for.... Christ, I don't know how far we went, but anyway, we slept ... got in a field for the rest of the night; there wasn't too much night left. I'll never forget, at daybreak we saw this little house near the railroad track and rapped at the door. We knew there was some-body in there because smoke was coming out of the chimney.

Finally, a black man opened the door, and do you know what his words were? "What do you want, white boy?" Never gave us a chance to say anything, just slammed the door. So we were walking down the track and I saw a cow. That was the closest I'd ever been to a cow and I went over there and I took the thing and I wet it with a little milk to wash the wound off. I had torn my shirt, part of it, to tie the tourniquet around.

We finally got to Hot Springs, Arkansas. In those days, that was a Jewish resort. We went to this Jewish hotel in Hot Springs and we came to the back and we told them we were from Brooklyn. We didn't dare tell them we were from Canada. Jesus, they fed us and took up a collection; it was enough for us for a room, and we did little odd jobs around there during the day and they fed us, but how long could you, you know, lean on them, really? And we got a little job at the golf course, did a little caddying. Then time to go for our tryout in Little Rock. Lasted one day. Too small. Mabline wasn't good enough. I was too small and he wasn't good enough.

Then we got a tryout at Memphis, and Doc Prothro, who later became the manager of the Phillies, he kept us till Opening Day, then he let us go. But he took me in the office and he said, "Look you're going to be a ballplayer." He says, "Right now, you're too small and you're too light." He says, "You go home and you do some kind of building-up program," and he says, "You contact me next year," he said. "You're going to be all right."

Well, that winter, I contacted Prothro again. He said, "Look, I can't use you," he said, "but I'll give you the name of the manager of this team, New York–Penn League, Binghamton, and he'll give you a tryout, and I'm sure you'll do all right there." So I went there in '32, spring training, and I was doing wonderful and I was ready to start the season, and all that, and the day before the season opened. They had a working agreement with the White Sox. The White Sox had a couple of ballplayers down there, and they had to play, so they let me go. But when they let me go, they told me about a new league starting up called the Interstate League, and about Eddie Murphy, the manager of Stroudsburg, who could use me. So that's where I went.

The league lasted six weeks, then it blew up, but I was hitting real good and anyway, when the league blew up, the owners came to us and said, "Look, if you go home now you got nothing to do." He says, "Why don't you all stay on and I'll put lights in the park and you'll play all the Negro teams, you know," and this is what we did. That was my first venture hitting against Satchel Paige, by the way. I played against some of the greatest black players. I remember there was Josh Gibson, a catcher. I'll never forget hitting against Paige. He threw three pitches. I couldn't get the bat off my shoulder. I was going to go home the next day. I said, "My God, if the pitchers are that good, I got no business, you know, trying to make it!" But I had quite a season, you know. I kept all my clippings, and that winter, through a brother who was living in Louisville at the time, I sent him these clippings and he got me a tryout with Louisville in the American Association for '33 and that's where I started.

Once in Cincinnati during the war there was a guy in the stands who was yelling, "Hitler will get you" and things like that, and Dixie Walker was playing right field and he said, "Now, Goody, don't say anything, we'll take care of that so-and-so." So they went and got the police, you know, the park police, ballpark police, and they took that guy and, boy, they gave it to him pretty good. Other than that, honestly, I can truthfully say that in the big leagues, you know, the class of people, the class of players, were pretty good.

My first games were in '37, Crosley Field in Cincinnati. Two left-handed pitchers. I know I got five for eight, or four for seven, either one. I think there was one hundred and thirty-two people in the stands. It was quite a nice feeling. I was leading the league in hitting in 1939 and one day when I was sliding back into first base I tore the ligaments down here. Now being left-handed, that was my hitting leg. So the trainer said I should be out at least ten days. Now, remember, I was leading the league in hitting, [Leo] Durocher was the manager, and he said, "Oh jeez, he's got to play, he's got to play." We had not only a trainer, but we had a bone doctor; I remember his name was Weaver. They said, "Let him rest and he'll be as good as new in about ten days." No, Durocher: "He's got to play, he's got to play, he's got to play, he's my leader." Little did I realize that I was the leader on the team.

Anyway, to make the story short, they used to give me a needle nearly every day and I played on a bad leg. I went from over .400 to about ... don't know what I went down to. One day we were in Pittsburgh. This is, I guess, near the end of June maybe, came to me and said, "We're sending you down to Montreal till your leg gets better." MacPhail was the president then. So I used a few choice words to Durocher. Anyway, I went down to Montreal and I was there a couple of months and got recalled, but I didn't report. I hit over .300 for Montreal. At least I think I did.

But here's where the dirty work came in. I should have been out for at least ten days. I didn't think that they'd do what they did to me. But anyway, in the winter of '39–'40, they sold me to the St. Louis Cardinals, but they didn't tell me they sold me to the Cardinals. He said he sold me to Columbus, but I found out later they actually sold me to the Cardinals. Anyway, I reported to spring training in 1940. Burt Shotton was the manager.

Branch Rickey always liked me. I didn't know it then, but you'll see later that....Anyway, I remember the first day I walked into spring training in 1940. Opening my mouth. Telling Durocher and MacPhail what I thought of them, I got a reputation of being, I don't know, a rebel or whatever. I remember the first day Burt Shotton telling me, "I want to straighten you out!" Well I was pretty small, but I was pretty tough, and I said, "Yeah, you'll straighten me out. I don't know why but you'll straighten me out," meaning, you know. Anyway, he put me through a pretty tough spring training and I didn't like it too much and so.... Anyway, the season opened, and after about five games he got on me and I was going to belt him and instead I said, "Aw, you take it and shove it," and I got dressed and went home, quick. The abuse I was getting, what for, you know.

And I was home a few days and the phone started ringing and it was MacPhail [the Dodgers had sold Rosen conditionally to the Cardinals], telling me what a glorious opportunity I blew. Told me, he said, "You know the Cardinals bought you and they were putting you to the test," and blah-blah-blah-blah, so I hung up the phone on him. Anyway, to make the story short, he kept calling me because, you know, I was worth some money. He says, "You can go anyway you want. Where do you want to play?" I said, "What's in it for me?" you know.

Anyway, I ended up in Syracuse. And I made good money. And I remember, at the end of the '40 season I could have gone back to the big leagues. I was disenchanted and I said, "No, I'll stay here if you'll give me so much next year." I stayed through '43. I was content; I was making good money there. Well, I was probably wrong, but you know. How do I put it? Looking back now, I was probably wrong. See, I was a big fish in a little pond, playing in the International League, and I was probably a little fish playing in a big pond, you know, in the big leagues. But I was making a big-league salary playing for Syracuse. No hassle. I didn't want to go back to the big leagues, let me put it that way.

It was funny how I did go back to the big leagues. It was really funny. The season for 1944. Now I'm dickering for my contract and for the first time he's hedging on giving me an extra amount of money, the guy in Syracuse. Leo Miller, his name was. He was the GM. I says, "All right, you put in my contract 10 percent of my sale price if I'm sold." Well, I guess he said, "Oh, Jeez, we can't lose anything by that," [laughs] so he put it in there. The season was a couple of weeks old and all of a sudden he calls me in the office one day and he said, "Look, I know you don't want to go back to the big leagues," but he says, "there's two clubs that want you pretty bad and they'll pay a lot of money." And he said, "You're going to make yourself a good bonus." You know, he didn't tell me how much they were going to make, you know. So I said, "Who are the two teams?" He says, "Cleveland and Brooklyn."

Well, I called my wife and I told her, I said, "Shall I go back?" She said, "Well, why not?" She said, "how many more years are you going to play anyway?" I said, "I don't know." It was a good deal for me financially. They got $75,000 from Brooklyn for me, so I got $7,500, and I told Miller, I said, "Look, I'll go, but my salary," which at the time was $1,200 a month, I said, "You're paying me $1,800 a month. Remember that." He said, "They can find out if they want." I said, "Well, let them find out, but..." Anyway, I remember walking into Ebbets Field and Branch Rickey was in the press box, the old Ebbets Field, and I remember him saying, "Welcome back to Brooklyn." He says, "You're going to like it here," he says, "I've always had faith in you." He says, "I think you're a good ballplayer and you will help this ballclub. By the way," he said, "How much were you making in Syracuse a month?" So I told him $1,800. Actually, I was getting that much, but part of the deal was under the table. Honestly, Rickey treated me real well. He gave it to me.

Played eighty-nine games in '44. In '45, I hit .325. Brooklyn had an outfielder, Red Durette, he was a center fielder at the start of the season. I don't know, we were playing the Giants, I remember, and I don't know how old the season was, two or three days old, and for lunch he ate some fish and got sick. So I played center field. I think we beat them 4–2 or something and I knocked in the winning run and I got about three hits or something. I don't think I missed an inning, outside of Rosh Hashanah, the rest of the year. As for hitting, that twenty-four doubles, that's wrong. That should be at least forty-two doubles, at least that many. I don't know where you got your stats from.

I won a lot of games for Brooklyn that year. As a matter of fact, I was telling you about Rickey. He tore up my contract in the middle of the season, gave me a new contract, gave me a thousand-dollar bonus.

I'll tell you, Durocher knew baseball, but as a person he wasn't too much. He was probably as intelligent a baseball man as you could find, really. But you meant nothing to him; I meant nothing to him. He wouldn't care about your feelings; you were just a chess piece really. I don't know. I didn't like him too much; I really didn't, but he knew baseball, he really did.

Branch Rickey called me in at the end of the season [1945] and he said to me, "I guess you'll be wanting a lot of money next year." I said, "Yes." "Well," he said, "how do we know this year wasn't a fluke?" "Well," I said, "we don't." I said, "I'm no youngster anymore. If I don't make money now, I never will." He says, "Well, I can't blame you for that." He said, "I'll tell you," he says, "I'll sign you at the money you want." We'd been talking and dickering a bit. He said, "But the first chance I get," he says, "I want to trade or sell you because I have three good young outfielders coming up." One was Duke Snider, one was Carl Furillo, and the other one escapes my mind. He says, "I think I would take a chance with them." So I says, "That's up to you." But I made a mistake in spring training, you know, in '46. I didn't get into good shape. You know, I was waiting for him to trade or sell me, and instead of working my ass off and getting into real good shape, I kind of dogged it. The result was, the season opened and about ten days later I was sold over to the Giants.

I used to buy the *Mirror* every day and I'd always read the front page and then turn over to the back page. I read the front page and I turn over to the back page, "Rosen sold to the Giants." Jesus, all of a sudden [laughs] it hit me. That's how I found out I was traded. My first games for the Giants were a doubleheader. I got about seven hits. I was up to bat about eleven times. I got seven or eight hits, on base by an error once and two walks. I hit a three-run homer to win the second game. But what happened, not being in shape and it was a muddy day, by the time the second game was over I walked down the center field there and I was walking about like this. I had what they call muscle seizure and I didn't realize it. I was afraid to tell Ott [Mel Ott, then the Giants' manager], you know, I was ashamed of myself, you know. I was ashamed because I wasn't in shape.

Anyway, I remember the trainer. I can't think of his name. Shaffer or something like that. So we were leaving to go on a road trip about three hours later after the ballgame. We're going to St. Louis, the Western swing. Saint Louis, Cincinnati, Chicago, and Pittsburgh, then back home. And Jesus, I don't know how I got by in St. Louis, but I did, you know, and then we went to Cincinnati. I got by there somehow. In Chicago, I was starting to feel a bit better, you know, I as working hard and getting my legs in shape a little bit. Pittsburgh, I was just starting to feel real good. I remember the first time up that day I smashed one that was a base hit. In about the fifth inning.... Sid Gordon, you know, he could have helped there a little bit, but what the hell. I dove for the ball and suffered a severe sprain of the outer clavicle. If I'd have broke my shoulder I'd have been all right, but I didn't. I couldn't run for twelve weeks because of the jarring motion. That put a finish on my baseball. I couldn't raise this arm up for five years like I'm doing now. I could get it up to about here, shoulder high.

You know who was a great ballplayer? I don't know how intelligent he was, but, Jesus, he was a real good hitter, was Joe Medwick, who played for the Cardinals and later Durocher got him for the Dodgers. He was a good hitter, strong hitter. Yogi Berra was a real good hitter, good hitter. Joe DiMaggio was probably the greatest.

Another of the greatest hitters, I say this sincerely, probably better than any day in and day out, was Stan Musial. But we were talking the other day; I was talking with somebody and discussing the great hitters of baseball that never gained maybe a lot of mention. There was one that played for the Cardinals, Johnny Mize. He was a great hitter. I don't think he was too smart, but by God, he could hit.

I had the good fortune to one year playing for Brooklyn, and Babe Herman was a utility player and he taught me more about hitting in a couple months than I knew in 15 years. He was a great natural hitter. He was the fellow that got hit in the head or something with a flyball in the outfield.

In the big leagues and in Triple-A baseball, you never got anti–Semitism, if you will. But I'll tell you, in my time I can recall down in Florida seeing "Restricted." The son of a bitch that owned the Syracuse ballclub. It was a German bastard. Name was Schindler, I remember that. I remember this one year I'd taken Molly [his wife] down to spring training with our son and I needed some money, and I remember going over to where he was living and I remember seeing on the lawn "Restricted." From that day on I couldn't look at him. I'll tell you, I never looked for anti–Semitism; I never carried a chip on my shoulder, but if I ran into anybody that was, boy, I would let them know one way or another, I'll tell you.

I think today at my age [knocks on wood], thank God, I've never been sick a day in my life and I still hit par fives on a golf course and two on a lot of them, still shoot in the seventies. Smoking cigars is one of my bad habits. I smoke about twelve a day. Very expensive habit. I drink a little bit. I never drank as a youngster though. But I have a wonderful wife. We're married forty-seven years and the happiest years of my life.

SAM NAHEM

Brooklyn Dodgers, 1938;
St. Louis Cardinals, 1941;
Philadelphia Phillies, 1942, 1948

(1915–2004)

Sam Nahem grew up in a Syrian Jewish neighborhood in Brooklyn where the first language was Arabic. A law school graduate and licensed attorney, he pitched parts of four seasons in the big leagues sandwiched around a military hitch. After hanging up his spikes in 1948, he moved his family from New York to San Francisco, where he was a longtime organizer and activist for the Oil, Chemical and Atomic Workers Union. He was interviewed in October 2003.

There's one joke I repeat, and it's always good. I was pitching for the Dodgers in spring training camp, and they hit the crap out of me. And that's a big job, because I have a lot of crap in me. The next day, a reporter for the *New York Daily News* says, "What are you doing now?' and I say, "I am in the egregiously anonymous position of pitching batting practice to the batting practice pitchers." That made the *New York Daily News* and its two million circulation. That was around 1940.

When I was a kid, we played in the sandlots; there were still sandlots at that time. One day I went for a tryout with the Dodgers with Casey Stengel. I drilled the Dodgers' best pitcher, Van Lingle Mungo—remember him? And after I finished the tryout, he [Stengel] put his hand on my ass and said, "If you can hurt that big son of a bitch, you must have something on the ball. We'll try you out in spring training." I told my mother I was going to play ball, and she said, "You're grown up already. What are you

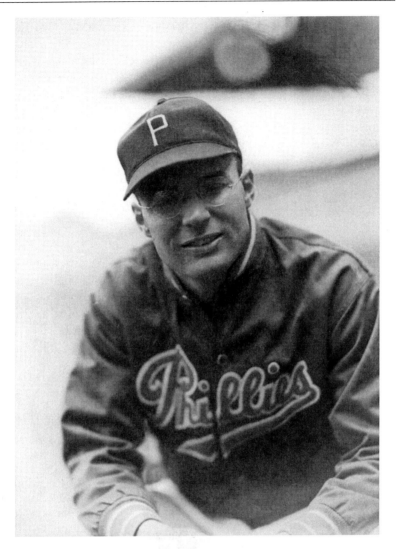

Sam Nahem, who pitched for the Philadelphia Phillies in 1942 and 1948, says he was the first to throw a slider.

doing playing ball?" And I said, "Ma, I'm going to make $150 a week!" She said, "Go play ball!"

By age twenty-two or twenty-three, I had already graduated from St. John's law school. I was the first Syrian Jewish lawyer and baseball player.

I went up gradually in the minor leagues to the big leagues. I had a sensational debut with the Cardinals. We had five rookie pitchers, all of whom made the big leagues later, trying for two jobs. So the manager called me in from practice to talk to me; he sent a batboy out. And I figured, "Oh boy, I'm done." And he said, "Sam, you're pitching today; it's your chance." Somehow I pitched the best game I'd ever pitched in the big leagues. There's something in the blood that inspires me in certain moments. It was a three-hitter, and I beat the Pittsburgh Pirates. I was on the Cards at the time, and Pittsburgh had beaten us by about fifteen runs the day before. It was quite a good debut. And the interesting thing is, with one really well-pitched game, you can stay in the big leagues for a year at least. Other teams may take a chance on you thinking, "At least he did it."

On the Cardinals were Terry Moore, Lon Warnecke, Mort and Walker Cooper. I remember I got a new concept of pitching watching Lon Warnecke, a veteran of twenty years. And I saw that it wasn't like how I pitched them: High, low, inside, outside. He threw low *and* inside, high *and* outside. He threw inside and he threw outside. This farmer had a theory of pitching far more complicated than me, a law school graduate and bar-passer first crack. And his theory was really fascinating. Balance is everything in hitting, and if you can get the guy just a tip off balance, that really does something.

I had just-above-mediocre stuff. Just enough to flash at times. Luckily, I'd made my impression and that lasted me for a year. So I managed to survive a little while. But if I executed what I understand now, I could have been quite a decent pitcher. I had enough stuff to be a fairly good pitcher.

I learned later they were stealing my pitches. They had coaches watching, and they found that when I pitched my fastball, my arm went up *so* high [he demonstrates] and when I pitched my curveball, my arm went *so* high [he demonstrates again]. They spotted it and it was easy to spot. If I had some decent coaches, they would have spotted it, too. We had coaches, but they caught batting practice. Now they have things really different. They have dossiers on every batter in the league. They know all the weaknesses and the strengths. It's a different game. I'm not saying it's a better game or there were better players back then. I don't know that.

College players are a big farm for Major League Baseball today, but they were not interested then. They weren't paying much: My first salary for the Cards was $3,200 from Branch Rickey. That was much less than normal jobs.

I heard a story about Jackie Robinson, where someone sneaked to his hotel room door, maybe even one of his teammates, and put his shoes out in front of Jackie's room to be shined. I was in a fairly strange position. The majority of my fellow ballplayers were very much against black baseball players, and the reason was economics and very clear. They knew they had the ability to be up there and they knew their jobs were directly threatened by these guys coming in there. So they very vehemently did all these things to discourage black ballplayers. But, you know, it was obvious to everybody that black ballplayers had the ability. Satchel Paige was one of the first to break the barrier and he finally pitched in the big leagues. But it was already obvious. Why shouldn't these guys be as good as white ballplayers?

There were only sixteen teams. The majority were afraid of seeing their jobs threatened by black players, even though they knew it was right. I did my political work there. I would take one guy aside if I thought he was amiable, and talk to him, man to man, about that subject in the way I felt could be most effective.

Anti-Semitism was there, but they didn't make it very vocal. I especially made sure I tipped as much or more than the other players. I was aware that I was a Jewish player and different from them. There were very few Jewish players at the time. I don't blame the other players at all. Many of them came from where they probably had never met a Jewish person. You know, they subscribed to that anti–Semitism that was latent throughout the country. I fought it whenever I appeared. There was this one guy who was always anti–Semitic, and I had to keep putting him now. I imagined he had it ingrained in him, for Christ's sake. Much of it was implicit: Jews and money. Jews and selfishness.

I played in South America. South America was bringing in players and paying them nice money in winter. They had leagues there and $600 a month was big bucks.

Day for a ballplayer consisted of chasing girls. And I remember then that even very almost-ethical guys would chase women. The class of women in big league baseball was higher than in the minor leagues. This was another reason to aspire to the big leagues. If I had a date, it'd be after a night game.

I wore glasses as a player. There were very few of us who wore glasses, very few. And I was bald-headed then. Or euphemistically, you could say I had dome hair, but only euphemistically.

How many of us regret that in their younger days they could have etter when a crisis arose, could have written better, could have done ? I could have been a better pitcher if I executed better. I was a smart pitcher out there, but at the last second, I wouldn't have confidence in my control, so I would forget to pitch high or low or outside and just try to get it over the plate.

I just didn't have that much confidence in my ability. I'd been beaten too much. What sport puts a player out there so when he's knocked out of the box the manager has to come out and get him? I used to propose a trap door lead right up to the toilet so when a pitcher knocked out, rather than have him face humiliation while walking from the mound to the bench you could just have a trap door. [laughs] Down and into the toilet. Yes, we look for realism. It had its moment in American literature. And I am the de Maupassant of baseball.

In World War II, I volunteered for the infantry, but I was "limited service." When the Bulge came, the opened it up to limited service — it was my eyesight — and I volunteered. I got across the Atlantic, but by that time the war had ended, so there I was entertaining troops. I led a group of integrated ballplayers and we played a team that was composed of strictly big league baseball players. We brought them all together and we played for the championship and my team won it. A lot of the teams were not integrated — and that was tough.

The only reason I had any fame is I was one of the first to use a slider. It's halfway between a fastball and a curve. You have to cut it, sort of. Burleigh Grimes was managing up in Montreal and he taught me the slider and that's where I got any fame I got. Burleigh Grimes was the last legal spitballer. [Major League Baseball outlawed the spitball in 1920, but pitchers who were using the pitch were allowed to use it until they retired.] I saw guys do everything. Spitball pitchers managed to get some of that spit on their fingers or kept some in their pockets — anything to make a living.

After baseball, I got married. My wife had never been outside New York City. I had two kids [and a third, after he moved to California]. Why not go out West? Some people I knew were out here, so I did. I got very interested in unionism, and I became a union leader for the Oil, Chemical and Atomic Workers of America. If you're from New York and Jewish, you're political.

I passed the bar the first time, but I never practiced law. I couldn't get into the area that I wanted to, which was civil liberties. At that time, law school was tough, and all the Harvard and Yale boys wanted jobs in civil liberties and all that. Here I was from the St. John's School of Law! I'm a left winger from New York, and my son Ivan is a big psychiatrist on Wall Street! My daughter, Joanne, is a psychiatrist and I have a son Andrew, who is a commercial artist. [Nahem's wife, Elsie, died of cancer in the 1970s.]

Baseball is one of those things in your life that passes and you don't go back to. It marks a period of my life that was there and now it's over. It was there, in my feckless youth. Feckless. Spell it right. I don't want to get the reputation of being a miserable rascal.

And mostly in the big leagues, I was not happy. You know, I wasn't a natural woman hunter and most ballplayers, even successfully married ones, were skirt chasers, they really were. I wasn't too happy at that. We traveled a lot; we didn't have a stable place to stay. One day I'd pitch OK in relief, the next day they'd hit the shit out of me. It's hard to be happy in something you're doing in just a mediocre way.

The last baseball game I went to was about twenty years ago. It was against the Phillies and I was with my brother who was equally as bald as I am. In the middle of the game, a foul ball went up and the catcher threw off his mask and he was bald! And my brother and I leapt up and yelled, "Hey baldie!" on the field.

Other fans around us didn't know what to think. Here are two bald-headed guys denouncing a bald guy. I'm offered free tickets all the time, but it's sort of like one of those things that's passed in life. About five years ago, a promoter offered me $1,000 to go back East to sign autographs. And that's the last real contact I've had with baseball. But who I am to complain if someone wants my autograph? What kind of egotistical ass am I? Shakespeare?

CY BLOCK
Chicago Cubs, 1942, 1945–1946
(1919–2004)

Maybe God looked down and said, "Block, you know, you should have been a helluva ballplayer," and he waved his hand, and whatever I was supposed to do in baseball happened to me in insurance. — Cy Block, interviewed in June 1987

My two brothers once took me to Ebbets Field. That day, I saw Dazzy Vance, and I fell in love with the Brooklyn Dodgers. And when I was ten years old, I decided I wanted to be a Major League baseball player.

I was raised in Brooklyn in a semi–Orthodox family. My mother was the matriarch of the family: my family brought everybody in from Russia. And every Friday night they met at my mother's house: all the sisters and the aunts and uncles, and we were brought up in a traditional way. I didn't go to the Talmud Torah [Jewish school]. I went to the regular school, but I went to the shul [synagogue], just like all the other kids.

I've always observed the High Holidays, and when I was with the Cubs and Rosh Hashanah came, I didn't play. I never played on Yom Kippur; that's a decision that you make yourself. Actually when I played ball, there were only about five Jewish ballplayers, and I normally would be the only Jewish ballplayer in the league, not just on the team. Everybody came to see the Jew second baseman. It was tough. Everybody was trying to knock me down, but that was part of making it. And I always felt that if I could play good ball and overcome it, they'd forget that they were watching somebody "with horns" or a Jewish player, and it worked out for me.

One of the few negative experiences I had, I was playing in Blytheville, Arkansas, in 1938. This pitcher knocked me down three times in a row. I mean, in those days they left your hat standing. I called timeout and I went over to the pitcher. I said to him, "The next time you blow me down, I'm dropping a bunt and you won't pitch for the rest of your life." And I had no trouble with him after that.

The next time I had a bad situation was in Augusta, Georgia, where Eddie Stanky was playing short alongside me. This guy came into second base and he really undressed me. He came in spikes high. I thought I was dead. He took my uniform off, but I didn't have a scratch. But he really undressed me. Stanky said, "He's mine." I said, "Nobody fights my battles." Stanky said, "That son of a bitch is a good ballplayer. He's gonna be back here." I said, "I'll take care of him." And about the sixth inning, here he came. I let him slide in, and I took that ball and I popped him right in the mouth. I knocked out six teeth, and then word went around: "Don't fool with the Jew — he fights back."

I had one guy who used to call me "Dollar Ninety-five," but that didn't happen much, no way. I never had that in the years I played. And I mean I played in Greenville, Mississippi; Paragould, Arkansas; Georgia. Fans are fans. You always have a few, but most of the fans in Paragould, Arkansas, were very good. The church even gave me a night. They gave it to me when I went back to Memphis to play for the Chicks. For thirty years, I corresponded with them. I had incidents, but that's part of life. Whoever says in life that's everything going to go smoothly?

My wife, Harriet, traveled with me eight years. We were married in 1943. She traveled with me all over. I had one daughter; she traveled with me for five years. My wife said that as long as I play professional baseball, she would only have one child. She wouldn't travel with more than one, and when I quit baseball, she said I could have as many as I wanted. We had two more after I quit. We had a few incidents when we traveled, when they found out we were Jewish. But most of the time, we were fine. We had very good experiences; whenever we got thrown out — we had maybe two incidents in the years when they found out we were Jewish and they asked us to move — the Baptists always took us in. That's why I voted for Jimmy Carter.

They were out to get me. It was that easy. But that was it. It's a matter of getting respect, and I got my respect. And then look, do you think I had it tough? Jackie Robinson — forget it! That man was a saint. Boy, what he went through! People used to walk up to him and spit on him. People on his own club never talked to him. So I had it easy compared to him.

I'll say this much: as a Jew, you couldn't participate in drinking, you couldn't participate in card games. I was a Dick Tracy. I just didn't want

Cy Block was an infielder with the Chicago Cubs in 1942, 1945, and 1946.

to get involved where they'd be in a position to say: "The Jew won in cards." I didn't need that, so I just stayed away.

In '42, Stan Musial and I were voted the two best rookies in the National League. I hit .364 [in 33 at-bats], but went into the service for those three years, and that was it. When I came out, I was just a cup-of-coffee ballplayer. I don't know; I just feel I have a deep belief in God in here [points to head] and here [points to heart], and I felt that I should have been a helluva ballplayer. But I never got that shot, and maybe God looked down and said, "Block, you know, you should have been a helluva ballplayer," and he waved his hand, and whatever I was supposed to do in baseball happened to me in insurance.

We were invited down to the White House for a reunion. Reagan used to announce the games for radio station WHO in Des Moines, Iowa. So six of us went down — Lennie Merullo, Bill Nicholson, Hank Borowy ... the Emil Verban Society [named for a journeyman Chicago Cubs player of the 1940s]. They had four hundred fifty people. They were asking me questions — it was funny as hell. In fact, one of the guys at the luncheon said to me, "Block, with your record, how come you really never got to play?"

Well, I came back out of service in the Coast Guard in 1946. The first day we opened up, Phil Cavaretta broke his ankle, and a kid by the name of Eddie Waitkus got a chance to play, and he became a star. Herman was traded to Brooklyn, and Lou Stringer, out of Los Angeles, got to play, and he became a star. Jurges pulled a muscle, and Lennie Merullo— out of Villanova — got to play, and became a star. And our center fielder, Charley Gilbert, dove for a ball and broke his thumb, and Andy Pafko, who nobody ever heard of, played.

And Stan Hack [then the star third baseman for the Cubs]? He played every day. That son of a bitch! It was unbelievable. I used to watch and watch, and I used to pray: "Let him break a finger!" He played every day. I used to get so desperate I'd go in the shower with Hack and I'd drop the soap. Maybe something would happen. So now 35 years go by, and this is the question they ask me. I never got to play; I played 17 games. What are you going to do? And in 1980, we have the Old-Timers Game and [former Cubs manager Charley] Grimm is the manager. He's eighty-five now, and he calls the lineup and he says, "Block, third base." And I said, "Grimm, what's with this third base? You haven't played me in thirty-five years." He says, "You're getting your chance. Hack is dead!" It took down the house.

During my time, there was Hank Greenberg, Sid Gordon. There was Cal Abrams, Mickey Rutner, myself, Saul Rogovin, Joe Ginsberg, Morrie Arnovich, Goody Rosen. There were maybe ten or eleven. That's all. Harry Danning. Harry Feldman was a hell of a pitcher. Lou Limmer played for me in Puerto Rico. He could have been one of the best first basemen in the business. All he had to do was not think. I had him in Puerto Rico and he's looking for signs, and I said, "Limmer, do me a favor. Just hit the ball." He hit thirty-seven homers for me there. Had a good year in Puerto

Rico. He was a helluva ballplayer; he never got a decent shot. Backup —
in between — he didn't really get a shot.

Cal Abrams was a helluva ballplayer. He didn't get much of a shot.
What call I tell you? He was hitting about .450. He went 0-for-4 and they
benched him. And at that time, Gil Hodges went 0-for-44 and played every
day. Abrams, if he had gotten a shot, he really would have been one of the
top stars. I liked Cal — good arm, good hitter. I would say Cal was the
same type of player as Willie McGee. Exactly the same type of ballplayer.
He didn't steal as many bases, but he had as good an arm.

AL ROSEN
Cleveland Indians, 1947–1956
(1924–)

For several years during the 1950s, Al Rosen was one of the best players in Major League Baseball. The American League MVP in 1953, when he narrowly missed the Triple Crown, Rosen was a feared slugger and run producer, a leader of the Cleveland Indians team that went to the World Series in 1954. During his career, Rosen made four All-Star teams and batted .285 with 192 home runs. He was also known as a tough guy who wouldn't back down from a fight. After injuries forced his early retirement from baseball at the age of 32, Rosen went on to a successful career as a stockbroker and baseball executive. When this interview was conducted in the spring and summer of 1978, Rosen was the president of the New York Yankees.

I was a Jew and I was well groomed, rather articulate, rather intelligent, representing a minority, doing so well that I was receiving all sorts of awards and recognition with plaques and dinners and the whole thing, and because I was handling myself properly it had to be a great feeling for Jews who were sports followers. Listen, you'd be amazed. I'm sure that if you look around, there are a lot of Al Rosen Schwartzes, you know. It's just something that happens, and it happened to me because that era was my era.

I was born in 1924 in Spartanburg, South Carolina, which was a small town at the time. About 50,000 people. It's grown dramatically since then. We moved through the South, lived for a time in Waycross, Georgia, Macon, Georgia, Jacksonville, Florida, and on down to Miami. At that time, my father and mother were not seeing eye to eye and there'd been a split. Eventually a divorce ensued and we wound up living in Miami with my mother's mother, my grandmother, and her younger sister, my aunt.

I had to be four or five years old because my younger brother, who is four years younger than I, was born in Miami.

We were better than poor and less than middle class. Of course, neither one of my parents went to college. However like most families in those times, we were very close-knit, and the money was pooled and everybody worked and somehow we survived.

It wasn't a kosher home. We observed holidays, and my brother and I went to Sunday school at Temple Israel, in the Northwest section. I was not Bar Mitzvahed or confirmed; my brother was. I had no contact with the Jewish community except Sunday morning when I had to go to Sunday school. My grandmother spoke broken English. She had been born in Warsaw. There was some Yiddish; there was some Yiddish around, mostly expressions as opposed to long dialogue. But that was it.

I saw my father last when I was eight, and the next time I saw him was in 1947 when I played in New York against the Yankees when I came up, and I hadn't seen him or heard from him during that period, so you know, both my brother and I lived without that advantage. I was asthmatic, and in those days you didn't have the sophisticated medicines and treatments, and the doctors told my mother that I would have to spend as much time outside as possible. I was very young, very young, when I was diagnosed as asthmatic. As a matter of fact, there were some very hairy moments where I was concerned because there were some times that there was some doubt as to whether I'd survive. Playing ball didn't aggravate it, though. I must have been in my early twenties or so when I finally got to the point that I just stopped taking the medication, you know.

I began to play at a very early age in semipro leagues, men's leagues, and it was because of playing in a men's league during the summer that I received a scholarship to a military academy, Florida Military Academy in St. Pete. You know, after all, only rich kids went to military school, and it was a tremendous opportunity. I was a little lackadaisical about my studies until I went to military school because things were very easy for me. My whole life revolved around football, basketball, baseball, and boxing, from the time I could first remember how to put on a pair of cleats. But when I went to military school, I was 3.8. I was good enough that they suggested I take the exams for West Point, and then I decided not to.

I met a man by the name of Herb Pennock, and Herb Pennock was a former Yankee pitcher, had been in charge of the Red Sox farm system, and that's how I got started. In 1941, I went to a spring training camp, a minor league spring training camp, and worked out with the Cleveland

Al Rosen won the MVP for the Cleveland Indians in 1953. A former amateur boxer, Rosen wasn't shy about using his fists to confront a player who made an anti-Semitic taunt.

Indians, was offered a contract, a Class D contract, with Thomasville, North Carolina, for $75 a month, with no signing bonus [laughs]. Elected not to do it. I went to the University of Florida — I wanted to go to school and I had a scholarship from a fraternity house there if I would compete in athletics—for one year and wasn't very interested and didn't do well, but when I went to the University of Miami I did very well.

After competing in athletics at Florida, I decided definitely I wanted to go into baseball. At that time, I contacted Herb Pennock, who sent me to Suffolk, Virginia, where the minor-league farm clubs of the Boston Red Sox were working out, and I was working out with a Class C team that was in one of the leagues up there. I forget which one, but they had a manager and a third baseman by the name of Elmer Yoter. After I worked out for about a week, Yoter called me up to his hotel room and said, "Son, I don't think you're ever going to be a ballplayer. You ought to get your lunch pail and go on home."

I never did know why he said that, but a bird-dog scout by the name of Frank Stein, who was the director of the local YMCA and had been following the workouts, and I got in touch with each other through one of the fellows on the team, and Frank couldn't understand at all because he thought that I looked like I had some talent, and he suggested that I go down, and believe it or not, it's the truth, to Thomasville, North Carolina, which was the team that the year before I had been offered a contract for $75 a month.

Well, I was going to go back to college in the off-season. I knew I was going to go into the service because, you know, of what happened. So I got on a bus, I forget, it must have been about four or five hours. I got off the bus, and as in most small towns in North Carolina there was always one industry, and I remember the Thomasville Furniture Factory being on one side of the tracks, and on the other side was a little town, about two square blocks really, the downtown area, and as ballplayers would tell you in those days, the place to go to find out anything about baseball was to go to the local café.

I walked into a place called Nance's Café, and I had my little bag and my shoes were outside. And when I walked in, there was a fellow who was not really ... he was not all intact, but he did hang around the ballplayers. I remember we called him "Sailor." And I said, "Where do I find the manager of the ballclub?" He said, "Why?" I said, "Well, I came down to see if I could get a job." He said, "What position do you play?" I said, "I'm an infielder." And Sailor took off out the front door and he came back about three minutes later and said, "Come on, I'll take you to the manager." And I went around the corner and there in the gas station getting his car filled with gas was the manager, Jimmy Guzdis.

I sat in the front seat with Jimmy and I signed a contract right then and there for $90 a month. I sent $20 of it home every month. I had room and board for $7 a week and they even threw in the laundry. I went out and put on a uniform, and I remember I got a base hit the first time at bat.

Once the season was over, I went back to school. After I completed a semester at the University of Miami, I think, or was it two, the V-12 program enlisted young college men for their officer training, and because of the large numbers you were left in your college or you were sent to a college where there would be a certain amount of ROTC training, and the University of Miami was one of those schools, so I remained right there. I finally went up to Plattsburg, New York, where I was in the V-12 program and was graduated an ensign, was sent to Fort Pierce, Florida, where we were put into small-boat training. Those are the small boats that you saw, the invasion, you know, carrying personnel and equipment onto the beaches.

I served aboard ship, made one invasion at Okinawa. We took the poor guys in to the beach and we were there on D-Day. I remember Easter Sunday when the planes were coming over. We made the one invasion and we were around Okinawa for seven days, and like everybody else who's ever been in combat, I was scared, but yet it's a different kind of fear because there's sort of a feeling that there's not a damn thing you can do about where you are. I really hesitate to discuss it.

I think that anyone who was Jewish in those days that wasn't deeply affected by the 6 million Jews that went to the gas chambers and ovens would have to be some kind of idiot, blathering idiot. So that yes, of course, it affected me.

I got my discharge at the Jacksonville naval station. I reported to Sumter, South Carolina, where Indians minor leaguers were supposed to report, in my Navy blues. I was still under contract to the Cleveland organization because the team I played for in 1942, Thomasville, was a Cleveland farm club. I was placed on the Harrisburg roster, which was a Class B team. But they made their cuts and the Cleveland organization said that I was to play at Pittsfield, Massachusetts. I went up to Pittsfield, very unhappy about the classification, and actually I was ready to quit.

And I went into a diner and there was a scout, a Cleveland scout by the name of Laddie Placek, and Laddie Placek and I sat down and had a cup of coffee and I told him that I was going to go home and he implored me not to. He said that you have all the abilities to be a Major League ballplayer, you'd be crazy, you just have to give it time and, you know, you can't be too anxious.

I was always looked up by, you know, Jewish families. I think there is a natural affinity amongst the Jews to remain close and to take care of theirs, and so they invite you to dinner and that sort of thing. You know, there's always, "Would you like to go to temple?" or "Can you come by for Sunday brunch?" Oh, I accepted, absolutely. Sure, I accepted invitations from people and I always enjoyed meeting people in the community. You didn't meet a great many now; don't misunderstand me. You'd do more in the Major League cities because you become involved in the community, you become involved in the lifestyle of the community. But in the minor leagues, it was just nice, people befriended you. They saw you as a young Jewish boy, that kind of thing.

The Jews have always had slang names attached to them, "kike" and "sheeny" and stuff like that, and sometimes offhand a guy will say it, that's not his feeling at all. It's just something he's heard and he's mad or aggravated. If he repeats it or he continues in that vein, then you realize that it's a different situation. But there are a lot of people that I consider good friends of mine that at one time or another have made what could be construed as an anti–Semitic remark. I didn't take it as that. Listen, we referred to DiMaggio as the "Big Dago." One day I took another player and Bob Lemon out to Park Synagogue for a father-son breakfast in Cleveland and both those fellows wore yarmulkes out of respect for the synagogue. That's the kind of relationship I had with them. I mean, I could say to Bob, "Hey, you got to wear the skullcap today," and he put it on.

Of course, I have, I've been judged because I was a Jew. After all, I was in the newspapers every day in every town I was ever in. Naturally, I'm judged as a Jew. My name is Rosen. I have a Semitic look. I certainly didn't expect anybody to think I was anything but a Jew. Sure you hear from the stands. Sure, you hear it, and you ignore it because all you do is provoke it if you take great offense.

I would not play on the High Holy Days. I just merely stated my position, and that was it. Nobody ever questioned me about it.

My first Major League at-bat was at Yankee Stadium in 1947. After we completed my season at Oklahoma City in the Texas League, I was called up by the Cleveland baseball club. It was my first meeting with Bill Veeck, who was then the owner of the Cleveland baseball club, and Bill requested that instead of flying direct from Oklahoma City to New York I fly by way of Chicago, and he met me at six o'clock in the morning, and if you know Bill Veeck, he lost a leg, and there he was, the owner of the ballclub, meeting me, gave me a check for a thousand dollars, which was more money than I'd ever seen. He took me out to breakfast.

I then flew to New York and I made my first appearance here at Yankee Stadium, and the first pitcher I faced was Joe Page, who at that time was the premier relief pitcher in baseball. I struck out, incidentally. I went to bat, oh, five or six, seven, eight more times during the season, then the next year I went to spring training with Cleveland. The manager of the team was Lou Boudreau, and he treated me with disdain. I don't know why. I can't get into another man's personality; I just don't want to comment on that. Lou was a man who liked veteran ballplayers around.

At first, you're a little awed. I must admit that when I walked up to home plate for the first time at Yankee Stadium, my knees were rubbery and I couldn't spit anything but cotton. I'm playing in the, you know, the great Yankee Stadium, and my first at-bat was against Page. But after a while you get to the point where you aren't overawed by it because now you're one of them, you're accomplishing and you're on a first-name basis and you realize that they're guys just like anybody else and they pull their pants on one leg at a time.

Forty-eight was my first spring training with the club but it was very frustrating because Cleveland had a fine third baseman by the name of Kenny Keltner, and I recognized that early on no matter what I did I wouldn't be a member of that club. I didn't expect it after I was in spring training for one day. I mean I knew that there was no way to do that. I recognized I was going to be optioned out to further my skills and I was sent to Kansas City. That was a Triple-A club, it was a New York Yankee farm club, and there was a deal that Veeck made with the Yankees: He acquired a pitcher by the name of Charlie Winslow, a right-handed pitcher, from New York, and part of the deal was that I would play the entire season at Kansas City, and I was led to believe that the reason was that the Yankees wanted to take a good, hard look with the idea of keeping me. But I had the kind of year there that Veeck couldn't trade me. I had a great year. I was MVP. I was a mediocre fielder, but I was working to improve that.

I was called up in August. I sustained an injury to my right knee sliding into second base and it was obvious I couldn't play anymore for Kansas City, so Veeck called me up, first of all, to make sure that I was getting the proper treatment on my knee, and, second of all, if I was all right and got better, that I could play a little bit for the Cleveland ballclub because they were fighting for the pennant. That was the year, if you recall, the Boston Red Sox and Cleveland wound up in a tie, had a playoff game in Boston which Cleveland won, and then the World Series against the Boston Braves. Even though I played, I was on the roster for the team that won the World Series, I still didn't feel a part of it, an integral part of it, because I hadn't been there all year and I hadn't contributed a great deal.

In '49, I was terribly frustrated because I thought I could play better than Keltner. I went to spring training again, stayed with the ballclub until July 3, sitting on the bench, not playing a great deal, but when I played I produced, and then on July 3 the decision was made to option me out to San Diego. In '49, Keltner got hurt, Lou Boudreau had gotten heavy, and the decision was made by Bill Veeck to move Lou Boudreau to third base and to play a young rookie shortstop by the name of Ray Boone at short. And Bill called me in and discussed it and told me what they were going to do, and of course I was terribly disappointed. But I went out and what happened was that Boudreau could not play third base effectively, Boone could not play shortstop effectively, Boudreau eventually had to go back to shortstop, and they wound up the season playing Bob Kennedy and Johnny Beradino, both journeyman players, at third base.

They lost the pennant by six games. Chances are, had I been there, they may very well have won the pennant because I thought I was ready. But because of the option rules and when you can send a man out and recall him and things like that, they couldn't get me back. You don't know whether we'd have made up the six games with my playing, but it is a fact that the following year I did the league in home runs with thirty-seven as a rookie. And I drove in well over 100 runs and hit close to ... somewhere around .288 or .285, somewhere in there.

In 1950, I went to spring training, didn't play at all. Keltner was still there, I was feeling very low, and on the barnstorming trip back Kenny was playing third base in Wichita against the New York Giants; he fell down fielding two ground balls. That night we went to Topeka, and at 10:30, Ray Boone and I walked into the coffee shop at the hotel, and Marsh Samuel, who was then the PR man for the Indians, said, "Congratulations." I said, "On what?" He said, "You're the third baseman." Well, I almost fell down because they had decided to give Kenny Keltner his release. Fortunately, I got off on the right foot and I wound up having a good season, which has been documented in the record books. I led the league in home runs, hit the most home runs of any American Leaguer in history in his first year. The team, unfortunately, didn't do well. We did better the next year.

Tris Speaker was at Cleveland when I first came up and he was tremendous. He was sort of a free lance. Tris was one of the great center fielders of all time and working for the ballclub, and he used to come down to spring training — and he used to be out at batting practice and things like that and we discussed hitting. I was very fortunate; one season that I

80

played there we had a coach by the name of Al Simmons, and Al was one of the great right-handed hitters of all time, played for the Athletics. I had the native intelligence to be able to sift through and to pick out those things that fit my style, I didn't try to be something that I wasn't, but there were certain things that Al Simmons taught me that I found to be very valuable tools in hitting. One was that you change your stance a little bit, you get different pitchers, different styles, different counts, how they like to pitch you in places like that, how you would adjust, maybe choking the bat a little more than normal, whether you would open the stance a little or close the stance or move closer to the pitcher or move off the plate a little, and he was a great one for that. And Tris Speaker was a great one who talked about how you level off your swing. Through conversation with him, I used to take a bat home and swing it 100 times a night.

Well, I developed what I considered a level swing, that kind of thing. Then, of course, Hank Greenberg was instrumental in my moving up on the plate, getting right on top of the plate, and his theory was that no hitter can handle both corners of the plate, so you have to make up your mind which one of the corners you're going to give the pitcher. His theory was simple: He said that they never could throw or they wouldn't throw curveballs on the inside part; they'd throw nothing but fastballs and sinkers in there, he said, but on the outside part they can throw sliders, curveballs, fastballs, and he said it made more sense, to him at least, to give him the inside part. If he made a real good pitch on you on the inside corner of the plate, you'd have trouble handling it, but you could handle everything else. And so, you know, I put all these things together and developed my own style. If you're going to ask for advice, you might as well go to the top.

Even when I was a kid playing high school ball, I had more power than the other guys, and even though I wasn't big — as a matter of fact, when I first got to the big leagues ... I'm only 5-10 and a half, but when I first got to the Big Leagues I weighed 175, so I was never known for size. They said you could always tell from my hands. I was strong in the forearms and hands and wrists, and I guess that must be it.

The black players on the team were treated shabbily. Particularly at spring training time when we traveled through the South on trains, and we played in some of these southern towns and sometimes we spent the night and they weren't allowed to stay in the hotels, they weren't allowed to ride in the taxi cabs — and it was a horrendous experience for them. And I always felt very badly about it and you might say, "Well, what did you do about it?" Well, there's very little that can be done in a situation like that. Sociological changes hadn't taken place in the South as yet, and therefore they were treated differently. They were revered on the ballfield for their exploits by the whites. But they were not treated as equals any other place. Those were the days when the blacks did not stay in hotels and they didn't eat in downtown restaurants with you. You know, it was a very bad situation.

The word "wary" could be utilized to describe the relationship between blacks and whites on the team. I think that the biggest problem on the team was the relationship between the blacks and the Latin Americans. Because so many of the Latins were very dark, but they didn't want to be known as blacks, and playing alongside the blacks, it's sort of pinpointed. I think the whites and the blacks got along better, although there was ... you know, there's never been a situation yet where ... at least at that time, where there was total acceptance by either party.

We were bridesmaids to the Yankees. Those were the years that the Yankees put together five consecutive pennant winners, '49 through '53. We felt very frustrated. We thought we had as good a club as the Yankees, and each year we would lose out to them by a game, two or three games. We finally broke that spell in 1954 when we won one hundred eleven games. But we lost four straight to the Giants. Well, I guess it wasn't our time on earth. Vic Wertz hit a ball in the first game against the Giants in the Polo Grounds that traveled well over 500 feet that Willie Mays caught, and then Dusty Rhodes hit a home run that couldn't have traveled 255 feet to win the game.

Oh, I was so emotionally drained [after the Indians' 1954 World Series loss] that my wife and I checked into the Statler Hotel in downtown Cleveland after the fourth game, left our children with my in-laws, and I took two sleeping pills and I slept for 36 hours, just tried to sleep it off. Oh, it was a horrible experience, I mean it really ... it's an unbelievable thing. I don't think people really realize the gamut of, the full extent of, the emotions that players go through. Particularly if they're expected to win and if they're winning players, I mean, it's tough to lose. Defeat is a very difficult thing.

Well, the first serious injury I had, the first thing that kept me out of the lineup, was in 1954 when I broke my finger. Prior to that time, I had prided myself in my ability to play every game, and I think if you'll check the record books, you'll find that I missed very few games until I broke my right index finger. I stuck it into a ground ball playing first base. I didn't get out of the lineup and let it heal, didn't put it in a cast, which I should have done. I played with it for a week or so, until finally it got so bad that I finally did go to a doctor and found out that the finger was shattered.

I was having a better year in '54 than I had in '53 and at the time that I got hurt they were already doing the usual thing about how many home runs you had in comparison to Babe Ruth. I was way ahead in the runs-batted-in column. The all-time record for runs batted in is 190, and I think they figured if I'd kept up my present pace, I'd have knocked in 220 or something like that. And I was doing great; I was hitting about close to .400. I was really putting the years together then.

After the injury, I found I was struggling to do things that used to come so easy. It was now getting to be a struggle. Couldn't grip the bat the same way and didn't feel that I had the snap on the right hand that I used to have. If wrap your right index finger around something, you'll find out that that really is the trigger point. I had what I considered poor years. Some people don't think so. I couldn't do the things that I expected of myself and I just didn't want to hang around 'till somebody else told me I couldn't do them, and I just felt that the time had come to make a decision, and I made the decision that I thought was best for me. One of the things that precipitated my retirement after the '56 season was because I felt it was time for them to trade me, and in fact they did have a deal worked out with Boston, which would have been very lucrative for me, but I was a stockbroker and we were building a home and expecting our second child and I just didn't want to move.

I worked for Bache and Company and, oh, I actually started my own firm with a fellow named Elmer Paul in Cleveland, who is exceedingly philanthropic and worked very, very hard for the Jewish community all of his life. Elmer and I formed our own firm on July 1 of 1973. I left there; on April the 25th of 1975 I joined Caesar's Palace in Las Vegas. I was director of branch operations. They have branch offices throughout the country and that was my province. We put together a group to buy the Indians, and had it not been for an eleventh-hour refusal of our offer, we may have owned the Indians.

When you get to be 54, you look back and you look ahead and I realize I'm getting older, so naturally everything that I said about my younger days, that was gone. I was a tough kid and I was willing to fight at the drop of a hat. You get older, you realize that you can't do those things anymore and what purpose does it serve, so you do things by example.

You conduct yourself in a way that people can respect you, you do more than if they can't respect you for your actions. When you give somebody a reason to dislike you by your actions then anti–Semitism will crop in.

I've never been what I considered a religious Jew. We observe holidays and have observed holidays and when my children were growing up they had a Jewish education. I served on the board of directors, board of trustees for the temple, I contributed money, I helped raise money. That was my way of showing outwardly that I was Jewish. I think that one of the things that I always wanted was to conduct myself in a manner in which people would say he's a man, not he's a Jew or he's white or he was a baseball player or a good businessman. I've always wanted to be considered the total of me.

I met George Steinbrenner out in Cleveland. We formed a group of young businessman; we called ourselves Group '66 because that was the year that we were founded, and we did an awful lot of good in the community.

The beginnings of my affiliation with the Yankees came last year [1977] at the All-Star Game. I sat with George at a roundtable during a party that the Yankees hosted prior to the All-Star Game, and he told me that Gabe Paul was going to retire and that I should come back and run the Yankees for him. And I didn't pay a great deal of attention to it until November, when George came out to a championship fight that we had, and we sat and talked. He was rather persuasive. I discussed it with my wife, the possibility of moving back East, but of course you're talking about New York and the president of the New York Yankees. You're talking about something that's far and above the normal kind of thing. So here I am.

MICKEY RUTNER
Philadelphia Athletics, 1947
(1919–2007)

Mickey Rutner was a good hitter — his lifetime minor league average was .295 — but he only played a handful of games in the majors. In 1947, Rutner received a call-up from the Philadelphia Athletics, batting .250 in 12 games. His trials as a career minor leaguer were the basis for Man on Spikes, *a novel written by his friend Eliot Asinof, better known as the author of* Eight Men Out, *about the 1919 Black Sox scandal. In January 2005, Rutner discussed his life and career. One of the interviews took place in a room in his house filled with souvenirs, including a photo of Rutner with legendary Philadelphia Athletics manager Connie Mack. Rutner's vivacious wife, Lee, joined in at times.*

We were playing the White Sox. I think it was the second time up, and there was a man on base. And this guy threw me a curve ball, and I hit it pretty good. And I rounded first base and all of a sudden the umpire gave me the signal and I was quite surprised. I got goose pimples running around the bases. (Voice cracks) 'Cause I all could think of was my name coming up at the pool hall where my friends hung out: "Rutner homers for Philadelphia." I also got a game-winning hit at Yankee Stadium. It was in the late innings. We had a man on first and second and I hit a ball past third base. And Rizzuto made a helluva play and he threw to second, but Pete Suder was on first and he hustled and slid into second and beat the throw. Rizzuto couldn't throw me out and it was a base hit, and the run scored from second. That was the biggest thrill of my life.

I just wanted to play ball — that's what I had my heart set on from the time when I was a kid. I grew up in the Bronx, around Crotona Park, where my idol was Hank Greenberg. His father owned our building that we lived in, and Hank would come home from spring training or whatever and hit and hit and hit. He was hard working, and smart, clean-living guy. He'd come home, drink a bottle of milk, and go right back to the ballpark and hit. And we'd shag for him when he come in from the Texas League.

My parents were struggling. It was during the Depression. My brothers were athletes: they played soccer in high school. I was a better soccer player than I was a baseball player. I really enjoyed the game. I used to follow my brothers around even though it was cold as hell. They were in this German-American league and I learned how to play, and then I was All-Scholastic when I played at James Monroe [High School].

I was the baby. I had two brothers and two sisters. My brothers went to Hebrew school, but I didn't. There wasn't any money around. I didn't care. I definitely was more interested in sports than I was in going to Hebrew school. I always knew that I came from Jewish heritage and that was it. I was proud [of being Jewish].

My mother and father, they spoke Yiddish. They'd yell at me in Yiddish. My parents didn't discourage me [from playing sports], but my brother started to work, and he was the only who would give me spikes or a glove and stuff. My father was in the dress-manufacturing business. They were from Russia, Poland. They were fans. They would come to watch me play.

I played shortstop in high school. But I didn't know what I wanted to be. In fact, Paul Krichell, the Number 1 scout for the Yankees, had me work out for the Yankees before one of the games. And he said, "Work out at third base." And I wondered why, but then I learned that I didn't have the range to go right and left. I realized he knew what he was doing, and that's where I ended up playing.

My brothers, who were my elders, always insisted, "Mickey, you want a college degree. When you get through playing ball, what are you gonna do? You have to have something to fall back on." Then that really held because after I got through playing ball I was offered a job with the town of Hempstead, and you have to have a college degree to qualify for that job. I went to St. John's on a soccer scholarship. In fact, my freshman year I played soccer, freshman basketball, and baseball, but they discontinued soccer and I concentrated on my baseball.

You knew you were different because before every game, whether it was basketball or baseball, they'd go into the church and say their prayer, and I'd say, "OK, fellows, say one for me and that was it." They knew I was Jewish — wasn't Catholic — but there was no discrimination.

When I was at college, I was intercollegiate batting champion for two seasons. I hit .430 and .450, and I had a pretty good record. A lot of scouts were after me. The Yanks were after me, and they said, "Mick, if there wasn't a war in Europe we'd be offering you $20,000, $30,000." Instead they were offering me $2,000 and $3,000. But Detroit made me an offer. I got a call from Mr. Briggs right from Detroit, and at that time their second baseman, Charley Gehringer, was at the end of his career, and I was playing second in college and I figured I'd take his place. I didn't realize they were sending me down to Winston-Salem in the Piedmont League.

I signed with the Tigers. I signed the contact, and they sent me to Winston-Salem, and I was going with my wife. We were kids, sweethearts. I called her and I said, "Lee, they just gave me a thousand dollars." I bought a convertible, a used convertible. I said, "Why don't you come down? We'll get married." So she came down with her brother — he didn't trust me alone with her. We drove to Virginia. They wanted us to take blood tests and wait a week or so. So one of the fellows on the team played in South Carolina, so he called somebody he knew, and we drove to South Carolina and we got there at four o'clock in the morning, and we got married by a judge and that was it.

Lee and I sort of grew up together. Her ambition was to be a dancer. My ambition was to be a ballplayer. In the summer, she would go with her group. I would go to play ball, but we always came back together. She danced with the Rockettes.

When I got there, they didn't give me the whole $3,000. They put me on the bench, and I pinch-hit once in a while. And they had me sign a release. If I signed the release, they'd let me play, which I did. I wanted to play. I was full of enthusiasm and I thought I was a helluva ballplayer but, you know, when they sit you on the bench, it was very discouraging.

They didn't give me the rest of the money. So I wrote to the president of the Baseball Association, and he got me my outright release. So one of the teams scouting me, a guy by the name of Eddie Glennon from Wilmington, got in touch with me. So I went to play with Wilmington. Class B Interstate League. Class B, but it was close to home and we had a good team and I had a pretty good season in '42. I had a good year at Wilmington. And I was supposed to finish the year with the Athletics, but Uncle Sam didn't allow me anything. They grabbed me, and I had to go.

In the same league — I made the All-Star team as a third baseman —

there was another third basemen at Lancaster who they took and he went up with the A's: George Kell, very nice guy from Arkansas. He never went in the service because, you know, in the Bronx, where I grew up, someone would call the draft board and say, "Mickey Rutner's playing ball and my son's in the service; why isn't he in the service?" But in Arkansas, they didn't do that, so he didn't go in the service." And he got a chance to go to the big leagues, and he did well.

There wasn't much you could do. There was a war in Europe, and Germany was killing all the Jews, and I wanted to get over there and do my part. Unfortunately, after that service I had to go back to Wilmington instead of going back to Philadelphia if I had just finished the season. That's the only regret I have — it would have made quite a difference. I had to go back and play for $250 a month, while in Philadelphia you would have made $2,500 a month.

They shipped me right into an invasion. They froze everything; I couldn't go to an officers training school. I couldn't do anything. I never got a weekend pass. I never got a furlough in my three and a half years in the service. They sent me right into an invasion: We went to North Africa and we invaded Sicily and we went up through France and we invaded along the Rhine River and then into Germany. I was in the 45th Division — the Thunderbird Division from Oklahoma — and they never knew what a Jew was. Very funny when you speak to some of those country boys. Thought I'd have horns. Like I say, I didn't let it bother me. I remember one guy said I've never met a Jew before: "Well, you met one now."

We landed in Sicily, and the Germans were attacking us. And they were up about 10,000 or above, and just below that our Air Corps came in with the paratroopers and knocked down forty-five of our planes. They didn't know they were ours. And the paratroopers came in, and the navy was firing — you can't believe the racket that was going on. The navy planes were just firing at these planes. They didn't know they were ours. But that was my introduction into combat in Sicily.

There were a few times that were pretty scary. In one area around Munich, there was a little German plane just peppering us until we got word to artillery, and they got rid of them. I had a driver, and we'd go out and do some reconnaissance. Once we were making an invasion, and I got on top of a truck and the German planes came over and I was sitting on top of the truck trying to shoot this plane down. But it was just a waste of time. If the navy didn't get 'em, nobody got 'em. I ended up in the hospital with malaria, but that was the worst that happened to me. I was lucky.

In 1947, I went to Birmingham. I had a good year. The people in Birmingham wanted me to stay there. The Sokol brothers [who owned a department store chain]. They said, "What's a nice Jewish boy playing baseball? Stay here for three years. We'll make you a rich man." But I had my dreams of playing baseball, so I didn't accept it. They'd call up and say, "You're gonna have dinner with us." And they got so friendly with us they'd say, "Lee, you go to the game and we'll take care of your kids."

I was a good hitter. I could hit. In batting practice, I'd choke up a little bit and try to meet the ball, hit it where it's pitched. And not try to follow through like you would when you hit a home run. I wasn't a base stealer. I was just a guy who drove in runs. I hit anywhere from third to fifth. I mean, if I was with the club and the cleanup man was in a slump, they'd move me in there. But I'd rather hit second. I'd rather hit behind the runner. I liked to hit and run. And I'd get on base. I like the small game. I didn't go for that big inning, where you had to hit a home run. Sometime they ask me how I compare to today's ballplayer: I say [they're] bigger, faster, richer. I read an interesting book called *Moneyball*: how many times you get on base, how many times you get hit by a pitch. It's all bullshit.

I'll tell you what happened: In Birmingham we were playing Nashville in the Dixie Series. The winner goes on to play the winner of the Texas League, and the score was tied, 2–2 or something like that 3–3. Going into the ninth inning and the leadoff man gets a double. And they walk me to get at Walt Dropo [later an American League player]. So what am I thinking when I'm at first base. I said, "My job is to knock that second baseman out if there's a double-play ball." First pitch, Dropo hits it right to shortstop. Shortstop throws to second base, I take him out, and the run scores. And we go into the Dixie Series. I won the game. But I ended up in the hospital — a broken collarbone. I really took him out. It got us into the Dixie Series. That's the way I played: to win. I didn't mean to hurt myself or the second baseman. I knew that was my responsibility to get the second baseman if I could. We both ended up in the hospital.

[One off-season] I was working with Cal Abrams in a service station — most of the time we didn't know where the gas cap was — and the phone rang and it was Hank Greenberg, and he said, "Mickey, we have a spot for you in the organization." I says, "I just got a call from [St. Louis Browns' executive Bill] DeWitt and he says I'm going up with the Browns." And he says, "I hope that's true." But years later, I met Hank in the Dallas airport, and he said, "What happened," and I says, "I never heard from

Mickey Rutner got a cup of coffee with the Philadelphia Athletics in 1947. He called a game-winning RBI he got against the Yankees at Yankee Stadium the "biggest thrill of my life."

DeWitt again." And he says, "Well, he's a goddamn liar." And I'm quoting Hank when he said that. They owned you and they could do what they want with you.

You never talked about [owner-player issues] because you'd become a clubhouse lawyer. That it was before [Marvin] Miller and the union. As a young fellow, you want to play ball, and that's all you want to do. You're stupid, and they like you that way. You're just a piece of paper. The funny thing is, when I played for Birmingham the general manager was Eddie Glennon. And he sent me a contract, and I was discussing it with him, and I said, "I had a good year last year, and you only sent me the same amount for the next season." And he said, "Mickey, there are ballplayers down in Cuba that'll play for only half of what you're getting." So they always had an answer for you to think about. Black ballplayers started to come in, and the same with them [baseball executives would say they'd play for less money].

Around March, you'd get a contract and you'd send it back and then you'd negotiate. And they they'd tell you, "If you don't sign it, then get yourself a lunch bucket." They owned you. They knew if you didn't play ball, you were unhappy.

In 1953 Dallas bought me, and Dallas was an independent club — the owner by the name of Burnett, a very rich man. So all of a sudden, I get a call from Dallas, and they said, "We just bought your contract." So they send me a contract, and it was less than I was getting at Louisville. And I wrote back and I told them that. See every March it was contract time. It's aggravating for a minor league ballplayer. Today they have all these agents. They have all their rights. So spring training rolls around, and I still don't hear from them. So I tried calling him, and they kept ignoring my call and so forth. So finally I speak to the general manager — I don't remember his name — and he said, "Mick, I'll tell you what: We'll give you your release, but I want twenty-five percent of whatever you get." So I said, "O.K. That's fair enough."

I get in touch with a guy by the name of Tommy Tatum. He was managing Oklahoma City. This is near the end of my career. So I said, "Tommy, I'm a free agent." He said, "Well, I could use a third baseman." So I said, "What can you do for me?" He says, "I'll give you $1,500 to sign and I'll give you a thousand a month," so I accepted that. And then once the season rolled around I kept hearing from Dallas. And I wouldn't answer the call and I said, "It's my chance to tell him to go to hell." After all these times he ignored me, now I'm ignoring him. He's not getting twenty-five percent of whatever I got. He never got it. I got a chance to screw him.

After I got to Oklahoma City, and I got the little bonus from Tommy Tatum and company, Houston needed a third baseman, but I said I had had enough. My third son was born, and I thought I may as well pack it up when I was still in one piece. So I said, "No thanks, I'm not interested." Lee knew that I had enough. When they trade you around like a piece of crap, you say what am I doing this for? You work hard, you play hard, and some of 'em don't appreciate it. Some do, but most of 'em don't.

How did I deal with people who didn't know Jews? By being a regular guy, and going and having a few beers with the guys and stuff like that. But then when religion came up, they always respected the fact that I had my own religion and my own thoughts. There were always remarks. They'd always say, "Those rich Jews up in the stands up in the park and so forth." I'd say, "Those rich Jews up in those stands are paying your salary." You know, you got to put them in their place. I got into a couple of fights.

I remember in the clubhouse one time, one of the guys was pitching and I musta made an error and he made some remark, so I went at 'em. I came out. Lee was waiting for me and my shirt was torn, but, you know, I got the satisfaction of going at this guy. They break things up. In baseball, they didn't fight. They have a scramble, and then they break it up and that's it. It was a little tough. You can't have rabbit ears, and I didn't have rabbit ears. I didn't try to get into any arguments.

LEE: Mick was good at ignoring it. Some guys had, you know, rabbit ears and it really bothered him. Like Cal [Abrams], he heard everything and he reacted to everything. It would eat his gut up, but Mick he was good at that. Mick would just spit and say, "Screw them."

MICK: Cal had a big nose.

LEE: The worst comments were when he played in Brooklyn were from the Jewish people. There's no anti–Semite like a Jewish anti–Semite. And they would pick on him. You would think they would have embraced him.

MICK: Even though he was leading the National League for one month when he was with Brooklyn, they'd yell, "Abie, Abie," derisively. It wasn't easy. Cal played for Mobile, when I played for Birmingham. [Fellow Jewish player] Cy Block played for Nashville. When Cal got on base, I'd start talking. "Cal, what are you gonna do this winter?" He'd say, "Don't talk to me. I'm not supposed to talk to you." He was afraid to even talk to anybody, especially me. There was no fraternizing.

LEE: Cal was skittish. And yet this other guy, Cy Block, would always travel with merchandise to sell.

MICK: He would go into a clubhouse after a game when they'd have a fight — and he'd go into the Mobile clubhouse and Chuck Connors would be there and he'd try to sell them some shirts.

LEE: Cal was just the opposite. Cal was nervous about these things. He didn't have the backbone to really spit in their eye, so he just listened and it ate his gut up. The Abramses and us lived in the same town [Hicksville, on Long Island], and when the guys went to spring training, May and I and the kids, we'd all go out to dinner and to the beach together and stuff. And during the Jewish holidays we would make gefilte fish together.

MICK: I regret not having been born forty years later. But I have no regrets. I really enjoyed it and met a lot of nice people. And I've got a nice family. I speak to a lot of people, a lot of young, honest guys, and they say their ambition in life is just one time to get up in a professional game and get up to bat, one time. And I did what I wanted to do, played for twelve years. My biggest thrill was playing in Yankee Stadium. That was your dream to make it to the big time. It was exciting playing in front of your friends and family. One of the guys selling hot dogs was a black kid that I grew up with — Frankie Haynes was his name. He came running down, and said, "Hey Mick, so glad to see you." And there he was selling hot dogs. There wasn't big money then. It's just the idea of being there. Today the ballplayers are mighty lucky that they have a union and all these different privileges.

I opened a dry-cleaning business, did that for a number of years. I made some money and then I sold it. I figured I'd retire, but then my neighbor who was a councilman said, "Mick, there's an opportunity in the town of Hempstead. They're looking for recreation supervisors. Do you have a college degree — it'd be perfect." So I said, "OK." So I did that. I did that for eighteen years and it gave me a pension. And luckily it worked out fine. Hector [Lopez] played for the Yankees for eleven years. He played for Minnesota before that. He was in four World Series. He never made more than $35,000 a year. And he was a regular ballplayer. He didn't just pinch-hit. He played one hundred games or more. We worked for the town of Hempstead. He was working at one of our parks as a laborer. And I used to go down and visit him 'cause I had to check the parks to see what kind of programs were going on. So I went back to the commissioner and said, "Look, we have Hector Lopez working at Lakeview Park. He was with the Yankees for eleven years. That's really degrading. How about having him come up here and become a regional supervisor?" So they brought him up and he and I worked together.

I've been a greeter [for the local minor league team, the Round Rock Express] up in the suites. Ushers have to run and down; my knee doesn't do that. But I'm the only one with a baseball background. So they gave me that important job in the suites. Up with the bigwigs. And the son, Reid Ryan, is a bright young man. He's the CEO of the club. He played a little ball but he never went too far, not like his dad. I see Nolan Ryan. He's a nice man.

They had me throw out the first pitch one day. And for a week me and my friend across the street, I'd throw to him to get my arm in shape. I wasn't going to get out there and make an ass of myself. I did damn-good, better than Nolan. Nolan had trouble. He threw it in the dirt.

The best pitcher I ever faced was a kid by the name of "Vinegar Bend" Mizell. He was a big, strong left-hander, and I loved to hit against left-handers. He had such a slow motion, but, boy, that ball would be on ya before you realized it. I found him tough to hit. The best hitter? Joe DiMaggio had the best form. He was just great.

I knew some good ballplayers. Joe Adcock. Let me see who else. Roy McMillan [later a longtime Major League shortstop] was the shortstop in Tulsa. I taught him how to chew tobacco. The manager at Tulsa was a great guy from Beaumont, Texas, Al Vincent. One of the smartest men in baseball, I thought. And we were working out one day, and he said, "Mickey, that kid out there, he's a hell of a ballplayer. Go out and talk to him. Teach him how to chew tobacco. Make him tough." So I went out and I said, "Roy, where you from?" So he told me what little town he comes from in Texas, and I said, "You ever try chewing tobacco?" He says no. I tell him, "Let me show you how to do it." So I give him a chew, and he always had a chew from that time on. So that's my claim to fame: I taught Roy McMillan how to chew tobacco.

MARV ROTBLATT
Chicago White Sox, 1948, 1950–1951
(1927–)

Marv Rotblatt had a short career with the Chicago White Sox, but he does have one Major League distinction: in 1951, Rotblatt became the first relief pitcher in baseball history to ride into a game in a bullpen car. What follows is excerpted from a June 1987 interview.

Basically, my folks were not very religious. And I went to Hebrew school very reluctantly. We didn't have very much money, and I went for about a month and I just couldn't handle it or comprehend it. So I went and told my dad and mother that I didn't want to get bar mitzvahed — that is at the age of twelve, going on thirteen, of course. And I guess my dad was kind of relieved because of the extra money he would save. It wasn't much, but it was enough. And I said, "I'm more interested in playing baseball in the summer, instead of sitting in Hebrew school for three hours a day." And it was an old, very religious rabbi or whoever did the teaching. So basically, my Jewish upbringing was very minimal.

Both my parents, especially my father, came from the Old Country — born in Warsaw, Poland — and didn't like me wasting time playing baseball. He was a "get-a-job" person when I was a kid. But my brother and I, that's all we did all day long. Till it got dark out, we were playing baseball. When I got into high school and was a better ballplayer, my dad still had no interest because he was trying to make a living. And when I got into college, my freshman year, the first game I got into, I got a shattered cheekbone — a line drive in the face. And my dad came down to visit me in the hospital. He said, "No more baseball for you. It's enough. It's too dangerous." And of course, it went in one ear and out the other because I continued playing at Illinois. And once I started to get some acclaim, *now* my dad would come down every weekend to watch the ballgames.

I wasn't a Koufax adherent [in terms of not playing on Yom Kippur]. Because I remember coming back from the House of David in 1947 and the semipro team that I played the summer prior to that — a team called the Ace Fasteners in Chicago — were playing against the champs of the league on Yom Kippur Eve. And they called me on the phone and they said, "Marv, we'll give you a hundred dollars, win or lose." Well, that was a lot of money in those days. I said, "Bet the money on me." The lights were so dark that night we came up with three runs in the first inning off Don Hanski, who used to pitch for the White Sox for a short time [1943–1944] and the money was passing hands, and we were getting like 3-1 odds, because they were the champs and we were like a last-place team. But of course I made the difference. So that night I pitched nine innings. Doug Meyer was scouting me for the White Sox, and I struck out twenty-three guys. They got one run — a home run — off me, but the other three balls I had to look to see who in the infield was going for the ball because that's how bad the lights were. So I looked a little bit like a combination of Sandy Koufax and Bob Feller that night. And that was on Yom Kippur. I picked up $400, and my conscience didn't bother me much. My parents didn't say anything about it. As I say, they weren't very religious, so I just said I was going out that evening and played a ballgame.

The House of David is not Jewish, although it sounds like would be derived from a Judaic background. They're sectarian — vegetarians, and it's against their religion to cut their hair or shave. They're in Benton Harbor, Michigan. They've been there for, I imagine a hundred years. To pick up money, they had a semipro baseball team.

Fans in the Southern Association were either bigots or didn't like black people. But other than that, they were OK. What happened is that the ballplayers were fine. There were some needles because, you remember, in those days, if a guy went to college he was a freak. So I ran into a lot of illiterate southerners, but most of the guys were pretty good boys. They needled me a little bit. The fans on the other teams would get on my case — the ones sitting in the cheaper seats, the 40-cent seats.

We did have an incident at the ballpark [Chicago's Comiskey Park]. If you remember, at that period of time, most of the neighborhood was Italian, not black, because this was 1951. And our bullpen was out in center field, with the bleachers right above us. And for about a period four or five days in a row, some punks from the area called me everything in the

Marv Rotblatt pitched for the Chicago White Sox in 1948 and 1950–1951. He remembers a postgame riot in Cleveland in which anti–Semitic slurs were used.

books—"sheeny," "Jew-bastard," etc. etc. And I mentioned it to one of my friends. So one day against the Cleveland Indians, out in the bullpen, all of a sudden there was a lot of rioting—and I find out that some of my friends and some of the Italian guys got into a real battle: lead pipes. They had the lead pipes; unfortunately, and the cops were called in. That was a weird incident. And I remember after the ballgame that day, Nellie Fox and I were getting on the bus at the same time, leaving to go to Cleveland. And Nellie said, "Marv, get back." It's like when they used to play catch with Jackie Robinson, Pee Wee Reese said, "Jackie, I don't want to get too close to you because there may be snipers around."

The White Sox front office, obviously, was anxious to have me be effective because they knew that there were a lot of Jewish baseball fans in the Chicago area, and if I had a good year, of course, with myself and Saul Rogovin on the ballclub, we did draw some extra people that were Jewish. I made a mistake because the Dodgers had been after me all my career, and they told me they would have loved to have a Jewish ballplayer play with them. The Dodgers and George Sisler wanted me very badly— and the only difference is that they wanted to sign me to a Triple-A contract and Red Ornsby, who was scouting with the White Sox, said, "We'll put you right in the Major Leagues, Marv, right out of college." I was short-sighted.

One of my teammates, Jimmy Baumer—came up with the Reds and the White Sox—for some weird reason nicknamed me "Pontiac." Now if you'll remember the old hood ornament with the cheap Pontiac. And they called me—let's see now—"if you had a nose full of nickels, you'd be a rich man," and "get that nose out of the way—we can't see the field." But I don't think it was really ethnically motivated.

I wouldn't have liked Saul Rogovin if he was Irish, let alone Jewish. [laughs] Saul was one of those guys that was all for Saul—and the hell with the team, frankly. Example: when he was pitching—and Saul basically was a quiet guy—when he was pitching, he was a cheerleader. I saw him, literally, walking up and down the dugout, saying, "C'mon guys! Let's get some goddamn runs!" When he wasn't pitching, he'd sneak out to the bullpen and lived up to his name: Somnolent Saul. [laughs] He didn't care who won as long as he did.

Saul was very funny. We'd have dinner—or breakfast—on the train, and if the eggs weren't done exactly two minutes and twelve seconds, he'd send them back. And then he didn't tip very much anyway. [laughs] Saul spent money like a man with no pockets.

98

One of the funny true stories happened on the Johnny Carson show: my mother heard and two of my clients heard it. One night, McLean Stevenson, who is originally from Bloomington, Illinois, was a guest on the Carson show, and they were trying to compile an all–Jewish baseball team. And McLean Stevenson said, "Johnny, the only two Jewish ballplayers I can remember are Marv Rotblatt and Sandy Koufax!" Carson quickly looked at him and said, "Who's Sandy Koufax?" I thought that was very cute.

CAL ABRAMS

Brooklyn Dodgers, 1949–1952; Cincinnati Reds, 1952; Pittsburgh Pirates, 1953–1954; Baltimore Orioles, 1954–1955; Chicago White Sox, 1956

(1924–1997)

Cal Abrams achieved the dream of a lifetime when he played for his hometown team, the Brooklyn Dodgers. Indeed, a New York newspaper once ran the headline, "Mantle, Schmantle, We've Got Abie." Reality with the Dodgers proved more difficult for Abrams, who was under a lot of pressure to produce. In fact, he's most remembered in Dodgers history for being thrown out at the plate while trying to score the winning run in a 1950 playoff against the Philadelphia Phillies. His best season came in 1954 while playing for the Baltimore Orioles. When he was interviewed in November and December of 1980, he spoke about playing for the Dodgers and his other childhood dream of being a professional dancer. His wife, May, occasionally chimed in.

When I was approximately three weeks old, my family moved into Brooklyn and I lived in Brooklyn all my life. I remember going to high school and listening to the ballgames, the Dodgers on the radio, and I recall very vividly the fans in those days were just as fanatic as they were when I was playing ball. As you walked along a main thoroughfare with stores, each store had its own crystal radio set sitting out front, and you never missed one word of the announcers as you progressed along your streets. In fact, I also recall a very crazy butcher at that time who was about to slice some salami for a woman when the Dodgers were up in the bottom of the ninth, two outs, bases loaded, and somebody got a base hit, whereupon the butcher took the knife out of the salami and started swinging it like a bat.

My father was in the trucking business for about forty-five years, and my mother was a housewife. But my mother, believe it or not, was a concert pianist. She and my aunt played in Carnegie Hall, she told me once together, a duet.

MAY: Your mother also used to play for silent movies in the theaters when she was first married.

CAL: My family was not very religious at all and, of course, a lot of it rubbed off on me, too. During the Jewish holidays, my parents insisted that I go to school.

MAY: But I must say that in spite of the fact that Cal didn't have a religious background and really was unaware of holidays and celebrations of holidays, he married somebody who had that kind of background. [laughs] You know, it's developed slowly, but he's really come to realize that this is a beautiful way of life. We're not very religious, but we know who we are.

CAL: Once we were playing a game and I hit a single, and Jake Pitler, the coach, who was also Jewish, came over and he hit me on the tuches, and he said, "Nice going, Cal, nice going, Abie." He says, "By the way, you're taking off the next three days, aren't you?" I said, "Why? No. I'm playing ball. We got three games." He says, "Listen you idiot," he said, "I'm going back to Albany to my house. It's the holidays, and if I go and you play, it makes me look like a dumbbell, so you better take off."

MAY: If you recall, we used to discuss it, but in those days being the only Jewish baseball player on the team was very difficult and you were afraid to say anything that would jeopardize your career, like, "Can I have a few days off because it's a Jewish holiday?" So whether I suggested taking off or not, he wasn't going to do it, until he had a little guidance from someone like Jake Pitler.

CAL: My father was what I always called a frustrated ballplayer, yes, and when I did make it I could see his nose shining and gleaming. And my mother and father, every time we went to spring training, would take off just so they can be near me and part of the scene. It was hard really because a lot of people said, "Ah! Wherever Mr. Abrams is, there's his son." You know, it wasn't, "Cal Abrams and his father."

Oh, I wanted to be a page boy, tap dancer in a chorus line behind the woman star. I loved dancing, I loved cartooning. But I think my first thing was dancing. I wanted to be in the movies, you know, the top hat and the cane, stand behind Fred Astaire while he was doing his routine.

I signed a minor-league contract prior to going into the service. This is with the Dodger organization and it was a contract calling for a fantastic sum of money. Seventy-five dollars a month. I don't regret going into the service. Number One, I came back with both arms and legs. I experienced a lot of awful things.

While in the service, being the property of the Brooklyn Dodgers, I used to get little fliers from Branch Rickey, Sr. "Hello, Cal, how are you? Enjoy reading about the Dodgers, what's happening, here's material, and we can't wait for you to come home," and so on and so forth, and this is the one thing that you look back at and you realize the team has a hold on you and you're thousands of miles away for years. You're a slave to a contract.

I have to tell you this. We loved chow mein and my father had a huge open house when I came home [from the service] and he cleaned out a huge garbage can and went to the Chinese restaurant and loaded it with chow mein, and everybody came in and got a big ladle of chow mein.

I came out of the service in, I think it was January of '46. In '47, I was with Mobile, Double A. I skipped A and batted .345, I think, that year. And the Mobile team had fellows that were all going to be Major League ballplayers. Aside from the fact that there was stupidity on the part of some farmers who lived down there, who didn't know that a Jew could be Jewish only, without being Jewish Protestant or Jewish Catholic, I got along with everybody because I was a comic, I was a clown. I enjoyed my life, I was in love with the game, I loved what I was doing, nobody can get under my skin, and as long as you're hitting, as long as you're doing well, nothing can go wrong for you.

We were in Mobile and I had just gone down from option, I was optioned out from Brooklyn, and I was shagging flies in the outfield and a farmer over there standing on the sidelines called me over and in a farm voice said to me, "Are you all Jewish?" and I said, "Yes, I am." He said, "Well, are you Jewish Protestant or Jewish Catholic?" See, then I knew what I was in for in little hick towns like Mobile. But I didn't let that get under my skin.

MAY: In Mobile, one family invited us to be their guests for Passover and, as luck would have it, he got sick, he got pneumonia. Do you remember, you had bronchial or viral pneumonia? Well, at any rate, he couldn't go. Do you know they sent the chauffeur with a complete Passover dinner for the two of us at our apartment in Mobile, Alabama, because we weren't able to attend the seder at their home?

The reason I came up to Brooklyn in 1949 was because Carl Furillo

Cal Abrams played for several teams in the late 1940s and 1950s. Raised in Brooklyn, he played for the Dodgers from 1949 to 1952, but found it difficult to live up to expectations.

had been beaned and I was immediately recalled, and I had all hopes and anticipations of playing with the team at that point, figuring that he was incapable because he got hit in the head. As it turned out, he was such a strong person that the very following day he was playing in the outfield, so I just sat on the bench and they couldn't send me down any more because I had used up my three options.

There was one time that I was even told to go pinch-hit for Pee Wee Reese, who had two strikes on him. Now, this is something that no manager in his right mind would ever do, but I can recall that day very vividly. After two strikes, he [Charlie Dressen] suddenly held the game up and told Pee Wee to get out and out me in there. And I popped the first pitch, I fouled it up, and then I struck out. Of course, I didn't get the strikeout, Pee Wee Reese got it, but as he walked by me when I was going up to the plate he was muttering something under his breath at me. Showing that he was a little bit mad at me, and I told him later on it wasn't my doing, it was the manager. But that's the way the season went for me.

It was a right-handed pitcher, and I guess he had made up his mind a little bit too late. Maybe he was thinking of putting a left-handed pinch hitter in, but suddenly it was strike one, strike two, and now he woke up to the realization that why not put in a lefty, or possibly why not put Cal Abrams in and hope he strikes out. There was a certain animosity, there was a certain feeling of discrimination possibly, but it was too early to tell. As the years progressed, I found out that it was so, that he did not particularly like the Jewish people.

In 1950 it came down to a playoff game for the championship of the league. We ended up tied with the Philadelphia Phillies' "Whiz Kids," and whoever wins the ballgame would be the champs. I was leading off the ninth inning, we were tie score, and I got a base hit. I was sacrificed to second base. Robin Roberts is nervous because Duke Snider is getting up to the plate, and he's concentrating so much on Snider that he missed the pick-off sign, but that sign had been relayed to the outfield. In center field you had Richie Ashburn, who got the sign flashed to him. He decided to run in before anything started in case they threw the ball to second and he bobbled it; he would back it up. Now Richie Ashburn was known to have the worst arm in the league. Therefore, he had to be very close in order to do anything about getting me out.

So as it was, Roberts missed the sign. He threw the pitch home, but only with half speed because Stan Lopata was getting out of the crouch, not even anticipating the pitch — and Snider immediately creamed it right over my head. Now I am running top speed toward third base and the coach, Milton Stock, at this point suddenly decided to look at where the ball went, and when he did that he was giving me the signs at the same time. With one hand, he was waving, "Go! Go!" and with the other he was biting his fingernails because he suddenly saw Ashburn throwing the ball before I even got to third base.

I rounded third as hard I could, still thinking that the game was going to be over, not knowing that Ashburn had already thrown the ball. But as I rounded third, I looked up, Stan Lopata was standing ten feet up from the plate, straddling the baseline. There was no way for me to go around; he was holding the ball. The man weighed 225, solid muscle, he had all his gear on him. I could try to jump over him or try to hold my breath, and maybe he'll miss me with the tag, which is what I tried to do, and he tagged me and in the following inning Dick Sisler hit a home run left-handed over the left-center field fence, and they ended up winning that game. Now the following day, even though the season was over, they fired Milton Stock.

The newspapermen, who did not even see Ashburn coming close, who did not see any of that, only were so intent in the runner, myself, going around. Some newspapermen said, "Well, Cal Abrams rounded third base too wide." Some said, "Cal Abrams got the slowest start from second base and he's not that good a runner," and all of these little incidents led me to believe that there was a little bit of anti–Semitism there. I was the scapegoat for a period of time, until one day in *Sport* magazine I actually read the legitimate story myself. Somebody, I don't know who it was, got ahold of the right story, maybe they got it from Richie Ashburn, I don't know, but they put it into *Sport* magazine.

If it weren't for the fact that Richie Ashburn threw me out at home plate, nobody would remember me.

My whole dream was to put on a Dodger uniform in Ebbets Field. To be able to put on a Dodger uniform and look at Jackie Robinson and play with Campanella and all of those guys, Don Newcombe. You know, it was a thrill, a thrill.

I recall coming out of Ebbets Field when I was playing ball and there would be at least a hundred kids standing near my car, and in those days we had the penny postcards. And they would all have a bunch of them and they would keep asking for your name and they would do whatever they would do with the cards. But I recall one boy who for about thirty days straight would ask me for my autograph, and the following day we were going on a road trip for two weeks, and I had to ask him, I couldn't imagine why. I said, "Look, I signed my name thirty times. Why did you need it every single day?" He said, "Well, I needed thirty Cal Abrams to trade for one Carl Furillo."

We were playing in Cincinnati, we were playing a three-game stand, and after the second game they told me to go across the hall and change uniforms and the last game I would be playing against Brooklyn, the reason being that they just sold me to Cincinnati. Unbeknownst to me at the time, Branch Rickey was the owner of Pittsburgh. He had tried to buy me from Brooklyn. Brooklyn did not want to sell me unless Rickey was willing to pay a million dollars for me because he had put that kind of value on me. So kiddingly, they said, "You said he's worth a million. Pay it and you can have him." Of course he said, "You're crazy." So he turned to Gabe Paul in Cincinnati and said, "Gabe, you buy Cal and I will make a fantastic trade with you," which is exactly what happened. Now when I got to Cincinnati I assumed, because Gabe Paul was Jewish, that he legitimately bought me for the Cincinnati club, so for the remainder of that season I played with Cincinnati and I think I had a fairly good year with them. And I did pretty good things for them, and right after that I was traded to Pittsburgh.

I just felt that my dream of being a Brooklyn Dodger was now shattered. That's all I lived for when I was in the minor leagues, to someday wear a Brooklyn Dodger jersey. You know, you go up a ladder one way or another. You're changing clubs, you're going to other clubs possibly, you're meeting different people and you have to go along with what you're doing. You're going to sit down and cry. You know you had to make a living. You know that you're married and have children, so you must do what you can.

There were four blacks when I was with the Dodgers: Joe Black, Robinson, Campanella, Newcombe. The four of them, they roomed with each other and they had to go into different hotels in the other end of towns. Like in Cincinnati, some black fellow would pick them up in a limousine and drive to the outskirts of town, and they would meet us at the ballparks because in those days the blacks weren't allowed in the Netherland, Sherry Netherland, Plaza and so forth. But I felt badly, I didn't think that's right at all. I associated with them because we had a rapport about being with each other. We kibitzed around with each other, but I didn't go out with them. I mean, I wouldn't go into the end of town to go dancing with the black people, but whenever we could we were together, clowning around and kidding around.

In the trains we would kibitz around, in the hotel lobbies playing cards together and ping-pong and pool, and jokes. Also putting me with Spanish-speaking ballplayers, because I did speak the language, would be very helpful to the ballplayer himself and I would always kibitz around with them. Like I would always give them the wrong definitions for words. I might tell somebody.... He'd ask me, "How do you say 'pleasant dreams' to the rest of the ballplayers in the train before we go to bed" and I would say, "Well, you just have to say, 'Good night, boobheads,'" you know, or something even worse than that, and they would all look at this individual and yell at him, and then he would say to me in Spanish, "You're no god-damn good."

I was playing right field one day, and Jackie Robinson was hitting and our first baseman that day was big, a strong ape named Ted Kluzewski. Naturally these fellows didn't know how I played, how I would play my position in right field. But Jackie hit a line-drive base hit to me, and I charged in and caught the ball as soon as bounced, and I had it in my glove. I also knew at this point what Jackie Robinson was going to do when he runs his bases. That is—and I'm not bragging—this is what a good ballplayer should know. I knew he would round the bag as hard as possible. If you slightly bobbled the ball, he would be off for second, but he was so good at stopping on a dime that he can get back.

Well, he rounded the base as hard as he could and I immediately, without thinking of getting an error or the responsibility of anything else, fired the ball as hard as I could at first base. I didn't care whether Ted Kluzewski was looking at me, I didn't care whether the catcher was backing up the play. I knew that I'm going to show Cincinnati and Gabe Paul that I'm going to play and not stick my tail between my legs and just ... because I'm not with Brooklyn anymore. As it turned out, he was stopping on a dime and Kluzewski was watching him, the ball went straight as an arrow, hit Ted Kluzewski in the chest, would have broken every bone in my body, but it just rolled off of him. Jackie dove back and got back to first base in time. As he touched the bag, he turned around to right field and suddenly I saw a whole mouthful of pearly white teeth. He was trying to communicate to me, I think, and because we had this little rapport going between the Jews and the blacks, he was saying, "You're a goddamn good Jew, and I respect what you had just did."

Sleeping Saul Rogovin. He was the only man I know of that could actually fall asleep before he pitched the ball. He had very heavy eyelids and he claimed he had a sleeping sickness. He would be sitting on the bench and suddenly be snoring. He could not stay awake. But he was a lot of fun and he was a good pitcher. But he was slow and fastidious and everything he did, he did with precision. Very slow, very casual. He knew what he wanted to do, if he could stay awake.

I recall one time that my wife and I went down to Vero Beach and I hadn't signed all winter, and I was anticipating asking Branch Rickey for a $5,000 raise because I had a fairly good season. When he got through with me, I couldn't even ask for a nickel because ... I was happy, you know, whatever he was going to.... But I held back a little bit and I said, "No, I'm not going to sign," and he said to me.... We had just gotten off the train from New York to Florida. He said, "Did you unpack your suitcase yet?" and I said, "No." He says, "Good. Tell your wife: you and she get on the train, go back to Brooklyn." I came back across the way and I said, "May, I didn't sign; he told us to go home." She said, "Go back there and sign that contract and kiss his big toe," and that's the end of that.

Paul Richards never had a rapport with any of the ballplayers. He never talked to any of them. He put up a lineup and that was it. I mean if he had something to say you went his room or in the clubhouse and he would blast you, but that was it. No rapport, and that is not the way you play ball. Charlie Dressen was the same way, no rapport. Fred Haney, a great guy. That was Pittsburgh. Jimmy Dykes, a great rapport with the guy. Rogers Hornsby, another one that was bad. These old-school guys, just ... "This is my job; I earn my living; ship up or get out," and you can't play for somebody like that. If they didn't have you, they would get somebody else, and if that guy wasn't any good, they would throw him out and get somebody else. You were a pawn, you were a slave, you were a nothing.

The year that I was batting .477, leading both leagues by many, many points, and we were playing Cincinnati, and some guy stood behind one of the other ballplayers from the dugout and would yell out as I was leading off, "You Jew son of a bitch, I wish I had your nose full of nickels," and I would yell out to who ever it might have been, "I wish I had it full of pennies and I would be a millionaire," and then I'd get a hit and then it would make me feel twice as good.

Whatever bat I picked up, whatever I did, it was perfect. It's just like *The Twilight Zone*. I knew that I would continue hitting forever, base hit after base hit. Nobody would ever get me out. I just felt it before the game even started, and it would have held true had it not been for my manager, who did not let me play three games in my own hometown of Brooklyn when we came back from the Western road trip. Charlie Dressen decided not to use me. Why, I didn't know, but I can only say it had to do with anti–Semitism. After all, if you were managing a ballclub and your leading hitter is batting .477, would you take him out of the lineup? No, of course not. So this is what I had to contend with and little by little my average kept going down.

One time one of the fellows on our club, a fellow by the name of Eddie Miksis, a utility infielder, for some unknown reason he called me a Bolshevik. Dressen, on the other hand, overheard it and reprimanded him, "I don't ever want to hear you say that against any religion whatsoever." Yet I know that Charlie Dressen, too, was anti-, very much so.

If you were helping a team win and it's coming close to the Jewish holidays, you had two thoughts. The fans may dislike you if you left the game, you know you're fighting with your guys to be Number One and win, so you don't know which was to go. I at that time would want to fight and win. God would forgive me for playing on the holiday. But then you come to Brooklyn and a fellow like Jake Pitler says, "Now, look, Cal, you're going home for three days because there's the Jewish holiday," but you don't feel right about it. Now if the team was a hundred games behind or, you know, last place, I wouldn't care. If the team is tied for first place and there are those three games are against the second-place team, I would want to stay and play and help them win. That's the way I felt about being Jewish.

I'm sure that the other fellows, unbeknownst to me, were saying or thinking things about it, yes, especially if I was hurting their club and I was winning ballgames. "Oh, that no good Jew, son of a bitch!" Sure. But they didn't come right over to me and say it because, as I said before, I had a good rapport with everybody.

In every town I did play there were Jews, and I think that deep down in their own hearts, win or lose, even if they were for the other team, they say, "Look at that, one Jewish guy playing in the Major Leagues. God bless him!"

Many people have said to me how come I left the game and why don't I become a manager or a talent scout or something or this and that, and my only answer to this is I did not want to live out of a suitcase anymore. I felt like a musician or a traveling salesman. You go to a town for three days and when you open up your suitcase everything is messed up and you have to send it down to press. When you're ready to leave the town you put your stuff in the suitcase, when you get it home it needs pressing again. I was sick and tired of this. I liked roots. I wanted to be with my family. I wanted to have my children growing up where I could see them every day. Plus the fact I was never one to love flying.

I wasn't self-conscious of being Jewish because, as I say, I was a kibitzer and a clown, and I had a lot of fun and teased and joked and everything else, so I got along with everybody. But I knew I was Jewish and I knew I stood out more so than the others and I also knew that I had to be twice as good as my opponents, because if the Jew wasn't twice as good, he was nothing. I think I was set apart a little bit, but I feel that God decided he was going to let one Jew become a ballplayer because he didn't have enough intelligence to make money elsewhere.

SAUL ROGOVIN
Detroit Tigers, 1949–1951;
Chicago White Sox, 1951–1953;
Baltimore Orioles, 1955;
Philadelphia Phillies, 1955–1957
(1923–1995)

I'd be sitting on the bench in the summertime, it's hot to begin with, the pressures are in me, with me, and all of a sudden I'd just fall asleep.— Saul Rogovin, interviewed in April 1982

I felt like the outsider as a Jew. I didn't feel like I was one of them, basically. Deep down inside I never felt that I was accepted, whatever accepted was. Now this wasn't a reaction from my teammates. This was an inward feeling, a deep, gut feeling that I was a Jew and a Jew is oppressed: A Jew is always oppressed. Be on your guard because basically no one likes Jews. That's the gut feeling. Get close, but not too close. Keep everyone at a distance. That was deep in my gut, and that's one of the reasons I felt like an outsider, and I guess I was an outsider because of that. It was a really lonely, very lonely, feeling. Being paranoid because you're a Jew? Yes, it was a lonely feeling.

Well, I guess as time goes by Opening Day still means something. It used to mean more, years ago, you know, when I first left the game, but I haven't been that close to the game as the years have gone by. I'm working and I'm busy doing something else. I watch the box scores, but there's always the feeling that you ... this time of the year that you'd like to go down to spring training, you know, that old feeling to get away from the cold and the wintertime here and join the club in the spring and ... it's something that stays with you. I replay it every spring, you know.

I wasn't really born October 10, 1923 ... that's a little baseball age. We take off ... some of us, at least I did, took off, oh, I'd say about a year and a half of my age, with the naïve expectation that you're more desirable as a younger player than an older player. I was really born March 24, 1922. I discovered that when you lose your fastball, it really doesn't make any difference. [laughs] I was born in Brooklyn and I went to Lincoln High in Coney Island. It was a predominantly Jewish and Italian area. My father and mother bought a little house there and that's where I started to play ball. We had an empty lot across the street and that lot stayed empty, oh, for many, many years and had a semipro baseball team playing across the street. I spent my youth in that lot, you know.

My parents came from Lithuania — Kovno and Vilna. I think that my dad came here in 1880-something, the latter part of the 1880s. I think he mentioned one time that he was seventeen when he came here. I was an only child. My mother gave birth to me when she was in her forties, early forties. My father was in his early fifties when I was born. So my memory of them was always of being elderly. They had been trying to have a child for a long time, and my mother told me that she had been to many doctors and finally she said that one doctor performed some sort of an operation and soon after that be became pregnant. But that was, I think, about fifteen years after they were married. So I was almost an afterthought, I guess. [laughs]

It wasn't a very religious home, but they spoke Yiddish. They also learned English, learned to speak English while they were here so many years. They couldn't write. Mom could write a beautiful letter in Yiddish. So could Pop. I listened to Yiddish and could understand them, but I didn't speak Yiddish in the house. I'm trying to think back to those years. The feeling was that I was out of touch, I guess. My feeling was that I didn't want to be Jewish. The feeling was that I wanted to be whatever an American was, that kind of a thing, and Jewish I associated with something foreign to me, possibly because of my parents being foreign, coming from a foreign land.

I started pro ball, the first four or five years, as a third baseman, first baseman. In '41, the Dodgers sent me to Valdosta for a look-see. They didn't give me a bonus. All they gave me was set of bus tickets back home. They had sent me North, and they released me from their club in Johnstown. In other words, Valdosta was a spring training camp, but a second camp was Johnstown, Pennsylvania. That was a Dodger farm in those days, Class D. That's where they released me from, from Johnstown, they told me to go home. Well, I wasn't able to go home. I didn't feel like it, you know, it was really a catastrophe for me. You're away and you're playing, and all of a sudden they won't sign you and, you know, it was really a traumatic experience.

Someone told me that Beaver Falls needed a first baseman. Well, I think I had $12, $14 on me. That's all I had. I took my last moneys, invested it into a railroad ticket and went to Beaver Falls. Wound up without any money, four o'clock in the morning, I'm at the Bradford Hotel in Beaver Falls, Pennsylvania, looking for the manager, whose name was Dick Goldberg, and I got on the house phone and called him. He signed me for $60 a month.

I wasn't drafted in the war because my folks were elderly — my dad must have been seventy-two, seventy-three — at that time, and I was supporting them at that time, so the draft board sort of gave me a break. They were lenient with me, and I wasn't going to question their wishes. [laughs] So I got a job, working in a defense plant, Brewster Aeronautical, playing ball there. And Dolly Stark, the old umpire, also was working there, and he thought I might be another Greenberg. He saw me play, saw me hit a couple of home runs, you know, and thought that I reminded him of Greenberg. I said this later in one of the interviews, "The way it turned out, the only similarity to Greenberg was that we were both Jewish."

Dolly recommended me to the Giants in training camp in Lakewood, New Jersey, where Mel Ott was the manager. And Gabby Hartnett was the manager of the Jersey City ball club at the time. I was signed to a Jersey City contract as an outfielder. It didn't work out. I didn't hit.

The Giants wanted to make a pitcher out of me. Well, of course this is hindsight, but I wouldn't let them do that. I had an idea: I wanted to play every day. I didn't like the idea of pitching. I liked the idea of playing every day, of hitting a ball, of ... I couldn't see pitching. Pitching was playing maybe twice a week or once a week, sitting on a bench, and it was a foreign thing to me and I couldn't see it. So I refused to do that and, in refusing to that, I passed up an opportunity of ... I would have been with the Giants, you know, ironically. From there, they sold me, when I refused to do that, they sold me to a Washington farm at Chattanooga as a third baseman. I played third base there for a number of years, for three years, before I finally turned to pitching.

The first game I pitched, in the last game of the '45 season, was a

Saul Rogovin finished first in ERA in the American League in 1951 with the Detroit Tigers and Chicago White Sox.

four-hit shutout. I'd never pitched before: I just stepped on the mound and never pitched before. Well, I had a little extra presence of mind because I'd already been ... I had played pro baseball for three or four years by then, so even though it was the first time I had ever pitched, I had some kind of presence, you know. And so from then on I was a pitcher.

At the end of the '47 season, I pitched winter ball in Venezuela. I needed experience and I got in touch or made connections with a professional team in Venezuela and I reported to the Venezuela ball club in the winter.

In Venezuela, I became the Number 1 pitcher on the club. We had a very strong league. They had players there.... Roy Campanella was in the league, Don Newcombe, Luke Easter. Right-fielder ... manager of the White Sox, I've forgotten his name. Larry Doby. A really fast, professional league, and also local players there, and, as I said, I became their top pitcher.

And one day, getting back to this incident, one day I had pitched, I had won a ballgame, the next day.... Not only was I their top pitcher, I was practically the only pitcher they had. So a couple of days later, we had a ballgame, and the owner wanted me to pitch that ball game with one day's rest and I didn't want to do that. I didn't want to take a chance on hurting my arm because my future, I felt, was back in the States and I didn't want to take a chance, and I said, "No, I need a couple of days between starts." He said, "Either you pitch or I'll have you thrown in jail." I couldn't believe that, you know. Still, you're in another country and who knows what happens in another country, especially in a Latin country, you see how volatile they are. So I thought I'd cover myself. I said, "All right." So I agreed to pitch, went out there, but couldn't throw very hard, tried to get by on a change of pace and another change of pace and a third change of pace.

Well, first thing you know, I had walked the first three hitters, and he must have thought I was throwing the game or something, whatever, and the first thing you know four policemen ran out on the field and they surrounded me on the mound. They had rifles, and it looked like something out of *Viva Zapata!* or something, you know. I couldn't believe it, I figured, well.... They had about 10,000 people in the stands. The stands were full. Figured it's a publicity gag, you know, because the crowds were going crazy out there. And they marched me. They said, "Vamos." I knew what that meant, and they marched me across the infield, underneath the stands, and I figured, "Well, they had their gag or they had their publicity stunt," and I was headed for the clubhouse. And then they wouldn't let me do that. The marched me through the streets, about five blocks to the local station house.

They didn't even drive me there; we marched right through cobblestone streets. It was a night ballgame and it was about ten o'clock at night, 9:30 at night, and here I am, surrounded by four policemen marching through the streets in my baseball uniform to this local station house. They booked me there. At the time, I couldn't even speak a word of Spanish. I don't know what they booked me for, and they kept me in the station house until about one o'clock in the morning.

Then they let me go, told me to go back to the ballpark. They put me in a cab, cab driver drove me to the ballpark, let me out, and here I am, one o'clock in the morning, nobody's at the ballpark, I'm there in my uniform. [laughs] So I had to scale the wall. So, at any rate, I broke the door down to the clubhouse and changed clothes, came back, and I was fit to be tied. The next day, the owner came to the hotel, apologized profusely. I said, "No, no, I'm going home. I don't want this treatment," you know. And he says, "Well, I'm really sorry." I said, "No, no, no." And finally he said, "Well, if you stay, I'll raise your salary," and he gave me a pretty good increase. "Well," I said, "I don't..." Well, I started to weaken a little bit, you know, swallowed my pride and stayed on. And so I spent most of the season there.

Spring of '49, I reported to Detroit. Tough ballclub to make. They had this great left-hander, what was his name? He was a little bit over the hill, but he was still a good pitcher. I've forgotten his name now. Had Virgil Trucks, Dizzy Trout, Art Houtteman, Billy Pierce, Ted Gray. Tough pitching staff to make. And so I kept reporting to spring, they'd send me out. I'd look good in the spring, but they'd send me to the minor leagues. Sixteen wins and 163 strikeouts: I considered myself the Number 1 pitcher in the International League that year, 1949. I should have been in the big leagues at that ... I wish I could have stayed on with Detroit. I might have had a good season. I don't know, but I might have. Of course, I still had to make the hurdle, maybe I wouldn't have made the jump, you know. I was very nervous the first time out, when he put me in with Detroit, before they sent me back to.... In 1949, the first thirty days I was with Detroit. He relieved with me one day, and they hit me hard and I lost the game. The he sent me away, sent me to the minors. So I don't know if I would have made the transition then or not. In the meantime, Paul Richards had gotten the job with the White Sox.

In 1950, when I was pitching against the Yankees in Yankee Stadium,

I hit a grand-slam home run. Talk about Frank Merriwell, right? First time I ever appeared in Yankee Stadium. We were leading the league all season and the Yankees were half a game behind us, and if we lost that game we would have been in second place for the first time in a couple of months, and he started me. Well, there were two men on, the score nothing-nothing in the second, two men on, men on second and third, and they passed Bob Swift, the catcher, walked him purposely to get to me, and all I was thinking about was staying out of the double play. There was one out. I was just trying to put the ball in play someplace. Even if I popped up, we had the next hitter coming up, lead-off hitter, so I just didn't want to hit a ground ball, because if I hit the ball on the ground, it was an automatic double-play, Rizzuto and Coleman and those guys, and so it happened, I was just trying to meet the ball. Eddie Lopat was pitching. Hung a high curveball and the first thing you know the.... Swung easily and the ball just jumped off the bat like a shot, you know, a home run, and really an unbelievable day, you know, all my friends were out there and all that kind of business. It was really an unbelievable feeling.

Around the fifth inning, they started to hit me. My arm started to tighten. Also, I hadn't pitched in so long, and it was such an important game and I told Rolfe — Red Rolfe was managing — I told him to take me out before that. The score was 4–3 at the time and my arm wasn't feeling ... it was starting to tighten and he jumped at me, he sort of felt that I was, I don't know, maybe shaking out or frightened or losing my confidence, and he says, "Get in there and pitch," you know. Well, I did the best I could, but it wasn't good enough. DiMaggio hit a home run; the next pitch, Berra hit a home run, back to back. Now we're losing 5–4. Then he took me out. Houtteman came in, pitched no-hit ball the rest of the way, and in the ninth inning we scored two runs to win 6–5.

I had a real good fastball when I came up. Later on, when I'd lost the real good fastball, I developed a change of pace and threw a slider, curve ball.

After my injury, I came back in '51, and meantime Paul Richards had gotten a job as the manager of the White Sox, and Paul liked me as a pitcher. Looking back at it, he was like a father figure to me. He was a young father that understood me because he was a ballplayer and so was I. So it was a special kind of relationship. As soon as I came to the White Sox, I became a starting pitcher with them.

Richards started me against Washington, and I pitched, I think, three or four great innings. I think I had a perfect game against them for about four innings. Then in the fifth inning, the bottom dropped out of everything. I think they scored four or five runs, he took me out, and I figured, Oh, here it goes. Here we go again, I'll never make a pitcher, you know. So he followed me into the clubhouse and he sort of told me.... He told me that if I kept pitching like that I'd win a lot of games. He liked the way I pitched that night, even though I'd allowed those five runs, and sure enough, the next time I went out there I pitched a great game and became one of their top two pitchers. That staff was Billy Pierce and myself. We were the top pitchers for them. Pierce hadn't yet reached his full potential. He was just starting to come in on his own, and I was at my peak at that particular time. I was 12–8, and I led the league in earned runs that year [1951]. Every loss was a tough game. So that was a remarkable year for me, really a fantastic year.

I started to take all this kind of burden onto myself and, hindsight again, totally unrealistic, taking on all kinds of pressure that I shouldn't have taken on. But it was there, and the more that I thought about it and the more I thought of how important I was to this ballclub, the more pressured I felt. First thing you know, that season, instead of winning sixteen, eighteen games or winning twenty games, that I'd feel I had a chance for, I wound up winning six [seven] games, losing eleven, in 1953 and looking so bad that they traded me. In '52 I had come back with a 14–9 record and had improved over the '51 season as far as developing as a big-league pitcher is concerned.

By 1955, Richards had taken over the Baltimore baseball club. It was their second year in the American League that year. They had joined the American League, and it was their second year there, from the International League. He had taken over and he was hiring ballplayers, everything was new over there, and I asked him to give me a chance, to take me to spring training. He took me to spring training in 1955 and I was able to throw. I made the ballclub and became a starting pitcher for them. I won my first game, I think. Yes, I won my first game, pitched a good game for them. "Hoot" Evers won the game for me with a single in the last inning, I think, or extra innings. Won the first game, looked great, and then proceeded to lose my next eight. Although I lost the eight in a row, I pitched solid ball. I could have won most of those eight games, but every time we walked out there we got shut out. They started to release the veterans when Richards saw that they were losing. Richards released me outright.

Well, here I am, half a season gone by, now I'm a free agent. My pension came into play. I only had three and a half years. I needed another year to be eligible for a pension, you know, and everything seemed to really ... this time it really dropped out of sight, everything. Well, I sent telegrams to all the big league clubs and didn't hear from any, except one ball club. The last day I heard from Philadelphia, report to Philadelphia, Philadelphia Phillies. They needed a pitcher over in Philadelphia. Robin Roberts was all pitched out. Curt Simmons had a sore arm. The ace of the staff was Murray Dickson, who was 42 years old at the time, and I joined them and did a good job for them, I became a spot pitcher for them. Mayo Smith kept me there for two and a half years, three years, and I got my pension.

My highest contract was with the White Sox. The most I ever made was $7,000 in a season.

I was married in 1954. '53 or '54. Married for a year and a half, married for a short while, and we divorced. Baseball didn't contribute to the divorce. It contributed to the marriage. I had that bad year in Chicago in '53 and I felt that I needed someone, I felt that ... I was looking for confidence, my confidence was at a very low ebb, and I was looking.... You know, I had seen the great players we had, like Nellie Fox, Billy Pierce, a few others I had seen, they were married men and I felt possibly ... maybe I needed someone in my corner, you know, needed rooting for me or something like that, and I think that.... That was one of the reasons that I felt I had to get married, I felt that would make me a better ballplayer. Not a very good ... really, not a very good reason to get married.

Wherever I went I made many appearances in the Jewish community as a speaker, you know, sports nights and B'nai B'rith banquets and things like that, and the question always comes up, did you run into any anti–Semitism? And truthfully, no. Well, once to my face from Russ Derry, an old Yankees outfielder. Played for Rochester at the time. He was closing out his career. and I was coming up. I was with Buffalo, and I had beaten them that night. I had pitched and beaten them and I had gotten him out easily, and he was high in the bar, local bar, that we were in after the game, a bar and restaurant we used to eat in. Late at night, twelve o'clock at night, and he had a few beers too many, you know. Had a few beers too many, and he started to curse and he claimed that I spiked him. There was a play at first base where I covered first base and I spiked him accidentally, and he claimed that I did that deliberately and he wouldn't let up, you know.

So finally he called me a "Jew bastard" before... You know, I tried to calm him down, but by the time, you know, he just wouldn't keep quiet and finally he called me a "Jew bastard" and I hit him, and the first thing you know, you know, there was a thousand people there, broke everything up. And he went his way, and I went my way. But that wasn't really ... I don't really consider that a ... I don't consider that an anti–Semitic remark in the.... Why? Well, in the context that it came from, that wasn't an anti–Semitic remark. He was just pissed off that they'd lost the game, he was pissed off that I struck him out a couple of times. and that's the way he had of getting out his feelings, and he probably honestly felt that I tried to spike him.

Someone on our bench rode Al Rosen one day. Al was playing third base for Cleveland and I remember.... I forget who it was. In fact, I didn't know who it was because I was at one end of the bench and the player was on the other end of the bench. And Al always killed us. I mean, it's another story like ... as I told you with Rochester about me pitching against Derry. Rosen always killed us, always beat us. Rosen [laughs] must have hit at .400, you know, when I was over there, he always hit about .400. [laughs]

So he grounded out one night, and as he trotted back in front of our dugout somebody yelled, "Well, we got you that time, you 'Jew bastard,' "or something like that, and Al ... Al was a tough guy, you know, Al was a fighter at one time, he was a club fighter, and Al stopped, you know, he stopped in his tracks, he didn't know who it was, and I looked myself because I didn't like it. It embarrassed me. I don't know who it was till this day and I didn't ask, I didn't want.... It was so unpleasant I didn't want to bother to ask, you know, I just kept quiet. And Al walked over to our dugout and he said, "That son of a bitch that called me a 'Jew bastard,' would he care to say that again?" you know, and everybody was just sitting there, you know. And I had mixed feelings. I felt very funny because here I am, I'm an opposing player and also I'm a Jew, you know. [laughs] I had mixed feelings over that. I felt good for Al, you know, I really ... oh, thatta boy, Al, give it to them, you know, and I also felt sort of disloyal, feeling for an opposing player, you know, funny feeling.

Narcolepsy is falling asleep while you're sitting up. All of a sudden, you're just out, you're just sleeping. Narcolepsy, the definition of nar-colepsy, "narco" is sleep, and so narcolepsy is uncontrollable sleep. Along with that is cataplexy, where you lose control of your muscles, coordination and muscles, and I did that a few times. I'd hit a line drive; a feeling of elation would cause a muscular reaction. I'd hit a line drive, you know, or a long hit, and you know the feeling of immediately, you know, the feeling of elation. I could barely make it to first base, I would stagger down to first base, my legs would go out from under me, and I'd just stagger into first base. I didn't know what it was. And so a doctor analyzed it as narcolepsy, whatever that is.

So the way it's turned out, it's more psychological, it's more psychological than.... As I've said, they don't know what the disease is, but there is a psychological background to it that.... First place, a true narcoleptic, it's a very debilitating disease. It's someone that falls asleep hundreds of times a day, that's half-paralyzed. I mean you can't get up, you can't move, something like that. That's a true narcoleptic. I'm not that way at all, thank God. But there's a similarity in the symptoms, that the pressure — and this is what I believe, looking back at it now — that the pressure that I felt playing ball.

This started when I was in the big leagues. That the pressures of, oh, possibly the marriage, the marriage and playing ball and the pressures of staying in the big leagues, worrying about my career, worrying about.... What didn't I worry about? You know, worrying about my parents, who were old when I was born, worrying about how they were while I was away playing. There was no one taking care, as long as they were all right, and thank God they were all right for practically all their lives. I wrote to them every day and I called them. I could have called them more often, I guess, but I didn't. But as long as I ... I kept getting letters from them, you know, I'd get a letter from them and I knew they were all right.

So all these pressures, I think, contributed to a certain breakdown, certain blackouts, a certain breakdown in my makeup, where if the ... I'd be sitting on the bench in the summertime, it's hot to begin with, the pressures are in me, with me, and all of a sudden I'd just fall asleep. Just out of a clear sky, I'd just fall asleep. I wasn't sleepy, but all of a sudden I'd get sleepy and just close my eyes, and then I was out. And then I'd come out of it. This would happen ... at the worst it happened maybe half a dozen times a day, which wasn't good, you know. It was embarrassing at certain times. Also worrisome. And as the years have gone by, I've gotten out of baseball, as I began to understand a little bit more about myself and what was going on, these things have eased up on me, these pressures have eased up, so I don't fall asleep anymore. I sleep less now than I ever did in my life. This physical reaction takes place once in a while when I get very angry. Then I get a certain physical reaction, but that lasts a second and then it's over with and I can handle that.

A sportswriter, however, Warren Brown, a sportswriter for the *Chicago Tribune*, at the time, took that as a ... when I had my bad year, took that as a take-off point, and claimed that I wasn't trying, that I was gutless, that I didn't give a damn. I have an idea that might have started ... it started, I guess, from my having a bad season and then the fact that I slept on the bench, you know, that I'd fall asleep on the bench, he picked it up and used it also as a.... Maybe that turned him against me, because he was very vitriolic in the papers against me. They should trade me, get rid of me, I don't give a damn about playing ball, that I don't care if I win or lose or things like that. And I believe he was very instrumental.... In fact, Frank Lane told me that usually they keep a player that's had a couple of good years for them. If he has a bad year, they don't trade him off that quickly. He said, "Usually I'd try to keep a player like you," he said, "but," he said, "Saul," he said, "you'd be amazed at the number of people who wrote in, that said get rid of him, he's no good and things like that, he doesn't care." These people picked that up from ... I think Warren Brown must have had a very big effect on them because they read it in the papers.

I can think of a couple of players that felt that I had no confidence in myself and didn't want to pitch, you know, and, well, I guess I can't blame them. I mean maybe it was true, you know. Maybe without Richards, you know, maybe with Rolfe there, was who was a strange manager to me after Richards, maybe I was afraid, maybe I was too cautious to go out there and really break my ass and take a chance and say, "Well, fuck next year. Let me go ahead and play now, and I'll worry about next year when it comes up," you know. Because when I finally did that, my arm did come around when I had the trainer manipulate it, where I wouldn't let him do that before. When I said, "Well, all right, the hell with it," then my arm did come around, see. But when I went to Richards I felt at home, that father image. I felt I was back home. I played with him for three years in the minors. So maybe they're right about that, you know. Maybe it's a good rap that I deserve.

Toward the late stages of it, it was starting to affect my playing, this worry, see, and so it got to the point where I started to take Dexedrine. I'd take just enough where it could tide me over a game. That upper would give me ... became a very strong thing to me. I couldn't take too much of it because that would keep me awake, I couldn't sleep, I had a bad reaction taking too much of it. But I cut down to just enough where I could get through a game and I needed that at that point. So that's how I got by, because this thing.... I felt tired, constantly tired. The pressures were wearing me down, instead of feeling up. No matter how much I slept, there were times I'd go out to the ballfield, I felt like I was up all night, see, where I shouldn't, shouldn't feel that way. That's when I'd grab that pill, that's when I needed it, and that's what kept me around two or three years longer.

I've done what I wanted to do in baseball. I wanted to do more, of course, but so does everyone else. But I've had a happy life, in spite of all the problems, and people have been good to me. I'm married again, I've got a good second marriage. Evelyn, my wife, Evelyn, supports me in many ways. I met Evelyn through a friend of mine ... oh, we went together about ten years before we decided to get married. So actually I've spent the last twenty-five years with her and we've had our battles, we've had our ups and downs, and one thing that we have that I recognize, that no matter how much we battle, we don't stay angry. So that's sort of an indication that it's pretty good.

I teach remedial reading in the New York City school system. All grades. Mostly, I guess, ninth, tenth grade. These kids are at the bottom of the ladder when it comes to reading. Some of them are reading on a fourth-grade reading level, third-grade, fifth-grade, and they're in ninth, tenth grade, eleventh grade, so it's very difficult. Verbally, they're fine, you know, nothing wrong. Reading? Forget about it. [laughs] A lot of problems when it comes to reading and writing. By and large, they like me. Why? Because I have a feeling for them, I feel, I empathize. I have a certain empathy. I like them. I don't like all of them. I mean, you know, some of them really make me angry and all that. But taking the whole picture, I have a compassion for them, I have an empathy for them, and I think they sense that.

How would I like to be remembered? That's a very difficult ... I guess ... I don't know. I'd like to be remembered as some sort of a strong person, a feeling of, there's a person that has a lot of strength, a lot of inner strength, a lot of guts or something or whatever you'd call it. But you know, it's a funny thing, there's another side to this. That I don't really care too much for that feeling, but it comes out of another feeling that on the other side of the coin is someone that's a young boy that's very frightened. That's the other side of the coin that brings out this kind of feeling. So it's really a cover-up of someone that's very, very ... I don't know what to say. Inadequate? Helpless? Hopeless? I'm not that. I'm that in one sense, but I'm not that in another sense. But I do have a lot of frightened feelings that are lying around that need dealing with.

LOU LIMMER
Philadelphia Athletics, 1951, 1954
(1925–2007)

In 1954, Lou Limmer was responsible for the last home run ever hit by a member of the Philadelphia Athletics before the team moved to Kansas City. During his stints in Philadelphia, Limmer was known as the "Babe Ruth of batting practice" for the prodigious home runs he hit before games. He also was a minor league star for many years. Unlike many Jewish Major Leaguers, Limmer was a regular synagogue-goer for most of his life. Despite suffering from emphysema, he agreed to be interviewed in January 2005 in Boca Raton, Florida.

I got along with most of the umpires. There was this one, Joe Paparella, he was a nice guy. We had a game in Detroit and Saul Rogovin was pitching and Joe Ginsberg was catching. I came up to pinch-hit. So Paparella comes from behind home plate, and he dusts it off and he says, "Boy, now I've got the three Hebes. I wonder who's going to win the battle?" And Rogovin throws the first pitch and I hit it into the stands and I round the bases and Paparella says, "I guess you're the winner, Lou." It so happens I wasn't because Joe Ginsberg stayed with Detroit and Saul Rogovin went to the White Sox that year and he led the league in ERA, and poor Lou Limmer, he got shipped to the minors.

I played two years in the majors, in 1951 and 1954. A few years ago, my wife and I went to see the picture *Bull Durham*. All of the sudden, they sent Kevin Costner back to the minors. I left. I went home. I didn't stay for the finish. That struck home. That hurt me 'cause I know I was able to play, and I couldn't finish. I never got the chance. Did I enjoy playing ball? I would do it all over again, even with all the heartaches I had.

I grew up in a big family — twelve kids, eight boys and four girls. I was the youngest. Three of them were born in the old country, in Austria. My parents moved here well before World War I, but they went back a couple of times.

In the old country, my father, Charles, was a Roman-Greco wrestler. My mother's name was Elizabeth. My father was a waiter. My two brothers, the oldest and next to the oldest, they were wrestlers. They had to make a few extra dollars, so they did wrestling on the side. And my brother Ralph was a contender for the middleweight crown, in boxing.

We had an Orthodox home. I mean strictly. Everyone was bar mitzvahed, except my brother Ralph. He was the run-around. You couldn't find him if you wanted to find him. He wasn't bar mitzvahed until he was seventy-three, in my shul.

We had a strictly kosher home. In fact, when I got married we were strictly kosher because her mother who lived with us thirty-five years — may she rest in peace — lived with us. But after awhile, I wasn't strictly kosher. But when it came to the meats in the house, everything was kosher.

When I was a kid, Greenberg played ball at nearby Crotona Park. I'd run in there and grab a bat and take it away from home plate — we called it jerking the bats. At that time, they had maybe only two bats to a team. But hey, man, I was there. I just wanted to be with the baseball players. Years later, Greenberg remembered me for doing that, but we had a problem. When the A's sent me down, he [Greenberg was then Cleveland's general manager] said Cleveland would pick me up. They wanted to buy me. I called him up and said, "Hank, the A's are sending me down. Here's your chance. They're looking to option me out." He says, "Well, Lou, I let one of their guys go by; they let one of my guys go by." Since that time, I didn't see eye to eye with Hank Greenberg, although he was a nice guy.

I was a left-handed pitcher, and a better pitcher than hitter, in semi-pro games. Well, listen, I was big for my age. In those times in semipro, guys would bet $5 a man or $20 a man, or their teams would bet against one another and put up a jackpot of money. I was fourteen. Well, one day, it was a late afternoon game on Saturday, and I said my prayers with my father, and I pitched that day. And I not only won and got $25, but I bet on myself, and I came home with $50. My dad called me a bum and said, "Where'd you steal that money from? Did you steal it?" I said, "No, I got it from playing baseball."

And he said, "You play baseball?" I said, "Dad, that's what I got." So Sunday, I had to say my prayers also. It made no difference what day of

Lou Limmer, a slugging first baseman who played for the Philadelphia Athletics in 1951 and 1954, recalls a few teammates who were anti–Semitic, as well as one who backed him up.

the week it was. And they called me from downstairs and said, "Hey, Bummy, come on, you gonna play ball?" And my father says, "You gonna play ball today?" And I said, "Yeah." And he said, "You go."

When it came time to join the service, I wanted to be in the Navy, but I couldn't pass the colorblind test. So I became a flight engineer in the Army Corps. One day in Biloxi, Mississippi, I was working in the cowling of a B-29 when a fire broke out inside as we were fueling. I jumped out of the hold and tore a muscle in my shoulder. That was the end of my pitching career. It's lucky I didn't get hit by the propeller.

After that, my shoulder would pop out. When I got up to the big leagues, they didn't know I had a bad arm. I couldn't throw too good. I threw underhand to keep my shoulder from popping out. Wally Moses taught me how to throw overhand when I got to the big leagues. They told me if I wanted to shut people up, shut them up with your bat. And that's how I got to the big leagues.

I thought the shoulder would get better, but it never did. I got out of the service in 1946 and went to work with my brother Ralph in the commercial refrigeration business in the Bronx. I was also playing sandlot baseball, and a scout for the A's saw me and invited me to Philadelphia for a tryout.

I worked out with them for a week, and one day I was in the batting cage and the regulars came out. This is why I love Sam Chapman so much. I was just out of the service and the regulars wanted to hit. One of their guys said, "Come on, you bush SOB, get out of there. We got to hit." And Sam Chapman comes up and says, "Let the kid alone. I might learn something," because he was in a slump at the time and thought he might find something. And he let me hit for another ten minutes. They were as mad as hell, but he was my hero.

Connie Mack — who was 83 at the time and still owned the team and was the manager — watched it all from the stands at Shibe Park, and he called me up into the stands. He said, "Listen, young man." I'm giving this to you slow, the way he talked. "Young man ... we like ... the way ... you play. And we'd like ... to have ... you join ...our organization."

I said, "Oh, Mr. Mack, that would be fantastic." And he said, "Well, we have a Double-A team and an A team, and do you know what that is?" And I didn't know what that was. I was just out of the Army. I didn't know nothing. I wanted to go to the big leagues. He said, "Well, you're not good enough for that." He said, "We have a Double A," and I said, "OK, I'll go to Double A." And he said, "Well, you have to learn a little more." Then he said to me, "Do you want to be a star in D ball or do you want to be a so-so in Double A?" I said, "I'll be a star in D."

The Phillies had given a couple of big bonuses a few weeks before, and I said to Mr. Mack — everybody called him Mr. Mack — I said, "Well, these other players got bonuses, and I think I deserve some more money, too."

Then he did his heart routine. He grabbed his heart and went, "Ugh, ugh ... we don't ... usually do that ... young man. "When I saw him do that, I got scared. I thought he was going to die. I said, "OK, OK, Mr. Mack. I'll sign, I'll sign." Right away, he got better. "Go see Ira Thomas up in the office. He'll take care of you."

But in the beginning, I thought he was going to die. And when I finished with him, all the ballplayers later told me that was an act with this guy. He gave me a bonus of $200. That was the whole bonus. And he sent me to D ball for $300 a month. That was a lot of money down there then. It was usually $75 a month. But he gave me a bonus of $200 and I had to pay my own way on the bus home.

When I played ball, wherever I went, I went to see if I could find a synagogue. That's the first thing I'd do. I'd open up the phone book and find out where the synagogues are. And that's where I found the apartments and homes for my wife and me to stay. In Lincoln, Nebraska, the Lincoln dairy belonged to Jewish people. And the hotel. And when I went to Omaha, the car dealer was Jewish. He knew I didn't have any wheels, so he gave me a car to drive around. I'm a married man with children, so what do you think he gave me? He gave me a Corvette. I said, "That's not for me. I'm not a single guy." So he gave me a station wagon to drive around.

In 1949 in Lincoln, that's where I had my neck broken. It was my first year at Lincoln, and I had a pretty good year. I slid into the third baseman, and the throw got away from him and the third baseman kicked me in the head and I broke my neck. I went blind for a couple of days. And my arms and legs didn't feel so hot.

They wanted to drill holes in my head to hold weights, but I said, "Oh, no," so they put a collar under my chin and they put a weight in the back of my head. And it stretched out my neck. It made my jawbones deteriorate a little bit, and every now and then they'll pop out of joint.

I took batting practice three weeks later, in my regular clothes. I didn't hit any out, but I could swing the bat. For a couple years, I couldn't hear myself breathe at the times I had the headaches. Then they went away.

In 1950, the A's thought I was ready, but they wanted to make sure, so they had an agreement with the Dodgers to send me to St. Paul, which was in the Dodgers organization. And in 1950, of course, Jackie Robinson was there and Gil Hodges was coming in and, again, I can't remember his name — the Rifleman — Chuck Connors was there. Afterward, they sold him to Chicago, but the A's didn't want to make any deals with the Dodgers. They wanted to keep me.

In spring training, I also stayed with Jackie Robinson a little bit. That was an experience because in those days, you know, they still had the restrictions. In some hotels the Jews couldn't stay, or in some other places the blacks couldn't drink water or they couldn't eat in restaurants. They had to go to other colored people's houses to eat. I went with him. I wasn't going to let him go alone. And I'll tell you what. The food was a lot better there than at the hotel. He was a pretty nice guy, Jackie Robinson. He was very intense. Very intense.

In Lexington, North Carolina, on the signs they had, "Jews, Niggers, and Dogs stay out." They were along the railroad tracks and some of the roads. "Jews, Niggers, and Dogs stay out." And when we traveled in Florida, some of the roads on some of the buses and they would have signs, "Jews and Niggers aren't allowed."

You're darn right it was worse for the blacks. But we had some of that experience, too. In Lincoln, my wife was sitting with a couple of ballplayers' wives who were looking at her. She said, "What are you looking at?" The wives said, "You're Jewish." My wife said, "Would you like to see my head? There are no horns." And she had to show them her head. These wives had been to college, too. That's what it was like in those days.

I was playing with Toronto at the time, 1955, and Castro was starting to come into power. We'd have batting practice in Havana, because Havana was one of the teams in the International league, and Castro would come down and work out in the infield. He'd catch and he'd play shortstop and he'd pitch. He wasn't too bad.

At that time, a ballplayer to get to the Major Leagues was a thousand to none. To none. They had the reserve clause and if you didn't like it, you could get a lunch bucket. Go ahead and complain. I knew I was going to be with the Athletics in 1951, but I got there at the wrong time. Ferris Fain led the league in '51 and in '52. In '52, they sent me back to the minors because I was the worst pinch-hitter in the world. I hit .159. But I knew I was a better hitter than that. And they knew it. In '52 and '53 I was in the minors, and in '54 I got back.

I pinch-hit for Joe Tipton on my first trip to Yankee Stadium as a player and I hit a ninth-inning home run off Vic Raschi. I never touched the ground. I started rounding the bases and Kermit Wahl was on in front of me, looking at the homer that went out, and almost passed him on the bases. He turned around and caught me, 'cause I would have passed him. He put his hand on my chest and he said, "Wait a minute, you bush SOB. Relax." And I said, "Hurry up, hurry up, get off the bases."

I wanted to get off. So we rounded the bases and I got into the dugout and [manager] Jimmy Dykes said, "You don't look so good." I was white as a sheet. "You better go in the clubhouse. I think you're going to puke." And I did.

I was so excited. That was the greatest thing in the world. Not only that, my family was there. When we were walking home up the hill after the game, kids asked me for my autograph. When I finished, my mom said to me, "You know, from you, I got nachas [Yiddish for pride]." That was the greatest thing that happened to me in baseball. Other than that home run, when she said that, that's what you're here for.

Other umpires, not that they were good or bad, but they put me in my place right away. We were in Yankee Stadium and, geeze, Cal Hubbard, what a monster. He played football. He was an All-American football player. He's in the pro football and pro baseball halls of fame, by the way. Anyway, Vic Raschi is pitching that day. And the first pitch is up here and he says, "Strike one." And I said, "Gee, that looked a little high, Mr. Hubbard." And he says, "Well, OK, now get in there and hit, bush." The next pitch is right down the middle. You couldn't put it any better. And he says, "Ball one."

And Yogi Berra jumps up and says that pitch was right down there and blah, blah, blah, blah. And Yogi Berra walks out to console the pitcher and the umpire comes out in front of the plate. And he says, "You see that, young man? I just wanted to let you know who's the boss. Now, you're on your own." The next pitch, I hit a home run. The next day, I come up to the plate and Yogi Berra says, "Hey, bush, you feeling pretty good?" And I'm standing at the plate, and he throws dirt on my shoe. And I say, "Hey, Yogi, cut it out, will ya." And I step in the box, and he throws dirt on me again. And I said to the umpire, "Hey, he's throwing dirt on my shoe." He said, "Shut up and get up there and hit, bush." I was a rookie. And I hit into a double play.

The worst anti–Semite was Joe Coleman and outfielder Dave Philley. They were both pretty good anti–Semites. Some of the people I knew from the A's used to tell me all the things that were going on behind my back. Ferris Fain wasn't too good a one, either, although I was taking his job. When it comes to Jewish ballplayers, I don't care what team you're on, somewhere along the line there's anti–Semitism. If you're a good ballplayer, they leave you alone. When the '54 season came along, I was one of the best.

Allie Clark was the one that took care of me when Dave Philley gave me a hard time. I wanted to challenge him and Clark says, "Wait, you're still a bush. You're still a rookie. I'll help you." He told Dave Philley to leave the kid alone, he's just a rookie. They got to talking back and forth and saying things to one another and they got to pushing and Allie Clark decked him. He knocked him on his fanny. Since then, Philley never bothered me. That was it. No one ever really bothered me. I got along pretty good. All the fellows used to do their crossword puzzles, and they'd run into a problem and they'd say, "Go see the Hebe. Go see the Hebe. He'll tell you." I was their father superior. I was their advisor. I didn't know from nothing, but they sent them to me. Jews were supposed to know everything. Good, let them think that.

In '54 they had Don Bollweg at first. He came from the Yankees. I'd pinch-hit in a game here and there. I wasn't getting to play at all. And only because he came from the Yankees. He was hitting a resounding .120. So they put me in and I hit .300 from June on. And I don't know if I led the team or tied for home runs [Limmer hit 14 in 316 at-bats, tying Gus Zernial for one behind team leader Bill Wilson].

That's the year Gus Zernial broke his collarbone and the fans applauded. Tough fans, but they know what they're talking about. At the end of the season, Eddie Joost said, "I'm sorry for not playing you." I said, "Thanks a lot." And that was the end. I got the last Philadelphia A's home run. That was in Yankee Stadium. And then I got the last base hit. I had no idea. I didn't find out until years later when I heard it on the radio. I thought I'd be back in the big leagues the next year, and I was done after that. When contracts were sent out, Lou Boudreau sent me a telegram that said bring an outfielder's glove. When he said bring an outfielder's glove, I said, "That's it, goodbye Charlie." I was done. I was a first baseman.

My highest salary was $7,500, and when I was sent down, they let me keep the same salary. I went to Birmingham of the Southern Association in 1958. In Birmingham, I helped pay for my kid's bar mitzvah. If you hit a home run in the playoffs, especially, they'd give you a $50 bond. And I hit twelve home runs. And they gave you a radio, too. In '59 they wanted me to go to the West Coast and manage and play on the West Coast for the Detroit organization. I said, "No, that's it." Besides, I had two young kids at the time, and my wife said it's time and my brother promised me I'd be a partner in his refrigeration business. And when I got home, he got married and got into a partnership with his father-in-law and his brother-in-law. I worked for my brother and I was going broke. So I went into competition with him after that.

The best players I saw? Joe DiMaggio. What an outfielder. What a hitter. Ted Williams. He was the greatest. And he was a good outfielder. They used to knock him, but he was a good outfielder. And Stan Musial. He was fantastic. I played against Mickey Mantle a little bit. He was a good one. And Chico Carrasquel at shortstop. He should be in the Hall of Fame before Phil Rizzuto. And Luis Aparicio was the greatest. Hank Aaron, I remember him when he was in the Sally League, a second baseman. I thought he was Jewish. With a name like Hank Aaron? Oh, sure. He was a hell of a player.

After baseball, I was president of my synagogue for five years. I spoke Yiddish. Oh, yeah. Because of my grandma. If I wanted to eat, I talked Yiddish. And my mother and father, when they didn't want us to know, they talked Polish. Yeah, Yiddish I understand very well. Street Yiddish.

I knew the other Jewish players. In New York, there was Cy Block, and there was Mickey Rutner and Cal Abrams and Sid Gordon and Saul Rogovin. There were six of us. We knew one another. We talked, we got together.

All the old A's, I see them on Old-Timers Day in October. The A's Society, it's like a cousins' club. You play in a lot of ballparks and they forget you. With the A's, everybody knows you. Everybody seems to like you. And you're a hero. You're actually a hero. They may forget your name, and they say, "Oh, yeah, I remember you." They never forget you.

ED MAYER
Chicago Cubs, 1957–1958
(1931–)

Ed "Eddie" Mayer, a southpaw pitcher, was interviewed in December 2005 in California. The interview took place in a small guest room stuffed with photographs of his large extended family and baseball memorabilia. Among his prize pieces is a trophy personally handed to him by Babe Ruth for being Most Valuable Player in a 1947 San Francisco teen tournament. The interview was updated in 2011.

My dad, Ned, was born in Hong Kong in '09, and so he got over here in '13 or '14. And he was playing ball by the late twenties. And he was very good. He was the third baseman for the Galileo High team. You know who the shortstop was? Joe DiMaggio! He played semipro ball. But this was the Depression, and I was in my mother's womb, so he couldn't chase his dream. But he instilled it in me. (He points at picture of himself as a toddler.) You see, that's me, and the bat is taller than I am!

They wanted me to play ball. My mother did want me to finish my education, and they wanted me to go to Lowell, which was the best high school at the time and probably still is. And I went to Cal, which was fortunate, because when I was finished playing I went back to Cal and got my teaching credential instead of spending the rest of my career as a bum.

You know, a lot of ballplayers, when they're finished playing, they don't do much. They don't have much to fall back on. I taught twenty-five years in Pacifica at three schools. And I enjoyed it! I'm not just a P.E. guy. I love math and science and Spanish, and I play piano and guitar. I like everything.

My grandparents were religious, and they lived in the Mission District over in San Francisco. And they insisted I go to Hebrew School. My father was never bar mitzvahed. They insisted I go to Beth Israel on Geary and Fillmore. It later burned down. But before it burned, they saved the stained-glass rosette. And, somehow, it ended up at the shul in Aptos, near Santa Cruz, where my son goes. That's the same place my grandson and granddaughter were bar mitzvahed and bat mitzvahed. It's an incredible coincidence. I'm not religious. I don't go to shul. But I am culturally Jewish, totally. And I know lots of Yiddish and love to play around, but I don't tend to the religious part.

We won that city championship — you can see the picture here under the clock. I'm the scrawny one with glasses. But I could really throw the ball hard. People played on all kinds of different teams. You'd play for a bar, a company: Double Play, Walter Gordon Realty, the Junior Seals. Look here [he points at a newspaper box score], I played on the same team as my dad. We were a man short, so he played third. He must have been about thirty-five. He went 2-for-3 and we won, 4–1. I bet you he was a little upset; they batted me higher than he was. I got 1-for-4, so he did better. But I also pitched!

[He unearths an old, handwritten score sheet.] You want to see how good I was? Here's my stats from the Gordon Realty team in 1952. I'm 15–2 with a 0.95 ERA in 142 innings. I could really throw. You see those numbers? Eighty hits allowed in 142 innings. And 174 strikeouts. This was a good team. You see that guy there? [He points to the team photo.] That's Jim Gentile, he became a big league star. At that point, I was throwing every which way. [He points to a dozen-shot montage of his sidearm pitching motion from a Cuban newspaper in the '50s.] But in Cuba, I was really effective with the sidearm. That's what caught the Cubs' eye. They gave me a chance.

I had signed up with the Red Sox, and I'd been on Red Sox farm clubs for three years. They had squads in San Jose, which was C ball, Greensboro, which was B ball, and at Montgomery, Alabama, which was A ball. I won thirty-four games in those first two years. And they didn't bring me up very fast. I was traded over to the St. Louis Cardinals, which is how I got to Omaha.

I did well there, and then they told me, "We want you to go to Cuba and play in winter ball." Well, I said, "OK." The problem was, I pitched 123 innings after having pitched all summer. After that, I was brought up to spring training with the Cards, along with Stan Musial and all those people. They didn't have room for me, so they sent me back to Omaha.

Ed Mayer, who pitched for the Cubs in 1957 and 1958, remembers segregated hotels for black players when he was a minor leaguer in the Deep South.

But then there was a trade, and I was the player to be named later. So, I was sent to Fort Worth of the Texas League. It was a combination team of Dodgers and Cubs. Larry Sherry was on my team. He's also Jewish. At the end of that season, the Cubs called me up.

We didn't talk about it [being Jewish]. Larry Sherry wasn't religious either. Nobody cared we were Jewish, to tell you the truth. Only a couple of nuts in the stands and one teammate with the Cubs, whom I won't name, who told us we couldn't go to that golf club or wherever the team was going.

I didn't suffer much at all [as a Jew]. Somebody yelled at me from the stands one time in Indianapolis. I couldn't go to a function at a country club they had when I was in spring training with the Cubs. And I couldn't belong to that frat at Cal.

I didn't know [about the anti–Jewish rules]. Everyone in high school wanted to be in their frat, and so I joined it. I was there a while, and somebody walked down from the Jewish frat and said, "Do you know you've got a Jew in your frat?" They came to me and apologized and said it wasn't because they didn't like me but they weren't allowed. So I walked right up the hill and joined the Sammies [the Jewish fraternity Sigma Alpha Mu]! Mostly, though, nobody cared what religion you were as a baseball player. They just wanted to know how you could do.

My salary was really pitiful compared to today's standards. Duke Snider was making $20,000 when he was a great player and $40,000 when he was MVP of the National League. And we had no agents and no leverage. We had to beg them for raises. It was tough. So, you know, $10,000 is good, really good money. The most money I ever made was in Cuba. You got good pay in the winter league.

But I didn't play for money! I didn't care about money. Stan Musial had a winter job. We all had winter jobs. Even the big shots. That's how it was. Now these jerks make five, ten, fifteen million. It's mind-boggling. Old farts like me just look at them, and [he shakes his head] they're selfish! They want to make more than the other guy! So what! How many lobsters can you eat at a time?

I have no respect for today's players. They're bigger, faster, and stronger than we were. But [he taps his head] they don't play the game the old-fashioned way. They don't hit the cutoff man. They don't call for the ball and they run together. You never saw that in the old days, and now it happens all the time. But they do make a lot of money and they do hit the ball a long way.

But that ball is juiced, I swear! I saw something, Greg Maddux was on the mound for the Cubs, and he bounced the ball on the mound, he threw it down and it bounced up like a rubber ball into his hands! [He points at his collection of old game balls from the 1950s.] These balls won't bounce! So if someone hits the ball, instead of going 280 feet it goes 400, and it's a home run.

We never had anybody juiced. Drunk? Yes. We had people drunk in my era. But nobody used any dope. I never saw any amphetamines. Look, we had arms like this. [He shows his arm.] This is what a normal arm looks like. Not a Sammy Sosa or Mark McGwire Incredible Hulk arm. Forget it, no way. In fact, we weren't even allowed to bowl or lift weights. They thought we might hurt our arms. Now they've disproven that, but in those days, we didn't do those things. We acted naturally. Now they have weight training and personal trainers, and they work out all winter. Which is fine. They're marvelous athletes, don't get me wrong.

I'm not a Giants fan. I'm a Cubs fan. I like the young players they have now. I wish their pitchers would be able to do what they can do. It's too bad. They have had chances, but they didn't do it. Maybe some day. Before I die, I'd like to see the Cubs win.

I was in the Deep South playing in Montgomery in '55, so I saw all the segregated bathrooms, dining rooms in hotels—guys on my team couldn't go and eat with us or stay with us. In Louisiana, they weren't allowed to take the trip. They couldn't play in Louisiana: there was a law about black and white players playing sports.

This is a bad incident: We were traveling from Montgomery through Georgia. And we stopped, and everyone wanted to buy a Coke. The machine was outside of a gas station, and there was a guy on my team from San Diego, a black guy who later became a famous pitcher, Earl Wilson. So, we all get off the bus to buy a Coke and Earl goes to put his nickel in the machine—a nickel, ha!—and the cracker attendant comes out and points a gun at him and says, "No N—is going to buy a Coke out of my machine."

I jumped in front of him and pushed him back on the bus and bought him his Coke. But that guy could have gotten away with killing a black man back then in the South. He could have made up a story. There was that kind of prejudice there, and the black couldn't do anything. Also, if the attendant knew I was Jewish, he would have shot me.

I think [part of the reason Mayer didn't make the big leagues until twenty-six] was that I was lax in not developing a good curveball until later. I had a good sinker, and when it was working I could throw it again and again all day, and they kept beating it into the ground. What else are you going to do with it? When I was in A ball at the end of that season, a scout for the St. Louis Cardinals got me on the side and taught me how to throw a good curve. As soon as I learned the curve, boom, boom, boom, I went right up. It took me an extra two years to get to the Majors. I didn't think I'd ever get there.

There were so many leagues! There were eight D leagues. There were four B leagues. You had to fight your way through. And there were only sixteen teams with twenty-five guys on each. There were four hundred big league ballplayers. That's it! Now they've got thirty-two teams. It's almost double the number of guys in the Majors. It's a lot easier to get to the Majors now. I think the talent level was higher in the old days. It's diluted now. We had guys from other places, too. Orestes Minoso from the White Sox. Tony Taylor. Vic Power from Puerto Rico.

I'll be honest with you. [My call-up] came out of the blue. It was an ordinary year with the Fort Worth, Texas, AA mixed team of Dodgers and Cubs, and all of a sudden they said you're going to Chicago. And I said, "Great!" Bing! All because of Cuba. They scouted me down there and I won a good, 1–0 game. I found out later there was a scout for the Cubs in the stands. I looked good that day.

I got to the Majors in the end of '57, and in '58 I had to go to spring training to try and make the team. And I did really well in spring training. I also had a very good move to first base. I picked off a guy and heard everybody go, "Oooooh!"

And then, finally, my arm wore out. I never had been a reliever. I'd always been a starter. A relief pitcher's got to warm up every day. Starter's in trouble, warm up, he gets out of trouble, sit down. Two innings later, warm up, pitch an inning. It's very tough to be a reliever. Very tough. Where the shoulder meets the bicep. I tore it up, tore it into spaghetti. And you can't fix it. So that was the end of my career. That was the end of it. Right now, I play tennis, but it's the racquet that gives me all my power. I still can't throw hard, and it's been — well, it's been more than fifty years!

I was losing it, losing the speed, losing the stuff. It was gradual. And as soon as you lose the stuff, they get rid of you. You have to accept that. You can't be bitter. You've got to be happy you just got the opportunity. And then I became not interested in baseball. I became interested in other things, what I was doing. Teaching and other things.

On my first day in the Major Leagues, I started against the Giants. That was one time I wasn't in relief. And then I dished up a home run to Willie Mays. But I did OK. I pitched five innings and we won the game. Somebody else got the win in relief. I got in two more games in '57 and twenty-three in '58. And then I got sent out. I didn't quit until I was thirty; I played in Portland in the Pacific Coast League and then Monterrey, Mexico, in the Mexican League. But I knew I didn't have it any more. So you accept it.

My dad had a business selling pipe-valve fittings and sinks and faucets. So I did that a while. And then I decided I wanted to be a teacher. So I went back to Cal in '67, and the head of counseling was the same lady who had told me to go play ball fourteen years earlier! So she worked it so every credential I had taken at Cal wasn't wasted. She plugged me into the right courses and I got a bachelor's and my credential. I did do some coaching for junior high kids, but no, I like academics. I love math, science. I'm almost eighty old and I'm still learning.

In '55, I was playing ball in Georgia. It was a night game and the lights are on and I was sitting in the dugout between innings. And all the sudden this disc slowly comes over the pitching mound. It's about 250 feet up and round like that clock. It's spinning slowly red, white, and blue on the sides. An oval disc, and then it stops motionless and silent. And then, after twenty, thirty seconds, whoosh! Out of sight without a sound!

Everyone in the ballpark from left field, to right field to center field saw that. Everyone. And there's nothing that we have today that can do what that thing did in 1955. Jimmy Carter had a quote in *Time* magazine that he saw the same thing in 1959 or '60. I'm telling you, it was there. Everyone saw it. There's no question in my mind about UFOs.

I was the winning pitcher in 1958 vs. Sandy Koufax. It was Jew vs. Jew, and I beat Sandy Koufax. That's an accomplishment. I pitched the equivalent of a no-hitter in consecutive relief appearances; 9⅓ innings of hitless relief. And, here, look at this [he pulls out the newspaper leader board from early in the 1958 season]. At this point, I had the second-lowest ERA in the whole National League.

Well, there was Bobby Thompson. He was famous for hitting that home run vs. the Dodgers. I was in the frat house watching that instead of going to school. And there was Ernie Banks. He was a great guy, nice as pie. You would never have known how great he was.

I was married, and my wife died after about twenty years of marriage. I married again, and my wife died again. It's a shame. Cancer is not a fun thing. My current wife, Younga, and I have been together for about seventeen years. We have four children, eleven grandchildren, and four great-grandchildren.

Younga and I are crazy about birds. We've seen more than thirty-five hundred species in 140 countries. We had a great trip to Japan to see the snow monkeys and the ice festival. But when it comes to birds, there's no place like Costa Rica. [He shows the world map marked with red dots for every place in the world he has been and blue dots for places Younga went before she met him. There isn't much open space on the map.]

I'm happy. I'm a very positive guy. I've got a better life than Bill Gates. Billy Crystal would have given his right testicle to have been a Major League baseball player. George Will? These are people who are famous, and all of them want to be baseball players. Every young man's dream is to be a ballplayer, and I lived it.

LARRY SHERRY

Los Angeles Dodgers, 1958–1963;
Detroit Tigers, 1964–1967; Houston
Astros, 1967; California Angels, 1968

(1935–2006)

NORM SHERRY

Los Angeles Dodgers, 1959-1962;
New York Mets, 1963

(1931–)

When they played for the Los Angeles Dodgers, Larry and Norm Sherry were the only Jewish battery mates in Major League history who were also brothers. Larry, a relief pitcher, starred for the Dodgers in their victory over the Chicago White Sox in the 1959 World Series, when he won two of the games and saved the other two victories. Norm, a backup catcher, is credited with helping to rocket Sandy Koufax to stardom by convincing Koufax to take some speed off his fastball in order to improve his control. Below is an interview they did together in 2005 with an addition from Norm in 2011.

LARRY: Fairfax High School was 98–99 percent Jewish; when they had the holidays, they'd say they'd hold classes in a telephone booth because there was nobody in school. I never thought about it because the school was right in the middle of a Jewish area. When I went out playing pro ball, that was the first discrimination that I ever heard; you heard guys

Pitcher Larry Sherry's most notable achievement as a Major Leaguer came with the Los Angeles Dodgers in 1959 when he was named the MVP of that year's World Series.

from the South badmouth the guys from the North. I thought the Civil War was over. They'd go at it. Out in the West, you never heard that.

You'd hear off-color comments about blacks; every once in a while a guy from the South would make a comment about something Jewish. It didn't make any sense. They didn't know what they were talking about — something they heard from their parents. That was first time I heard any kind of discrimination. The first time flying, TWA to St. Louis, when I got off the plane, was the first time I ever saw black and white restaurants. That was a shocker — they had the separate drinking fountains. I didn't know that existed.

NORM: In 1951 in Fort Worth, they had white and colored restrooms, drinking fountains, and blacks had to sit in a section along the right-field line.

LARRY: Even in spring training in Vero Beach, the Dodgers had their own barber shop. They had to do that because a lot of guys couldn't get their hair cut downtown.

I had an incident managing in the minor leagues. Two black kids — good kids. We were traveling from Mobile to Florida. Pulled into a restaurant to get something to eat. Told them to get something quick to eat, we want to get on the road. Saw two black players getting on bus. Said, "You guys ate quick." Walked in, coach told me they wouldn't serve them.

I told the players that the bus leaves in five minutes. Owner of the restaurant was mad: "You ordered a lot of food." I said, "You serve all my players or you don't serve anything. That was 1970 in Mobile. Didn't do any good. Two guys — that's got to hurt them pretty good. You think 1970, you couldn't walk into a place and get a sandwich? We stopped somewhere down the road.

Only one who kidded me when I was coaching was [Rod] Carew, he was married to a Jewish gal. I can't recall any of the guys making any comments.

NORM: There's a lot of kidding. There's none of it said where they tried to hurt you.

LARRY: They're yelling at you because you're trying to beat them. They're mad about the way you're playing the game. Maybe they don't like the way you're throwing inside. The comments that you throw back at them are related to the game, not to your culture. There might have been some players who did that, but I don't recall ever hearing that. I can't recall any slurs. The name Sherry doesn't sound that Jewish.

NORM: I don't recall any Jewish ballplayers I played with other than you and Sandy.

LARRY: They had two doubleheaders on July 4 and 5, 1959. They needed a starting pitcher. I was in St. Paul. I was pitching pretty good. My record was only 6–7; I was pitching pretty good, lost two 1–0 games. Lost a fifteen-inning game. Never do that now — and I lost to Bob Gibson in Omaha. Well-pitched games and I had a couple of shutouts. They called me up. I got beat 2–1. [Ron] Fairly and [Wally] Moon, never forget it; misplaced ball in the outfield — two unearned runs scored. I got beat the ninth inning in my next game, 2–1. Then I won next nine in a row, counting two in the Series. One of those was a shutout — the only one I pitched in my career.

Being in the right spot for them to call me up and then making a good showing was lucky because I started the season in '58 with Dodgers and was there for about thirty days. Didn't pitch very well. They sent me to Spokane. Norm had a helluva year there. We both had our girls born on the same day, June 14, in Spokane.

I had a bad year in the minors in 1958: 6–14. It's dejecting because you're building yourself to get to the Majors, and then you don't make it and you go down. It's very depressing. They had two Triple-A teams with a lot of players; you feel your chance to get back up is very limited. Not like it is now. I went to winter ball in Venezuela. You were there, too. Norm helped quite a bit with my pitching and my delivery. I came up with a slider. Then getting that call in '59 put everything together.

NORM: He's being modest. We went to Venezuela in the winter. He was struggling along and struggling along, just like he'd done in AAA ball in Spokane. When he got that slider going, he got better and all his pitches got better and his command got better and his confidence rose. You could see the difference is his attitude: now he was going to be a pitcher. His pitching got better. You could see it in all of his pitches.

LARRY: Charlie Dressen had a lot to do with making me a reliever. [Clem] Labine was the Number 1 reliever; they weren't counting on him. They were using Art Fowler. Art was what, 38, and I think they burned him out in first half of the season. Labine just wasn't getting the job done and they didn't really have anybody. Right in that span of '58, '59 is when Don Elston, Von McDaniel, and myself and Elroy Face in Pittsburgh all became what they call a short reliever. That's where that started to develop. Dressen's idea was that I threw hard and the shorter breaking ball that I had now. They were always worried about my control. I remember seeing

Norm Sherry, who caught for the Los Angeles Dodgers from 1959 to 1962 and later for the New York Mets, helped Sandy Koufax with some advice during a spring training game.

an article, "Now the Dodgers Have One." Dressen's suggestion after I threw the shutout: he said, "If you're going to win the pennant, you better put him down there. He's got a strong arm. Put him down there to close."

I remember coming in a lot of games the last three weeks of the season. More I think about it, the playoff game in Milwaukee almost tops the Series. That was the best hitting club in baseball the last two years. They bring me in the second inning with the bases loaded. We're up 2–1, little drizzle coming down. Here comes this rookie kid and the whole season is on this one game. I shut them down for seven and ⅔ innings. That's quite a lineup.

NORM: I remember afterward the writers come filing into the clubhouse, asking, "Who is this kid?" That was some turnaround at that point in your career. It really elevated you. I'll go back a little further. I was playing Triple A and then I came back; every time he pitched he was that much better, that much better. I kept saying, "Is that my little brother? Look how good he is." When he pitched in Milwaukee, that was unreal, really something to behold. Then he went in the World Series and pitched even better.

LARRY: It [The Chicago White Sox] was not as tough a lineup. It was the first time there was not a complete game in the Series. I was the first pitcher to finish all four winning games; [Keith] Foulke did it in 2004 and [John] Wetteland did it in '96. From '59 to '96, no one had ever done it. Both those guys saved all four games. I got two saves, two wins.

Some days you'd go out like Drysdale used to say, five fingers and a prayer. Don would go out and take the ball no matter how he felt. You'd feed off your teammates: you'd feed off Drysdale and you'd feed off Koufax. Podres was a different type. John was quite a teammate. I was right-handed, he was left-handed. Alston would come out in the seventh inning. John would say, "Bring in the right-hander, I've had enough." John was beautiful; he's thinking about winning the game. John never worried about finishing a game. Drysdale and Koufax always wanted to finish.

I was hardly home that winter. I was traveling, sending the trophies home. I had an agent, temporarily, to set up all my appearances in New York because that's where the money was to be made. In California, they'd asked me to go somewhere and then the agent would call and they'd want to give me a couple hundred bucks. I was getting one thousand bucks for every appearance: in New York that was the standard fee. So I spent the whole month of January pretty much in New York and traveling around. I did a show, *What's My Line* Canadian style, in Toronto. They were pretty sharp: they guessed it. I was on Ernie Kovacs' show, Ed Sullivan's show. All they do is just announce you, you stood up. They had a few other Dodgers. I met Nixon in Washington.

In Boston I rode in the car with Stengel and Durocher. We were going to a banquet. This guy owned two newspapers, paid pretty good money—

146

cash. You think I could get a word in with those two guys— not a chance. It was unbelievable; they were going at it.

Then, in '61 Norm was responsible for getting Koufax turned around.

NORM: Koufax had to pitch. We didn't have extras. We had a split-squad game [in spring training] and we were going to Orlando to play, I guess, the Twins. There weren't a lot of guys going over there that day. Hodges was the guy that run the team, and Koufax and a couple of other pitchers, and one of them failed to make the plane over there, so we were short one pitcher as it was. We didn't have a lot of extra players. I think there were just enough to play the game. On the plane going over there, Sandy was talking to me and he said, "You know, I'd like to work on some things. I'd like to work on my curveball and my change-up." I said, "Yeah, we can do that. I'll just call for a bunch of 'em, and, you know, you work 'em in there." That's what we decided to do.

So now the game starts, and we hit first and then we go back on the field. And I started out by calling a curveball for Koufax and it's a ball. I called for a change-up and it's a ball. I called for another curveball and it's a ball. I called for a fastball and it's a ball. And now he walked the guy, and another guy came up and I called for a curveball, a changeup, and he not throwing any strikes and he's getting a little frustrated. Then he throws a fastball and it's a ball, and he walked the next guy, too. So now you've got two guys on and he hasn't thrown a strike yet. That I can remember now, this is how I picture it in my mind.

So now the third guy comes in to bat, and he starts shaking me off. He doesn't want to throw the curveball and the change-up, he wants to throw fastballs. And he's rearing back and firing. And each one's getting higher and higher than the last one, and he walked the guy on four pitches. Now you've got the bases loaded, and I went out to the mound, and I said, "Sandy," I said, "You know, we're short of players. We don't have a lot of guys here. We don't have a lot of extra pitching." And I think Gil came over and told him, "You're going to have to go as long as you can. We need you to throw some innings." And so I said to Sandy, "Why don't you just take something off the ball? Throw it over the plate and let 'em hit it. If they hit the ball, we got a chance to catch it and get some guys out. The way it's going now, they're not even swinging." So I went behind the plate, and he winds up and throws the ball and strikes out the side.

Walking off the field, I ran up to him as we were going into the dugout, I said, "Sandy, you know you just threw harder by not trying to than when you were trying to." I think that registered in his mind, that

147

maybe he didn't need to grunt and groan on every pitch and throw as hard as he could. He became a guy as time went on, that he could throw the ball wherever he wanted to and throw nothing but strikes. He became the greatest pitcher I ever saw.

LARRY: Norm was closer to him [Koufax]. Norm roomed with him and knew him. The only thing I thought the early part, '59, '60, to me he was hard on himself. You saw the great brilliance through the years; but then in '61 you just saw him put it together. I was fortunate to play five years and sit in the bullpen or on the bench with Drysdale and Koufax. Whatever comparisons you want to make — Schilling, Johnson — I don't think two guys will ever equal those two guys. To watch the hitters try to hit when he's on.

NORM: Koufax — you look at his earned run average, right at two or less. Today, I don't see anyone at two or less.

LARRY: Sandy maintained it through nine innings. The hits per nine innings, the strikeouts, and the walk ratio. The worst thing if you're the manager now is the number of hits and walks per inning — five hits and five walks; you can't win a lot of games putting two guys on base. Koufax didn't do that.

NORM: Hitters come to the plate and say he should be in his own league. They just couldn't come near him.

LARRY: Koufax was left-handed, so it was hard to learn from him. He was difficult when you go over hitters in a meeting and you discuss how to pitch to them; Sandy would say down and away. He'd throw the 12-to-6 curveball. He didn't help me much that way as far as how to pitch to a hitter.

I remember Zimmer arguing with Podres: if it came down to one game you needed to win, who would you give the ball to: Koufax or Drysdale? Ed Roebuck was sitting there, too. You had to put both of them pretty close. I think the choice came out Koufax.

When I worked as a closer, I worked multiple days and I worked multiple innings. I worked first game of a doubleheader in '62 and pitched seven innings. Davis got a base hit in the fourteenth inning and we win the ball game. Otherwise, I think I was going out for the fifteenth. I worked seven innings in relief. I shower, go down into the bullpen. I was sitting there. In the second game, they called to bullpen to see if I could get up and throw, figured I couldn't pitch the next day. I had been sitting two hours and stiffened up. They thought nothing about getting me up and getting me in the ballgame.

148

Being in a pennant race, I wouldn't refuse to pitch. That takes it toll. It took a toll on me. I think it cost me a few years; definitely. I hurt my arm in '62 and starting losing velocity. By '66 I had dropped under 90 miles an hour. The main thing I lost is the movement. Then you don't get the strikeout when you think you should. You see the guy foul it or hit it, you know you're not throwing as hard.

I didn't have a good year in '63; again Dressen played a part because he was managing in Detroit and he asked for me. I guess they felt I was expendable. That hurt because you feel you put in a lot of time and did a lot for the organization. You feel you have some worth. When you get traded, you say, "Well, I have to prove myself again over there." That was part of baseball.

At that time, American League umps still wore the outside protector and they were over the top: the low fastballs were harder to get. They couldn't bend over as easily. I couldn't believe some of the fastballs they'd call a strike and the hitters didn't want to say anything. But you didn't want to pitch up there. You couldn't get the curveball ... the umpires were bad on the overhand curve. Runge, the older one, was over there, and he'd called a wide strike zone The hitters know which umpires call which pitches. I had to learn that and I had to learn all the hitters in the American League.

In the '59 Series, it worked out to where we were traveling on that holiday [Rosh Hashanah]. Sandy asked me about it. It hadn't been a problem because the season in the minor leagues was over. That was the first time that came up. It didn't make any difference because the holiday was on Friday and we didn't play until following day; there were no night game. He was not going to be in uniform, I know. That was the thing that came up with him in Brooklyn; something did, yeah. If he wants to tell you about it, he'll tell you. I'm not going to. The other one in St. Louis, I did sit out. He took a flight back and I stayed behind in the clubhouse.

After all the years of him [Norm] warming up and catching me in practice and the year in '58 that we played and even in winter ball where we had some battles down there, it's like having your favorite sweatshirt on. I never shook him off. He'd put the pitch down and he'd have to hurry to get up; I know what he's going to call; I'd already start my windup. Every once in a while, he'd pause, he'd have to slow me down. I knew exactly where he was going. Every once in a while he'd put his glove down on other side ... I'd have to shake my head — just to change the side of the plate, not to change the pitch, just the location. It was very comfortable.

MIKE EPSTEIN
Baltimore Orioles, 1966–1967;
Washington Senators, 1967–1971;
Oakland Athletics, 1971–1972;
Texas Rangers, 1973;
California Angels, 1973–1974
(1943–)

Mike Epstein, a left-handed slugger, had perhaps the greatest nickname of any Jewish Major Leaguer: "Super Jew." Epstein earned a World Series ring with the Oakland A's in 1972. While a member of the Washington Senators, he played for Ted Williams, launching a relationship that led to a second career for Epstein as a hitting instructor. He was interviewed in August 2005.

I had an Uncle Irving. Everybody has an Uncle Irving. He lived in the Bronx and took me to a baseball game when I was five years old. He had only daughters, so I became his son. In those days, you could exit Yankee Stadium by walking onto the field, and one day I stopped at first base. And he said, "You just stopped," and I looked up and said to him: "This place is so big and one day I'm going to play here. It turned out to be prophetic."

Anyway, there was this manager for the San Jose team, Rocky Bridges. When I was going out to my position at first base after I'd hit this homer that say carried 500 feet, and he was in his dugout and he said, "You lost that one, Super Jew." And the clubhouse kid was picking up the bats and he heard it, too. So the next day in the clubhouse all of my undershirts had "Super Jew" written on them.

Slugger Mike Epstein played with the Washington Senators from 1967 to 1971 and was known as "Super Jew." After the Munich Olympics massacre in 1972, Epstein, along with teammates Ken Holtzman and Reggie Jackson, wore black armbands to commemorate the tragedy's victims.

Well, I really had two debuts. One when I came up from Rochester to Baltimore. I pinch-hit against Gary Peters of the White Sox. I wasn't really nervous. I thought it was strange that I'd been called upon to pinch-hit. But that was Hank Bauer, my manager. He liked to give you a tough initiation. I hit a tremendous flyball. This was '66 [when the Orioles went on to win the World Series], so I got up only a few times.

The next year in spring training, Hank Bauer came up to me and said, "I don't care how good you do, you're not going to make the team. These are World Champions, and I'm not going to change anything." I mean, I had a good spring. That first month, I didn't play at all. The first month, they had a cut-down day, and they called me in with the general manager and Bauer and some others, and they said, "We're going to send you down to Rochester."

I look back on the two games when I hit four consecutive home runs. My last two at-bats in a night game, then the next two at-bats the next night. So I tied a Major League record. I'll tell you an interesting story: It's my fifth at-bat, and the count goes to 3–2, and I wind up hitting the ball over the right field screen over by the line, and the first-base umpire is Bill Kunkel. And Kunkel is trying to watch the ball, and he's running down the right-field line and called it a foul ball. Now I would've had the Major League record, and running down the first-base line and that ball curved foul way after it went by the foul pole. So I say to Kunkel, I said, "Jeez, Bill, that was a fair ball. You just deprived me of a Major League record." And he said, "I didn't know that." So anyways, that was unbelievable.

In those days, you were almost like a novelty: Wow, a Jewish player. Unlike today, where there are quite a few Jews in the big leagues. But I didn't personally run into anti–Semitism. I was 6 feet 3 inches, 230 pounds, so nobody ever said anything to me. But if we went into a restaurant, some of the players would expect I had "short arms," that I wouldn't pick up the check. Even though that wasn't true, it was something they'd heard.

I did not play on the High Holidays. In fact, when the Israeli Olympians were killed in what was it, 1972, Kenny Holtzman and I were in Chicago playing the White Sox, and I got a call from an old teammate, and he said, "Did you hear what happened?" We just walked around Chicago. We didn't say anything. We just walked around Chicago all day. That really affected me. And the next day, we wore black armbands. Reggie Jackson wanted the publicity, so he did it, too. But we just felt so vulnerable that something like that could happen.

My biggest disappointment is not being the kind of hitter I thought my credentials showed I could be. I was a good left-handed power hitter, but I always thought I could've done better. As it turned out, I had vision problems, and even corrected it was like 20/15. Some guys had perfect sight with no corrections. But based on the career I had in the minors, I thought I should've done better, and that's what led me to my ten-year relationship with Ted Williams. I wanted to find out why I didn't hit better.

In 1980, I was in the metals business and I had some customers in Florida, and I was in the Tampa airport and I called Ted Williams and I said, "I'd like to see you." So I went up there and spent the day with him, and we started talking about hitting, and I said, "I always thought I could be a better hitter," and he said, "Well, you should've been." And that started a mentoring relationship.

And while he couldn't really explain some of the things that he said happened in a swing, he could point me in the right direction. He knew more than anybody. And he thought he could teach me and he thought I had the ability to explain hitting. And he said that anybody who can talk about the learning process for years like you can has got to offer instruction to others.

The last time I saw him was in San Diego. He was being honored. And I had my wife with me, and we knock on the door of the hotel there, and he answered the door in his undershorts and he said, "Jeez, I don't know you'd be bringing a woman!"

I really didn't have any intention of doing the hitting company on a day-to-day basis. But in '99–2000, Ted said, "I'd really like you to put out a tape or something," and I said, "Ted, I'm retired, and I'm too old and don't want to do that." And he said, "Then I taught you everything for nothing. I'm asking you to do this." Then he called me again afterwards and asked me, "What have you done on the hitting tape?" And I said, "I haven't done anything." And he said, "Then I wasted ten years of my life."

So when somebody says that — a good friend ... so I put out a video-tape, got an Internet site. I did it to get people to remember him, and all that knowledge he had about hitters down through the years. And one day in the mail a letter of endorsement showed up totally unsolicited.

I think I regret that. I left baseball when I was 31. As a player, I would have done things differently. I wouldn't have questioned so many things that went on in baseball. A lot of people don't realize that I was going to sue baseball over the reserve clause. When I was sent down to Triple-A by the Orioles, and they said, "We don't have a spot for you," I thought they were depriving me of my right to earn a living. I questioned that and I quit for a month. I guess if I had to do it all over again, I would've kept my opinions to myself. The other thing is, I thought I could earn more money doing something else.

RON BLOMBERG
New York Yankees, 1969, 1971–1976;
Chicago White Sox, 1978
(1948–)

Like Andy Cohen and Cal Abrams before him, Ron Blomberg was hailed as baseball's Jewish savior in New York when the Yankees signed him in 1967. Blomberg enjoyed the notoriety and adulation from the city's Jewish fans, which included endorsement deals that he received because of his Jewish background. Blomberg later had a short stint with the Chicago White Sox before retiring at the age of thirty. Injuries helped to prevent him from reaching stardom, although he was a lifetime .293 hitter. On Opening Day 1973, he became the first designated hitter in the Major Leagues. He chronicles that historic event in his ghostwritten autobiography, Designated Hebrew, *published in 2006, from which this is excerpted with permission.*

I was relieved — and a little dumbfounded — when Ralph [Yankees manager Houk] asked me, "What do you think about being the DH?" "Skipper, I don't really know too much about it," I replied. "What do I have to do?" "You get up to bat, you take your four swings, you drive in runs, you come back to the bench, and you keep loose in the runway," Houk told me. "You're basically pinch-hitting for the pitcher four times in the same game. I can't play you in the field because your leg is so bad, but at least this will give us an opportunity to get your bat into the lineup."

If Ralph thought I could help the team the most by being the DH, it was fine with me. I loved to play in the field, but I also knew I was more valuable to the club at the plate. When we arrived in Boston, the papers printed the probable lineups for Opening Day [1973], and there I was hitting sixth for the Yankees.

After the National Anthem was performed, I couldn't sit still, so I ran up and down the runway track between the dugout and the clubhouse to stay warm. Several of my teammates were in the clubhouse, trying to keep warm. Trying to work up a sweat, I did a few sit-ups.

My team was busy heating up the basepaths. With two outs, Matty Alou doubled to center. Murcer and Graig Nettles followed with walks, which brought me to the plate with a chance to give the fans a look at a DH in action. Tiant was throwing a lot of junk that day, trying to confuse the hitters with his deceptive windup. I asked Carlton Fisk, who was catching that day, what Tiant was throwing. "He's throwing it right by you," Fisk told me. But Tiant couldn't find the plate. Just as the previous two hitters had done, I worked him for a walk, driving in the first run of the game.

I finished the game 1-for-3, but we lost the game 15–5, as the Red Sox pummeled us for twenty hits. I went into the clubhouse, where guys were hanging around as usual enjoying cold cuts from the postgame spread, and was surprised to find thirty-five or forty reporters waiting for me at my locker. Up until then, the significance of being Major League Baseball's first DH was totally lost on me.

Marty Appel [then the Yankees' assistant public relations director] ran up to me and demanded I turn over my bat. I protested: "Marty, I can't give you my bat because this bat has good wood in it. This is my bat." But Marty was persuasive. "We're sending it up to Cooperstown, to the Hall of Fame," he said. Photographers snapped photos of me, and I added my Number 12 jersey to the pile of memorabilia Marty was sending off to Cooperstown.

The fact that one at-bat earned me a lot of notoriety — not to mention a question in Trivial Pursuit — might be a bit unfair to others. But that's not for me to worry about. Besides, I have a designation that is far more important than my being the first designated hitter. When I die, I'm going to have the following inscribed on my tombstone: Ron Blomberg, the first DH, Designated Hebrew, in the game of baseball.

I was born in Atlanta, Georgia, where my father, Sol, the son of Romanian immigrants, moved to from Asheville, North Carolina. My mother, Goldie Rae, worked with my dad in his jewelry store on Alabama Street, where I hung out a lot as a kid. We lived in a middle-class neighborhood with only a handful of other Jews. So most of my friends, neighbors, and classmates were not Jewish.

I was strong mentally as well as physically. I had no choice, as growing up a young Southern Jew was not easy. In my late teen years, Lester Maddox, a former proponent of segregation, was the governor of Georgia. A synagogue firebombing occurred just three blocks from our house and made national headlines—as depicted in the movie *Driving Miss Daisy*. There were constant Ku Klux Klan marches, with Klansmen wearing their pointed hats and giving out pamphlets that were anti–Semitic, anti-black, and anti–Catholic.

My religion even made playing the sport I loved a worrisome affair. On some of the youth teams I played on, plenty of my teammates didn't know what "a Jew" was. But some of them did, unfortunately, and they were Klansmen who regularly attended meetings and cross-burnings. They knew I was Jewish — on Rosh Hashanah and Yom Kippur I went to services — but they never confronted me. As a gifted athlete and the team's best player, I was looked at as the savior of their team. Professional and college scouts came to our games to watch me play, and that gave teammates who were good enough a crack at athletic scholarships as well. So they never confronted me to their face, but I saw the KKK hoods and pamphlets in some of their parked cars. It was common to see a shotgun in someone's car, and I knew that after a game they might be headed to a cross-burning. It was intimidating at times.

But no amount of intimidation — whether direct or indirect — was going to keep me from being respectful of my religion and my parents' wishes. Growing up, I went to Hebrew school twice a week. Most Jewish kids disliked Hebrew school and tried to get out of attending, but I didn't mind going because I was proud of being Jewish. I often had to attend Hebrew school, hop in the car right afterward, change into my baseball uniform, and head to a game. I wasn't an Orthodox Jew, but I did observe the High Holy Days. I put on the yarmulke and tallis [prayer shawl] and remained in the synagogue all day long.

Of course, I was a kid and screwed up from time to time. On one occasion, when I was around the age of twelve, I played golf with my cousin instead of observing Rosh Hashanah. I knew I was making a mistake, but I really wanted to hang out with him. My rabbi saw us on the golf course and told my parents, who reprimanded me. I felt bad about that poor judgment and never let it happen again.

Despite my small family, over one hundred people attended my Bar Mitzvah. On my cake was a picture of me wearing a Yankee uniform, complete with pinstripes. That was unheard of for a kid who grew up in the South, but I was pretty outspoken about wanting to play for the Yankees.

Ron Blomberg was the first designated hitter to bat in the American League, which he did while on the New York Yankees in 1973.

Most of the gifts I received were of the sporting variety, including lots of baseball cards. Like most kids, I collected baseball cards to put them in my bicycle spokes. Yankee players were my favorites: I had lots of Mickey Mantles and Art Ditmars.

Being a Jewish athlete and a guy who loved the big city, New York was the only place to play sports. It was a great opportunity for me. Before

I even signed my contract, many New Yorkers were contacting me, begging me to play in the Big Apple. They wrote to me: "We need you. We want you to be our Messiah." The fans of New York were hungry for a star Jewish player to represent them.

As a Jewish ballplayer in Atlanta, I didn't receive much coverage related to my religion. But I knew that things would change in New York City. After I signed, the Yankees flew me up to New York with my parents for a press conference and a get-acquainted tour. I had never been on an airplane before. Nor had I ever seen a limousine, which took us from the airport to the hotel. I was all wide-eyed, especially when I saw the marquee of the New York Hilton: WELCOME, FIRST-ROUND DRAFT PICK OF THE NEW YORK YANKEES, RON BLOMBERG.

The fellow who checked me in at the Hilton was a Jewish man named Mort, who turned out to be a big memorabilia collector. When he was introduced to me, he said, "Ah, a landsman," meaning a fellow Jew. I signed something for him, probably the first time I was asked for an autograph.

We checked in and they carried my bags. I had an entourage, maybe twenty-five or thirty people met me in the lobby, most of them Jewish people wearing yarmulkes. Some of them were Chasidic Jews. I had never seen a Chasidic Jew prior to that day. I was so naive — I thought they looked like Pilgrims.

Even the taxi driver who took me to the stadium was Jewish. When I mentioned my name, he said, "You're the baseball player." It was a wonderful feeling; it seemed like everyone knew who I was and was expecting me. When I went to the Stage Deli, they put my picture up on the wall and I became very good friends with the owner. I sat in the seat where Joe DiMaggio used to sit and was served by the same waitress, Clara, who had served Joltin' Joe. I ate a corned beef sandwich that must have weighed twelve ounces. Later, the Stage even named a sandwich after me. It was a reuben, with corned beef, pastrami, cheese, and Russian dressing.

The grand finale was yet to come, however. At Yankee Stadium, my reception was even warmer. I was interviewed by Walter Cronkite, who was in the broadcast booth with Phil Rizzuto. I remembered seeing him on TV, but I never watched the news. I was eighteen years old, and Walter Cronkite shook my hand and sat down with me for an interview. That was my first major interview with anybody in New York City. The date was June 20, 1967.

The Yankees were playing Detroit that day, and the team placed a sign on the scoreboard that read; WELCOME FIRST-ROUND DRAFT PICK RON BLOMBERG. I was watching the game in the broadcast booth with Rizzuto, and the fans in the grandstand stood up and applauded in our general direction. Rizzuto told me to wave to them, so I did, and they cheered louder. I was living a dream. God gave me three wishes, and the first one was to play at Yankee Stadium.

I sure made the ushers happy. Most of them were Jewish, with names like Hymovitz or Lichstein, and three or four of them told me they never thought they would ever see a Jew play baseball in Yankee Stadium. They had tears in their eyes and said to me, "You little Yid, you're someone I can look up to now. Thank you for coming."

But the bubble burst quickly: the next day, I headed back to Atlanta with my parents, and began packing for my first minor-league assignment to Johnson City, Tennessee. I was just out of high school and nervous as could be, but my uncle, Mitchell Thorpe, calmed me down. He was the mayor of Johnson City. Uncle Mitch did a lot for the city and he loved baseball. In fact, he owned part of the team.

As a Jew playing in a small, southern town, I was a novelty. There wasn't a lot of understanding in the rural South. Most people know about Hebrews from Bible study, and everybody knew that Jesus was a Jew. But comprehension ended right there. I honestly think some people were surprised that I didn't have horns. On occasion, I heard phrases like "Jewboy," "Jewin' me," or "Jew me down" [when talking about money]. But I never confronted anyone. I knew they were just uneducated about my religion and didn't know what they were talking about. They had heard these words from their parents or friends, and were simply conforming to what they had already experienced. The words hurt, but I couldn't risk any confrontation.

Growing up down South, being Jewish meant you held Jewish beliefs, but you didn't necessarily practice the religion. Upon my arrival in New York City, I felt an incredibly intense, brand-new connection to my religion: I felt as if I were one of the chosen, simply because of how I was viewed and treated by the city's Jewish population. I was easy to spot — thin, with blond hair and blue eyes. I often wore Izod t-shirts, which were popular then. When I walked to and from the stadium before and after a game, fans were very friendly to me, waving or asking for autographs. Most fans knew that I stayed at the Concourse Plaza in the Bronx, and they were familiar with my route to and from the stadium.

I also received lots of fan mail: thousands of cards and letters. Every

Jewish mother in the world wanted to introduce me to her daughter, and each letter included a photograph. Jewish girls were writing to me, saying they wanted to come to the stadium to meet me.

My transformation from naive Jew to one conscious of his religion and its impact on others was a speedy process. During my walks to and from the ballpark, I often stopped to eat a delicatessen called the Roxy. I would usually enjoy the postgame spread at the stadium, but then have dessert at the Roxy. They had a delicious cheesecake, the sort of treat we were never given at the ballpark. Horace Clarke, my roommate, and I ate at the Roxy nearly every day when the Yankees were in town. The other customers of the Roxy were almost all Jews—little kids in yarmulkes and their parents—and they would read Jewish newspapers and magazines. I had never even *seen* a Jewish paper before arriving in the Bronx. Spending time at the Roxy opened my eyes, and I felt a major closeness to its patrons.

Trailblazers like Koufax shared their wisdom with me and impressed upon me the importance of taking my religion seriously. I met Koufax when he appeared at Yankee Stadium on Old Timers Day. I went up to introduce myself to him, but Sandy already knew who I was. He said he had followed my career because I was one of the few Jewish players in the big leagues. He reminded me to always wear my *chai* [a piece of Jewish jewelry that symbolizes life] around my neck with respect—and that's exactly what I did.

I also met Hank Greenberg, the best Jewish hitter of all time. We spent a weekend together at Grossinger's, which was then a Jewish-owned Catskills resort in Liberty, New York. He talked to me about all of the anti–Semitic incidents he encountered during his playing days. During the 1930s, he was the only prominent Jewish player, and so he endured a lot of abuse from players, managers, and fans alike. People were upset and anxious during the Depression, and needed to vent; Greenberg was an obvious target.

Riverdale, the portion of the Bronx where I lived, was 95 percent Jewish and was home to around ten synagogues, from Reform to Conservative to Orthodox. It was an ideal area for me to live, and only strengthened my bond to the people of the city. If a young man from the South moved to New York City by himself, he would likely be overwhelmed and intimidated. But if he went to New York City as part of a family, he would feel comfortable. I felt like the whole city took me in—they were like family to me. Unlike my stay in the low minor leagues, I did not feel uneasy due to my religion.

One Sunday morning in 1973, I found out just how large my impact was on the city's Jewish population. I drove into the players' parking lot at Yankee Stadium at around eight in the morning. I knew we would have a full house that day because it was "Bat Day"—a popular giveaway at the gate—but I noticed an unusually large number of people hanging around. As soon as I stepped out of the car, a policeman came over and said he needed to escort me into the stadium. There were a couple of hundred fans asking for autographs but the cops wouldn't let me sign for them.

I asked, "What's wrong? What's happening?" But they wouldn't explain the situation to me. I was escorted into the waiting room outside the Yankee offices, which were also full of security people. There, I was told that Rabbi Meir Kahane, the founder of the controversial Jewish Defense League, was coming to the game that day with a legion of his followers. I was aware of other Jewish organizations like the B'nai B'rith, but I knew little about the Jewish Defense League. I soon found out that it was a radical Jewish organization, considered by the FBI to be a terrorist group. The security personnel at Yankee Stadium were worried that the members might run out on the field and disrupt the game. They told me not to take batting practice for security reasons. I agreed, but mentioned that I was going to be playing right field that day. They said they would put extra security people in that area of the stadium.

Prior to that day, I had always spoken with the fans out in right field — many of whom were part of my fan club — before or during a game. But I was a little worried that day when I saw a lot of activity in the stands during the game's latter stages. There was a bit of commotion among the fans in that area, and I saw one man in particular who was wearing a yarmulke causing a stir. But security put a stop to it. The members of the JDL in attendance were waving to the fans and yelling at me. I waved back.

A security guard sat on the bench with me during the entire game, but nothing ever happened. It turned out that the JDL wanted to present me with their "Jew of the Year" award. Eventually I received their plaque: they gave it to somebody to present it to me. The Yankees would not allow them to present it in person. They wanted nothing to do with that group.

Being a Jewish Yankee was definitely a different experience than most of my teammates ever experienced. I received gifts from Israeli military leader Moshe Dayan and Israeli political leader Golda Meir. On one occasion, I even met Ambassador Simcha Dinitz, who used to attend a lot of Yankee games.

On the road, I often experienced a similar sense of belonging. Before a game in Boston, which also boasts a strong Jewish population, Red Sox executive John Alevizos asked me to meet with a friend of his. Alevizos had been my minor league general manager while I was with the Manchester affiliate and was also a college professor at Harvard. His friend entered the locker room wearing a yarmulke, and told me he was a rabbi. The rabbi said that I was a "chosen person" and that he felt like a "chosen person," too because he was in my presence. In many ways, I did feel chosen. I attribute that feeling to my success in baseball despite my injuries, and to my becoming the first designated hitter.

Even before I met that rabbi, I had made it a point not to play on the High Holy Days. I never played on Rosh Hashanah or Yom Kippur. Growing up, I went to Kol Nidre services on Yom Kippur and stayed in the synagogue all day. I came home for an hour, then went back to the Yizkor services and stayed there. Then I broke the fast with my family.

In 1973, we were playing a day game against the Cleveland Indians late in the season. Rosh Hashanah started at six o'clock that night. The game was tied with two outs in the bottom of the ninth inning, but we had a man on third base. I had had to make the decision: quit the game for Rosh Hashanah or get a base hit. The Cleveland pitcher was a lefthander named Tom Hilgendorf who threw seeds. I got a clutch base hit to win the game — the biggest hit of my career. I cherish that at-bat more than anything else in my life.

That game-winning hit made me a lot of new fans, too. I had told all the reporters that Rosh Hashanah was my holiday. And Ralph Houk supported me, saying that he would never stand between a player and his religion. I never had any trouble with any of my managers regarding my religion. The reporters jumped on the story—calling me the "Sundown Kid"— and from that day on, it felt like I was idolized by every Jew in New York City.

The Yankees made every effort to market my religion for the team's benefit. It didn't matter to me; I was proud of my Jewish heritage. Thanks to the team's efforts— and my good relationship with the press— my popularity within the Jewish population continued to soar to new heights. I was a hit at every delicatessen in the city. I'd go to the Stage Deli and they would refuse to give me a check. I was invited to Bar Mitzvahs, clinics in the Borscht Belt, synagogues, and countless speaking engagements on behalf of the B'nai B'rith and other organizations. I was contacted by every Jewish publication in the country. Rabbis would tell me that I was "part of the tribe."

I was a true celebrity. I appeared on the Jerry Lewis telethon, *The Ed Sullivan Show*, *The Tonight Show With Johnny Carson*, and *Good Morning America* when McLean Stevenson was the guest host and Alan Alda was also a guest. I had my likeness hung on the wall at a pair of famous restaurants: Elaine's and Sardi's. I was living a fantasy.

I always anticipated a downfall to my fame as a Jewish ballplayer, some sort of hatred spawned by anti–Semitic bigots. But such actions happened only once in a while. Although Hank Aaron received a hefty amount of hate mail as he was approaching Babe Ruth's record, I received only a handful of anti–Semitic letters. Every so often, a letter would arrive with no return address and a swastika or Ku Klux Klan sign inside. A few pieces of mail were addressed to "Jew-boy" or had a swastika on the envelope. I didn't even bother to open those. If they were death threats, I was better off not knowing about them. I tried never to engage someone who wished harm upon me. That's why I never got into an argument with the occasional loud-mouthed fan.

Through my stay in the South during the early portion of my minor league career, I would occasionally hear abusive taunts from the crowd. I played ball in plenty of small coal mining or tobacco towns, and the townspeople looked at a Jew almost like an alien. In their eyes, I was quite different from them. In Winston-Salem, I hit a home run against Bill Lee, who later pitched for Boston. As I rounded the bases, I could hear someone shout from the stands: "Sit down, Jew-boy, you got horns!" I never looked up; I just touched home plate and returned to the dugout. I felt like I was above such fans and their actions.

Another memorable incident occurred while I was playing in Manchester, New Hampshire, which I thought was a very liberal, progressive town. I was good friends with a Jewish radio host from the town, so it came as quite a surprise when I had a bad experience in a local restaurant. I went into a seafood restaurant by myself, and the maitre d' sat me in the back of the place. I told him, "There are seats up front. I'd rather sit there." But the maitre d' declined. When I asked him for his reasoning, he replied: "This was where I was instructed to put you so that you will get good service."

I could see what was going on. It was no secret that I was Jewish, as the press in Manchester had profiled me on several occasions. I recalled that I had often gone out to eat with black teammates in certain towns, and we were often placed at the back of the restaurant. But now I was in New England, and ordered to sit in the back, *by myself*. No one said a word about my religion — but they didn't have to. I received the message loud and clear.

There were other unpleasant incidents in the minors. But thankfully, things went a lot more smoothly in the majors. Possibly, that was because people in bigger cities had more exposure to Jews and were more open-minded. In all the years I played in the majors, I never once heard a derogatory comment from a fan in the stands. Not even in Boston, where the fans were pretty hostile to the Yankees, or in Chicago, or even in places where they had too much to drink.

Too bad my teammates didn't react the same way: a couple of players were definitely anti–Semitic. I heard a couple of them refer to me as "The Jew" or say that New York City is "just a Jew city." They didn't dare say such a thing to a writer — only in talking amongst themselves. If I would have said something to the press about what I overheard, it would have become a big story. But I kept quiet because I respected my teammates as ballplayers. If they did not respect me as a Jew, that was their problem. I did not want to create any additional friction in the clubhouse.

After the newspapers reported that I was going to observe Rosh Hashanah and Yom Kippur, a couple of my teammates weren't too happy about my decision. One of them came up to me and asked, "What are Rosh Hashanah and Yom Kippur?" I told him they were High Holy Days for Jewish people. He replied, "What are you? A Seventh-day Adventist?" I told him I was Jewish and I intended to respect my beliefs. Too bad he couldn't do the same.

I guess some of my teammates were envious of me because I was receiving a lot of attention from the press. When I joined the team, it was centered around Bobby Murcer and Mel Stottlemyre. I could sense some of my teammates thinking, "Who is this kid getting all the attention? What has he ever done?" They were right, of course, but I didn't go *looking* for the attention; the writers came to me. They were nice to me, and I spent time with them, which was a no-no. Some thought I was cozying up to them, looking for publicity. But I just liked to talk, and the press came to me because I was talkative and gave them something to write about.

Despite my occasional popularity issues in the clubhouse, I was beginning to find additional demands on my time due to my popularity with fans. Elston Howard introduced me to Sheldon Stone, his agent and attorney, and we became the best of friends. Sheldon soon became my agent, manager, and attorney. He arranged bookings for me, and soon I was averaging three per weekend, although we once did as many as six. He had me traveling all over the place. I also did a few TV commercials and endorsed a few products for print advertisements.

Everything I needed came free of charge. If I needed some shirts, I went down to the Garment District, gave somebody a signed baseball or picture, and left with bags full shirts and pants. I received meals on the house and rarely paid taxi fares. I was even waved through tollbooths. At that time, only the top players got commercials or enjoyed such perks, and I wasn't a top player. So some additional resentment built up among the players because of the opportunities I was receiving.

I was an easy target: I was the only Jewish player on the Yankees until Elliott Maddox came aboard in 1974. Then Ken Holtzman joined us in 1976. The first time I met Elliott, he was wearing a *chai* and said he was going to convert to Judaism. He was black, and so this news shocked me. I had never known anyone who converted to Judaism — let alone a black man who undoubtedly had a good deal of discrimination to contend with. We talked about it and he said he believed in the faith. We became very close friends.

Holtzman was an introverted, intellectual guy who loved to read. When we acquired Kenny in June of 1976, I was excited. I was the first one to shake his hand when he joined the team. We became close friends as well. Having supportive teammates to lean on helped me forget any misguided discrimination I encountered from other teammates.

Following the 1974 season it was time to ask for a raise. Negotiating a contract with Gabe Paul was a long process, requiring a lot of meeting and back and forth. Feeling pretty good about my chances, I went to see him, accompanied by my agent Sheldon Stone. I was coming off a decent year, and I started the conversation by saying, "Why don't you trade me?" Paul replied, "No team will want you." Then he laughed and said, "We'll never trade you. You're the token on this team."

He meant — the Jewish player. Not too many people know this, but Paul was Jewish, too. It was a secret in baseball. Due to his religion, he felt a connection to Sheldon and me and often joked with us. He also looked out for me, making recommendations on my behalf. But when it came to business, he wouldn't kid around.

Just as it was in New York, my religion appealed to [Chicago White Sox owner] Bill Veeck as well. He told me there were other Jews on the team, including Steve Stone and Ross Baumgarten. "With your personality," Veeck told me, "and all the Jewish people in Chicago, you're going to be a perfect fit."

I found Chicago to be a beautiful city with terrific people, including a large Jewish population. All the synagogues contacted me and I visited many of them. I met a lot of people in Skokie, the home of many Holocaust survivors, and found a condo in a very exclusive address downtown not far from the Chicago River.

White Sox manager Bob Lemon had been the pitching coach of the Yankees in 1976, so I was already familiar with him. He brought me into his office and said, "I remember watching you in New York. Don't worry about anything. You are going to play here and you won't have any pressure." I was friendly with many of my new teammates, including a lot of the black and Hispanic guys on the team: Ralph Garr, Chet Lemon, Lamar Johnson, and Jorge Orta. I was closest to Bobby Molinaro; he and I would have fun arguing over whether to go out to eat at a kosher deli or a pizza joint.

But to my dismay, I didn't blend in to the Chicago clubhouse as well as I had hoped. There were four or five guys on the team who never spoke to me and would not associate with me outside of the ballpark. Even though he was Jewish, my relationship was not good with pitcher Steve Stone. He did his own thing. In addition, there were a lot of born-again Christians on the team who held regular prayer meetings. They didn't accept that I was Jewish and didn't want me to get involved, even though the meetings were supposed to be nondenominational.

ELLIOTT MADDOX
Detroit Tigers, 1970; Washington Senators/
Texas Rangers, 1971–1973;
New York Yankees, 1974–1976;
Baltimore Orioles, 1977;
New York Mets, 1978–1980
(1947–)

Elliott Maddox is truly one of a kind: an African-American Major Leaguer who converted to Judaism during his baseball career. Maddox was known for his outspokenness. As he notes in this March 2005 interview, he wasn't afraid to bring the race issue into the clubhouse.

My first time up in the World Series in 1976 I got a hit, which a lot of people have done, gotten hits in their first time up. And most people, they'll get a single, some will get a double, there are those who get home runs. But I bet not many, on their first trip, playing in a World Series, get a triple. That's what I did. Off Don Gullett. And I was playing in a brace, the brace was under my uniform, and I could barely move because the brace was huge, it was bulky: It weighed about five pounds. And I remember coming into third, we're playing Cincinnati and I did a headfirst slide, and Rose, Pete Rose, is playing third. And I look up and he's looking down and I said, "Did I look like you going in?" [laughs] And he just starts laughing. I'm curious as to how many people got triples. But more than anything I will bet I'm the first and only black Jewish ballplayer to get a triple in his first at-bat in the World Series.

Jackie Robinson? I'll put it this way. The only autograph that I ever got as a kid. As a matter of fact, the only autograph I ever asked for from anyone until I was in my twenties was from Jackie Robinson. Not only did he give me an autograph but it was in a small spiral notebook, and he signed three pieces of paper, little pieces of paper. And I always remembered that. It was after he had retired. He came to my community in New Jersey and gave a speech, and I asked him for that and he signed those pieces of paper. I never ever saw those pieces of paper again until both of my parents had died.

And as far as Jackie Robinson, to me, I think about it all the time. I think about that actually every day: Every day I think about what is owed Jackie Robinson and the fact that he doesn't get enough recognition. I mean a lot is owed to a lot of people — baseball players owe a lot to Curt Flood — but American society owes a lot to Jackie Robinson because he was the leader of the civil rights movement in my opinion. Because here was a guy who took America's cornerstone, the foundation of American society, which is baseball, and he integrated baseball.

My mother and father migrated from Georgia following, actually during, World War II. My father was in the Coast Guard and was stationed at one point in Sheepshead Bay, in Brooklyn. So my mother, who was pregnant at the time with my brother, came up north and never went back. And when he went off to Europe, well, mostly the Pacific Theater, she went to live with relatives in Cleveland and Detroit.

When my father came back, some of his brothers and sisters had come up to New Jersey, so that's where he went — Vauxhall, New Jersey. It's basically a borough or a section of Union, New Jersey. Vauxhall is predominantly African American. Union is predominantly white.

Oh yeah, baseball was an important part of my life because in high school, tenth grade, I remember I was the starting third baseman on the baseball team as a tenth grader, and my town has produced some very good ball players, great high school teams. If you mention high school ball in New Jersey, Union High School will be Number 1. Anyway, so I made the team, starting team, third base.

I remember as a kid, we were in Georgia and we stopped for gas at one of these out of the way dirt-road gas stations. And my father was asking for directions and this was the first time I ventured out of the car to go to the bathroom, and I was about four, maybe five, at the most and I saw a water fountain for the first time marked "Colored" and I didn't know what it meant at first, then I realized and I was pissed. Then I go back and my father's in the middle of trying to get some directions, and

Elliott Maddox, who played for several teams including the Washington Senators, converted to Judaism while playing for the New York Yankees in the mid–1970s.

the guy wouldn't give him the directions, and the guy at the gas station was white and he was giving my father a hard time. And I started to say stuff to him and my mother was, "Shh, shh, no you can't say that down here, you can't say that here. You can't say that." And I'm going, "Well, he can't do what he's doing." And so eventually I ended up becoming involved in the civil rights movement and things that were going on even when I was in high school.

My father was Baptist, my mother Methodist. It was the Baptist church that my brother and sister and I went to as kids. My first coach in Little League, I was an eight-year-old, and my brother was also on the team, coach's last name was Shapiro and he was a great guy, and I always felt well liked by him. Like he just accepted us into the family and I'm thinking, Wow, this is all because of baseball, this is baseball? This is great. I'd go over to his house and play. He lived in another area of town, not too far away from me. But we'd go over there and play with his kids, who were also on the baseball team, and that was fantastic. And then later as I met more and more people, as I think back, I wasn't going to other guys' houses, other homes of white players and their families, and as I think back it was because of the fact that upbringings in families, Jewish families and black families, you're more willing to accept people for who they are, and so it just turned out that most of my friends or really all of my friends in those early years were either black or Jewish.

And then when I got to high school, there was a kid named Ron Meyer who was in my homeroom, and as homerooms go, whoever's in your homeroom in tenth grade is going to be in your homeroom in eleventh grade, is going to be in your homeroom in the twelfth grade, and you have homeroom in the morning, you have homeroom in the afternoon. Well, Ron, every time we were in homeroom, it was his duty. He must have felt it was his duty to talk to me about Judaism.

I started to see the parallels between Jewish society, Jewish upbringing and Jewish history and that of blacks, primarily blacks in this country, but blacks in general. It was extremely similar and then being somewhat of a historian, when I went off to college at the University of Michigan, we had hundreds of history courses to choose from, and you would have history of Islam, Buddhist history, Judaic history, Christian history. So one of the courses I took was the history of Judaism and that's when things all really got rolling. Talk about slavery, the Exodus, etc., etc., coming out of Africa, you may want to call it Egypt.

The dream of becoming an orthopedic surgeon kind of fizzled after my sophomore year when I was drafted to play baseball. I went in the first round of the draft. I finished college one semester a year. I'd go to fall semester. Start a few weeks late, a month late. At first, I was playing for the Detroit Tigers, so that was fantastic. I'm on campus, just forty miles away, and I could keep up with my classwork, compared to being in Texas for the Texas Rangers, and going to school at the University of Michigan. I had no idea what the class assignment was, getting my books, but I still continued with school, and I graduated.

It was good with the Tigers. I was rookie of the year for them, and then the manager was fired, Mayo Smith, and Billy Martin came in and I was traded immediately to the Senators, who after a year became the Texas Rangers. Ted Williams was the manager in Washington. He was the manager of the team the first year in Texas as well.

Ted and I had our political discussions. They were very interesting. They were very interesting. Ted didn't like me for a long time. He didn't like me. As a matter of fact, Ted hated me. [laughs] I shouldn't say that. I think Ted disliked me, but he respected me and we eventually came to like each other to an immense degree. Because he found that I was the only guy on the team who could stomach him as far as most things in life. Because I would sit next to him and ask him questions. About baseball history, about hitting, he just didn't like the fact that he would say, "Well, in baseball it has to be done this way about such and such and he was clear cut. You have to do it this way," and I would tell him, "Ted, that only applies if you're about six feet four with great reflexes, tremendous eyesight, fantastic eye-hand coordination."

That's when I knew he liked me. No one could affect him like I could affect him. And when you dislike someone they don't get to you that quickly, that easily. Ted would say, "You go up, you get this. The pitcher's gonna throw you such-and-such pitch in a certain situation, blah, blah, blah, look for it when you get it, turn your hips, move your hands through and so on and so forth." And I would come and say, "Ted, that only applies if you're six-four, have great eyesight, fantastic hand-eye coordination, extremely talented, strong upper body and, in closing, you have to be white," and he just looked at me, "You really piss me off. You're pissing me off." And then I would say, "But what about Henry Aaron, he doesn't do it that way?" He'd go, "I don't want to talk about him." And he'd start talking again about some hitters who he felt did it his way that were successful only because they did it the right way, which was his way. And I'd say, "But Roberto Clemente doesn't do it like that either, and he didn't want to talk about that." And another one that I used was Willie Mays. "He doesn't do it that way." And usually by the third person he would just walk away. He'd just walk away from me. "I don't want to talk to you." And you know I'm trying to tell him there's more than one way. "I don't want to talk to you."

That was Ted. He was something. He was a character. I mean there were a couple of times when he and I had to be separated. He would become so infuriated. He would actually come after me, want to fight.

Seventy-one, spring training, '71. You've got to remember this is coming out of the sixties. We're still in the era of demonstrations, campus demonstrations. We're still in Richard Nixon time. Vietnam. I was thinking I was going to be drafted anyway. I showed up in Pompano Beach for spring training, leave the college scene, big Afro, college attire, looking like Jimi Hendrix with the tassles hanging down. And which just irked Ted to no end, my coming in dressed like that. And I looked around and guys had things up in their lockers, little stupid things. A day later I went out and bought some stuff to put up in my locker. In the back of the locker was a large poster with Huey Newton sitting down and Eldridge Cleaver next to him. I don't know if you remember that picture.

A huge banner in the back of the Black Panthers. On the front of the locker, right above the opening where your name is, I put up a poster, fourteen inches long, maybe five inches wide: Free Angela Davis. And I can't remember what the third thing was, but that was also odd. Went out on the field, actually I was sitting at my locker when the news reporters came in that morning and all of a sudden, flash bulbs. I go out on the field and then someone comes over to me, "You have to go back to your locker and take all that stuff down." I said, "Why, everybody has stuff up? You have to take yours down." I said, "I'm not taking them down." I said, "If everyone takes all their stuff down, I'll take mine down."

Was I labeled from that minute on? I was labeled. I poisoned the waters, from that moment on, and I had nothing but aggravation. It was terrible. They made life miserable for me. I was threatened to be sent to the minors. That was a constant threat. Now I'm getting back to some things I really don't even want to get into.

The black players supported me. The white guys, the liberal white guys, they weren't sure what they should do, so they didn't do anything. And they were so-called older and wiser, and so they knew that in sports, in many areas of life, in business, you know you got to toe the line and I wasn't about to do that. So they said, "Well, maybe we should stay out of this." And anyway, so some of that is in a book, a couple books. Ted later that year said I was trying to undermine his authority.

In October, September, of '69, I was with the Tigers, I came down to Clearwater, Florida. They called it the Instructional League. And there were four blacks, one Puerto Rican, playing on the team. And everyone was staying over on the beach, on Fort Lauderdale beach, and guys had all gotten motel rooms, every player had gotten a room and the four blacks and Puerto Rican were to sleep in cars for three days. I said this is not going to work. I said all these places can't be full. Every time they had a vacancy: "We just sold, just rented out, the last room. That's it." We got together, we were talking one day about what we were going to do. And everyone said, "Well, let's contact someone."

I said we should call George Campbell, Joe Campbell, he's the general manager of the Detroit Tigers. "Well, call, call Campbell." "I don't want to call him." I said, "Well we have the manager, he can call." Manager of the team didn't want to do it. "Elliott, you call, we'll sit here in the room, you call, you get him on the phone; he'll talk to you." I called him. I told him who it was; I'm the first-round pick. "Mr. Campbell, this is Elliott Maddox. We're tired of sleeping in cars, we're not going to sleep in cars anymore." I didn't want to start saying, because once I start I get on these rolls and it just keeps going and going and going. I can start out kind of timidly, but then somewhere around the middle of the sentence I'm building up this animosity and by the end this is what's going to done or, but, lo and behold, we had rooms on the beach within two hours. One of the places was a place that already told us no. Wow, someone must have just checked out. Huh? [laughs] I am a smart ass.

Oh, God. The plague had followed me. Billy Martin shows up in Texas in the middle of September of '73. He had been fired in Detroit. Bob Short, the owner of the team, said this will be a great publicity coup for Texas: "I'll get Billy Martin." So he fired the manager that we had who was in his first year of managing who was really good, got along with him great, Whitey Herzog. Just his first year of managing, so he had not built up his reputation yet. But everyone liked him, we'd run through walls for him. Guy knew what he was talking about. But the owner wanted Billy Martin. So they bring Billy down and that's when I knew with Billy and me it was oil and water.

That got me to the Yankees. That was great. Because now, whenever I would go to Yankee Stadium, as a visitor, having been a Yankee fan, and a baseball fan, I would feel, I would actually feel, even when I would go there to watch games, I could actually feel. It's like the spirits of former ballplayers. But putting on the Yankee uniform, being in that clubhouse, being a player, there's an added burden, not really, responsibility, yes, incentive, to performing well. Because you have to carry on tradition and if it's a Yankee uniform you're putting on, then obviously you are capable of carrying on the tradition.

The following year was coming along even better. April was good, May, I had a bad two weeks in May. At least for me it was a bad two weeks. Then I got hot again, but then I got hurt on Friday the 13. June 13. Catching a ball. I hurt my knee the play before that. Someone had gotten a base hit, to right center, that's when I hurt my knee. And I walked back to center field and I'd gone over to right center and I walked back and I said, "Something's not right." I put my hands up, calling for time, and no one saw me. And the batter hit the first pitch to right center so off I go to right center, caught the ball for the second out of the inning. Run scored, runners at first and third, caught the ball for the second out. And as I was going down, I knew I was going down, I did throw the ball back into second base to keep the runner from being in scoring position. And it was like being in a cartoon when the guy gets hit in the head with a big club and the stars are going around in circles around his head. I saw the stars. I never felt pain like that.

I remember the trainer, Gene Monahan, came out, and he held my upper leg and took my foot and turned it and laid it flat on the ground. And I'm looking at it and for a moment I was exercised out of my body and the medical side came out, the student, and is it supposed to do that? And he just looks at me like, "Well, I guess it can do that because it's doing it." He said, "I think we need to get you off the field," and he said, "Don't try to get up and walk." And he had a cart and I'm wondering why I can't walk off and he's got this cart, they put me into this cart, and I go in and they're icing my knee and I'm lying down on my stomach, and Catfish Hunter comes in and he tickles the bottom of my foot, the leg that the ice is on. And what's your first reaction when someone tickles your foot? You jerk — ohh, it was like I destroyed my knee again. He thought that was the funniest thing he'd ever seen. Oh gosh, he just stood there and laughed and laughed and laughed. I remember standing up to walk up to him, to face him, and that's when I found out I couldn't walk. I put my foot down and boom.

All the ligaments were torn. What happened was because there were no ligaments I stepped and the bone just slipped right off, no support. I remember going, "How did I do that?" I was amazed by it, and I wanted to do it again. It hurt like you wouldn't believe, but I said, "This can't be," and I did it and fell again. And that's when they helped me back up on the table. When they took me to the hospital they put me in a cast, they took an impression of my leg to put me in a cast, but I had to go back the next day because they told me my knee was going to be swelling. They put on a cast, but the cast was to help me for that night. When they took the cast off, again I wanted to see if I could walk, again I fell.

Anyway, they weren't doing scopes at that time. And George Steinbrenner, being the owner, doctors report to Steinbrenner. And then Steinbrenner decides what should be told to the player. So for two and a half months, there I was with torn ligaments with nothing being done. Because he was hoping I could get back out on the field wearing this brace.

I didn't get back until late '76. And I was never the same. They didn't operate. I got hurt June 13. They didn't operate until September 3. By that time, the ligaments were shot, they were gone. Three days after surgery, staph infection, I almost lost my leg. And then baseball wasn't as much fun. I stayed in the outfield. It was easier for me in the outfield.

In 1980, which was my last year in the majors, I played third. And that was the reason it was my last year. Because the constant bending that finished off my knee. I could have played a couple of more years had I been in the outfield in 1980. Joe Torre, the manager of the Mets, kept coming to me, "I need you to play third base tonight." It was funny, it was a day-to-day thing. "I need you at third base today. You've got to do it. You've got to help me out." And I said, "Joe, I don't want to play third. You have other infielders. Let them play third. I should be in the outfield. This is killing my leg." "Just for tonight, just for tonight." "OK, Joe, last time," cause Joe and I were close. As players we were friends, and he became manager and that was part of the reason why I came to the Mets as a free agent. And he asked me to play third. I said, "OK, Joe, one last time." I must have said that one hundred times. It was like an Abbott and Costello skit.

Whenever Jewish holidays, the High Holy Days, would fall during baseball season, I would take off Yom Kippur, I wouldn't play. There was a game, I wouldn't play. And managers—Torre, let me think who, I had Billy Martin as a manager once during the High Holy Days, Earl Weaver and who else did I have, Torre. None of them had a tough time, none of them had a problem with my taking time off. Torre knew about it beforehand. Torre knew I was Jewish. As a matter of fact, I remember one time Joe saying, coming up to me a few days before, maybe it had been even a week before, he said, "OK, I see such-and-such is coming up, you won't be playing, right, because I've got to figure out, you know, work on the lineup, so you're not going to be here, right?" And I said, "Right." So he was good. So yeah, I would take those days off.

Billy Martin was anti-most things. His being an anti–Semite was another one of his character flaws, of which he had many. There were quite a few in the baseball world, in the sports world. Just as there are far too many in public life, in life in general. Way too many.

I was talking about places in the South that I had traveled to and some of the experiences, whether it be thinking about going to college there, or spring training in 1969 or I played in the minor leagues in Rocky Mount, North Carolina. As you drive into Rocky Mount on US 301, there was a billboard at each end of town, you are now in Klan Country. Huge billboard. Wonderful, the South.

So anyway, with converting, my conversion to Judaism. What I did, I want to just throw this in. Some people want to know, why'd you do that, why'd you convert? Because I am a religious person, I'm not a Bible or Torah quoter, I'm not gonna throw scriptures at you. I believe in what I believe. I don't believe you have to go to a building or a structure necessarily to be considered religious. Your beliefs are within you. And how you obey them or live with them determines how religious you are. And what I believed in for most of my life is much more aligned with the Jewish faith than with Christianity. And I felt I should give my beliefs a name. And well, my beliefs do have a name, they did have a name, it was called Judaism. And not being one to be afraid to stand up and take responsibility or whatever you want to call it, or tell the world what I am, I converted. It was only right that I did it.

And I used to think, "Oh boy, my mother. What am I going to hear on this one?" She was, "Is that what you're wearing? You're not wearing that out of my house. You go up and change right now." And I was already twenty years old and, "Oh no, you're not wearing that." She was fine with it. Because she knew I had problems with Christianity. She said, "Well at least you believe in something." She came right out and said, "I have no problem with it." That was that.

As for converting, well, I mean I wasn't that really close to the rabbi. I can't remember his name. I happened to go into a synagogue in Queens one day [in the summer of 1974] and talked to him. Told him I want to convert. I was close to a rabbi in New Jersey, the one who married me. But he was Reform, and I thought if I'm going to convert I should learn something. Orthodox wouldn't have me. So I thought I'd go through Conservative, which was good, great. For someone who loves history and I love to learn, it was ideal, fantastic. It was a very special process.

Someone said, "Oh, can I see that chain," then they go like this, like, "Oh, why are you wearing that?" Now OK, now it has come up, now it's part of the discussion. But when I was playing baseball, everyone put a number on the bottom of their bat, but what do I put on my bat? A Jewish star. That's what I put. It was cool. But anyway, I say it didn't change things much, but actually it did. One thing's for sure. I was no longer a member of just one minority. I had options now. At that point I had options. I could be Jewish, I could be black, I could be a black Jew all by myself, I could fit in over here, I could fit in over there, I could sit by myself and twiddle my thumbs. It is funny even to this day, especially in New York, to be around a group of Jews and everyone's talking and what not, and they don't know I'm Jewish and all of a sudden I start speaking Yiddish, and everyone turns and like did that just come out of your mouth? Oh, gosh.

The stereotypical black mother, the stereotypical Jewish mother, you will never see in the same room at the same time because they are the same person. There's really no difference and the similarities are mind boggling. How they rear children. It's eerie, it is eerie, the similarities.

I know I've met some black Jews, New York City, there are a lot, there are a lot in New York. Large congregations of them, a lot. Talk about Rastafarians, they will stop me for the teachings of Hailie Selassie and we'll get into Judaism. They feel a kindred spirit with Jews. A former brother-in-law of mine was, or is, Rastafarian, and we were like this, and when he first found out the fact that I was Jewish, he made a beeline for me, you know, he wanted, "Come, let's go sit down, you and I are gonna..." we would always, we'd just sit down and talk. One of our relatives in Louisiana, he lives in Switzerland now, when I was around, I was only there for a few days, I spent most of my time with him. That was great. A lot of black Jews.

Life after baseball. I've done so much and I've done nothing. [laughs] I was offered a chance to go work for the Yankees and I didn't want to do it. Gene Michael asked me to come back in 1990 to coach. But I'd been out of ball for like ten years and he wanted me to come back. And I did go back. But in August of '91 I moved my family here, to Florida, to Coral Springs, right by Fort Lauderdale, have to do spring training, and that was the time Steinbrenner started building the facility in Tampa and I said, "I'm not going to Tampa." My son was about to turn five, and one evening I was going to put some garbage in the dumpster, and just come back to the apartment and he grabbed my leg and doesn't want me to leave, kept saying no. I said, "I'm coming right back." He says, "No, no, you're going on one of those trips." He thought I was going out on a road trip and he would not let go. And that touched me so much the next day I resigned. I got to be around to raise him.

I was on Wall Street for seven and a half years, first with Rothschild, then with Oppenheimer, an investment banker, in the shadows of the World Trade Center. And after that I started a dessert shop in New Jersey, I went into coaching, had a few businesses, trucking business and down here I did counseling.

I was the Broward County, which is the District 11 for the state of Florida, I was the senior foster care counselor for eight years. And for the year trained all the foster parents in Broward County. But then I became a single parent, I realized that I had to stop doing that or my son would end up being one of the kids I would have to counsel, because I would go out at 2 a.m., you know, these kids don't have any parents and they looked to me as a parent figure. I've got eighty kids that I'm working with. In 1989, I had the privilege of going to Poland and started up little league baseball over there. I drove to the Warsaw Ghetto, which was eerie, from a historical sense, that's the Jewish side of me, just as when I went to Germany I went to Dachau. Didn't really want to do it, but I had to do it, so I went and found that I've done those two. Now on my black side, which also liked me going to those two places, wants me to go to the Ivory Coast. I forget the name of it right now, but it's where the slaves were taken from. Then I'll go to Nubia [Egypt].

JOSE BAUTISTA
Baltimore Orioles 1988–1991;
Chicago Cubs, 1993–1994;
San Francisco Giants, 1995–1996;
Detroit Tigers, 1997;
St. Louis Cardinals, 1997
(1964–)

Jose Bautista played parts of nine seasons in the Major Leagues during a twenty-year professional career. Bautista is the son of a Dominican Republic Catholic father and a Jewish mother who immigrated to the Dominican Republic from Spain. Signed by the Mets in 1981 as a sixteen-year-old, Bautista made it to the majors with the Orioles in 1988. He retired following the 1999 season, and then pitched one more season in Mexico. As of late 2010, he was working for the Chicago White Sox as a roving instructor for Latino players. Bautista told his story in May 2006, while working as a coach at extended spring training in Florida.

There were some stories I read that said my mother was from Israel or she was a Holocaust survivor who ended up in the Dominican Republic. No, no, no. That's not true. My mother — her name was Gloria — and her family are from Spain. I don't know when they came to the Dominican Republic, but she came with her parents when she was a little girl. I never got to meet my grandparents.

My father, Joaquin, is Dominican. He was a carpenter and we used to help him. He is around eighty years old and still lives there. My mother died young, when she was forty-nine, in 1983. My mother, she's the one

179

who is Jewish. My father is Catholic. I don't have a really good story about how they got from Spain to the Dominican. They didn't talk about it too much.

Yes, they were all Jewish in Spain. My grandfather was Jewish Spanish. First, every Friday they do Shabbat. My mother always did that. And we celebrated Chanukah. On Chanukah, we got all kinds of presents. Yes, there are other Jews, especially in Santiago, where I was playing. There was a family named Washman that I remember. But there were not many.

I grew up in a little town, in a little country, too. No one knew I was Jewish. You know how kids are, especially then. Being Jewish was a big thing. My parents had to have everything quiet because the Dominican is mostly Catholic and people believed we killed Jesus. My grandparents told my mother to keep it quiet. So they kept it really quiet and that's how we grew up.

On Chanukah, she had a real beautiful menorah, silver. It was beautiful. She always took care of it. She said, "That's coming from your grandpop and this and this." My mother only prays every Friday. I still do it, too. I still call my wife when I'm away coaching and she lights the candles. And my brother-in-law, he says prayers over bread and the wine every Friday.

No, most of my brothers don't follow any Jewish customs. We are four boys and two girls. Two of them live in the United States, one brother and one sister. I have one brother who tries to be Jewish. I don't know why I'm interested. My momma said she could see I was really interested when I was very young. She'd say to me, "You especially want to continue to learn." That was when I was little. Maybe it was because I was curious about everything. I would ask questions. But when I was with other kids, I didn't say I was Jewish.

There are two synagogues in the Dominican, but I didn't have a Bar Mitzvah. Not many have them in the Dominican. So really, I don't have the background. But I did have Bar Mitzvahs for my sons. Sure, I did. I wanted to build a synagogue in the Dominican some day, but I don't live there anymore. I live in Florida. Some day, though, maybe I will build a synagogue there. It's in the back of my mind.

I do remember when I became thirteen. My mother said, "You're a man now. And you can do a lot of things." Even though my father was Catholic, he respected my mother's religion. I used to go to a synagogue in Santo Domingo and Santiago some, but we always prayed in the house. We had Shabbat and Chanukah and all that at home. We didn't have the

Jose Bautista, a pitcher for several teams, including the Baltimore Orioles, in the late 1980s and early 1990s, was born to a Jewish mother of Spanish heritage and a Catholic father in the Dominican Republic. When Bautista was a child, his family kept quiet about its Jewish background.

chance to do too much Christmas. My dad eventually divorced my mom and he had kids with someone else, and they had Christmas. We saw that and asked him if we could have Christmas too, but he said no.

When I became interested in baseball, I liked Sandy Koufax because he was a good pitcher and we've got the same religion. From my point of view, I think he's one of the greatest. I also liked Mario Soto, because he's from the same town as me, Bani. I followed him a lot when I was little. I always said I was going to throw harder than him. He threw hard, too. He threw 94 m.p.h. I hit 95 m.p.h. Juan Marichal was big in the Dominican, but he was from way out in a little town.

You want to see people like you who do well. There weren't that many Jewish players. There used to be a pitching coach for the Marlins, Wayne Rosenthal, who played a little bit in the majors. He was the pitching coach when they won the last World Series. We played a little bit at Oklahoma City in 1991. When we played together, we tried to help each other. He's really smart. He didn't play much in the majors, but he made it as a pitching coach. We talked about our families all the time.

I signed a baseball contract with the New York Mets when I was sixteen. It was for $2,000. The Yankees wanted to sign me when I was fifteen, but my mother and father said no. I was throwing like 87–88 miles an hour. I didn't sign. I was crying then, too. I wanted to be a baseball player. I signed with the Mets and they sent me to Kingsport in the Appalachian League in 1981. It was a rookie league. I didn't know English at all.

I spent a long time in the minor leagues—seven years—and I almost was released after my third year. The Mets wanted to release me, but the pitching coach said no. He had them send me to Columbia in the South Atlantic League, and I won thirteen games. I continued to play, but nobody called me up. It was one of those things. They said I was too young. I never thought I wasn't going to make it. I won fifteen games at Lynchburg of the Carolina League in 1985, the year after I won thirteen at Columbia, and I still didn't get called up.

Then the Orioles took me. I threw one game with the Orioles on national TV against Oakland and I won, 4–2. And they sent me back to the minors. They said I had an option. They tried to ruin my life a little bit. My wife said, "Don't worry about it." One time I had an argument with my manager, Frank Robinson, and they sent me down to the Miami Miracle in Class A. I ran my mouth a little bit. I shouldn't have done that. They still paid me the same money I was making in the majors. I had already been with the Orioles for three seasons.

I was 8–2 with a 2.71 ERA in Miami. That year, they messed me up. They sent me to Texas for a little bit, and I didn't want to go there. I said they could release me. Then, I went back to Baltimore. That was in 1991. I finished the year in Baltimore, but was given free agency at the end of the season. I never was traded. I was always a free agent. That was good. I picked every place I went.

Usually, I started slowly in spring training. But that year, I had to earn a job. I played almost every year in the Dominican, but I played even more that year. I wanted to make the Cubs. I made the team. Shortly before I joined the Cubs I married my wife. I met her in 1988 in Miami. She had two children from a former marriage and we have two. I consider all four of them mine.

No one knew I was Jewish until I was with the Cubs, in 1993. Jimmy Banks, he was our traveling secretary. He's Jewish, too. One year, for some reason, he said to me, "I got to go do the Shabbat." I said like, "You're Jewish?" He said, "Yeah." I said, "Me too." He said, "You?" I don't think he believed me. I said, "Yeah, my mom." Coming from the Dominican, everybody thinks I'm Catholic. Our public relations girl was Jewish, too. After that, everybody knew I was Jewish.

I bought this Jewish star in 1987 and I always wear it around my neck. And I wear my number, 38, that I wore in Chicago. It was the same thing when I met my wife, Lea. She is from Venezuela. I met her at an event for a Venezuelan ball player in Miami. I don't even remember why I was there, and for no reason I just started talking to her. I didn't know if she was Jewish or not. This was about 1988 when I was with the Orioles. Then the conversation got to religion and she said she was Jewish. I said, "Me, too." We got married a few years later.

When I was with Chicago and everybody knew I was Jewish, we had a game in Pittsburgh on Yom Kippur, but I asked to stay at the hotel. I didn't even watch the game on television. The other players always joked I couldn't be Jewish. They look at my color and don't believe it. I told them, "I know, I don't believe it, either." In baseball, players are making jokes all the time. I remember Tony Muser was our bullpen guy when he played. He watched me one day and said, "Jose, you're rushing." I said, "No, I'm not Russian, I'm Jewish." He said, "No, you're rushing out." I said, "No, I'm not Russian. I'm Jewish Dominican." I finally understood what he was trying to say, but he kept joking with me. Later, when I saw him with the Padres, he'd say, "Jose, you're Russian."

The fans really didn't know I was Jewish until it came out in some of the papers, especially in New York. You have to be Jewish to know who's Jewish. In New York, the fans would see the articles and say, "Jose, you Jewish?" and I'd say yes and they'd say, "Shalom," and they'd invite me to their homes. I'd give them my number and they'd call. Sure, I went to their homes.

Chicago was the best place for me in the majors. I liked to pitch in Chicago. Wrigley Field was really sharp. I had my best year there in 1993, and I pitched there in 1994, but we went on strike that year. I signed with San Francisco after that. Chicago offered me a one-year contract, but San Francisco offered me two years. I would have loved to stay in Chicago, but San Francisco made me a better offer. I was one of those pitchers, every time they give me the ball, I'd be there. They used to tell me I had an elastic arm because I could throw every day and not get hurt. Once in a while I'd get hurt, but I'd still pitch.

In 2000, I pitched in Mexico. They wanted me back the next year, but I said I didn't want to pitch anymore. And I retired.

I played two years with Barry Bonds in San Francisco. Bonds liked me, for some reason. I was born July 26, 1964 — not July 25 like it says in most record books—and he was born July 24, 1964. He used to say we should celebrate our birthdays together, but I said, no, no. He liked me, though. One day in the morning, for some reason, I was kind of a grouch. His locker was near mine, and I was just trying to put my uniform on and Barry came in and he passed by and he sat down and he say to me, "Hey, you, you're not going to say 'Good morning' or something?"

So I turned around and I say, "Enough. I don't come in here to make a friend. I just come in here to work." So from that day on, I was his best friend. He was really nice to me. He'd call me in the room and say, "Hey, let's go eat." For me, he was a really nice guy. But the way they raised him — his father Bobby and his God father, Willie Mays—was to have some distrust. Bobby Bonds and Willie Mays weren't always treated well. They had to work hard, and still it wasn't always enough. That's what they told Barry. They went through a lot of bad stuff and the way they were raising him was the same way.

I played with a lot of good players. One of the best teammates for me, was Matt Williams. He not only was one of the best teammates, but a nice person, a great third baseman.

I don't know why there seem to be more Jewish players today. Some Jewish players today go to school and go for it. Parents wouldn't let them go, but now, they're more open-minded. Before, the parents said, "You go to school and do this." Now, the kids say they want to do this. My mother wanted me to go to school and my father said, "You can play baseball." So I went to school and I played baseball outside. If you want to do baseball, you do it the right way, he said.

We belong to a synagogue in Davie, Florida, Pembroke Pines. I really turned to the Jewish thing when I found my wife. Because she's always doing things that are Jewish.

When I retired, I said, "I'm not going to do nothing for now." My wife said, "You're not interested in coaching?" Well, maybe I was, but not now. Well, she said, "We'll do all the papers and send them out." Within two weeks, three teams called.

I'm teaching what I know. I just want the guys to throw strikes. Jim Lefebvre of the Cubs came out once to see me, and I didn't understand why he was coming to the mound. This is in 1993. He said, "Jose, I want you to throw some balls. Not strike, strike, strike, strike. I want you to throw some balls, too. If you throw 99 percent strikes, you'll be OK." I started to mess around up in the zone. I didn't like to mess around. I didn't like to throw balls. If you're going to hit me, OK. I go right at them.

This is my third year in Idaho Falls. My wife goes with me part of the time, but my youngest daughter had a bad experience there. She went to a carnival and got dizzy and got a fever. When she went to the hospital, they asked her what religion she was. There are a lot of Mormons there. My wife wanted to know why they asked. Why does it make a difference?

I don't know what answer they gave, but my wife didn't like it, and neither did my daughter. My daughter doesn't want to go back. I don't know why it matters what religion you are. We're all the same.

JESSE LEVIS
Cleveland Indians, 1992–1995, 1999;
Milwaukee Brewers, 1996–1998, 2001
(1968–)

I was like, "I'm not Sandy Koufax. I'm not at that level. I'm a
Major League player trying to make a living, make a career."
— Jesse Levis

I grew up in Northeast Philly. I went to Northeast High School. I was drafted by the Philadelphia Phillies out of high school, but I elected to go to school, college, and I went to the University of North Carolina and had a lot of fun down there in Chapel Hill. Northeast Philly was very Jewish back in the seventies and early eighties, until we moved out of there. We grew up Conservative Jews, belonged to Oxford Circle Jewish Community Synagogue, but now it's a big church. It's not a nice site when we drive by there, but it was a good neighborhood, a lot of good athletics, a lot of good kids, a lot of playing in the streets, a lot of Wiffle Ball games.

That's where I learned to how to play the game of baseball. My brothers and I, when I was 5 years old, would play a lot of Wiffle Ball out in front of our house. My brother wanted me to be switch-hitting. He thought I would be a catcher. I guess he knew speed didn't run in the family, and he turned me around and I started hitting left-handed and just kind of forgot about hitting right-handed.

A big memory was when I was twelve years old and the Philadelphia Phillies won the World Series, their only World Championship [until 2008]. We were diehard Philly fans growing up, and that was a big thrill. It almost felt like I was part of that team growing up because I was so involved. Each win, each loss, I felt like I was a part of it, and it really

186

inspired me to move on and really go after my dream. My brother Jules and I, after the Phillies clinched the National League Championship against the Astros, there were tickets on sale that evening at the Vet, at the old Vet, and my brother and I and a couple other friends, we went down to the stadium. They were going to go on sale the next morning at five o'clock in the morning or something really early, so the line started at midnight. They set up tents and everything. I was like twelve years old. My brother was fifteen and my older brother was eighteen.

I wound up falling asleep at the Vet on the sidewalk. My brother woke me. I guess he watched me while I was sleeping. We got the tickets and we went to Game Two at The Vet. It was a win. It was exciting. It was a come-from-behind win against the Royals that night, and we were sitting up in the 700 level and it was a lot of fun. My mom, my two brothers, and me went. It was a good time.

There were non–Jews in our neighborhood, as well, but predominantly, it was a Jewish neighborhood. When I was probably ten through fifteen, I started to go to other playgrounds, separated from my neighborhood, to play against better competition, and I became friendly with some of my teammates who were non–Jews, but I always had a bunch of core friends that were Jewish growing up.

I was a kid that lived and breathed baseball all the time. Out back in our driveway, we had a wall, and I would go out back and I'd practice throwing and I'd practice my footwork. I was really insane, looking back and hearing what people say about the way I acted. It was kind of a little strange, but I really believed that I had to work above and beyond to get where I wanted to go, and I needed to do that. I would get up at 7:30 in the morning, and I'd take swings out in front of my house because there was a tree that I could visualize a pitcher standing there and I could work on my swing outside, where my mother would kill me if I started swinging the bat in the house.

I knew I wasn't blessed with the unbelievable Barry Bonds talent. You know, I was a short white Jewish guy that couldn't run. I didn't have slow feet behind the plate, but I couldn't run. I could swing the bat and I had a good arm. So, I knew I really had to work hard if I wanted to be a big leaguer. The first day I got back there [as a catcher] in Little League, I think I was eight, I just remember everybody saying, "It's so hard" and "How do you keep your eyes from blinking every time a guy swings?" It just became like a natural thing for me and I really felt comfortable back there at such a young age, eight years old.

When I was fourteen, I went to an open tryout camp the Phillies would hold annually at Lincoln High School in Northeast Philly. I just went. You had to be sixteen, but I went with my older brother, who was sixteen at the time or seventeen. I just wanted to see how I could do. I told the scouts I was sixteen. I wound up doing really well. The scout who wound up drafting me out of high school was the guy from that camp; so, for four years, he followed my career and he drafted me.

I was tutored for my Bar Mitzvah. My older brother went to Hebrew school and went the whole way, but my parents were divorced by the time I was of age to do that, and it just wasn't the thing for us to do, but we went to synagogue on all the High Holidays and my bub, my bubby, was very religious. Both my father's and mother's side were from Russia. My bub was in Russia. She escaped to Norway and then came to the States. Also my father's side was Russian and they came over here. I don't think Levis was our original name. I just can't think of it right now. I think that my great-grandfather when he came here was Levis' boy; like, he worked for somebody named Levis and he became Levis' boy, and I think he just took his name.

I mean, I couldn't play on Yom Kippur and all the High Holidays, which I needed to be playing those days, but I couldn't. I guess the first time it became an issue was at the Instructional League when I was a minor league player coming up with the Indians. I was faced with practicing and playing games at the instructional league in October and I wound up practicing that day. It wasn't something where I could just go in and say, "I need the day off. I'm Jewish and this is a High Holiday for me" because at that time, they probably would have said, "Hey, either practice or get the hell out of here." There wasn't another Jew there at that time. That was the first time I was faced with it.

There was one situation in 1996 where we were in Baltimore. Actually, it was a make-up game from earlier in the season. We were rained out, and it was a scheduled off day, which was Yom Kippur. It was late September that year and they scheduled it for that day and we went to Baltimore. I wasn't in the lineup. I went there. I didn't tell my manager, Phil Garner, "Hey, I can't play today. I'm Jewish."

He had no idea. He just wanted to win the game, like any manager. I was fasting, too, and I wasn't drinking water; so, I was trying to keep things together.

In the seventh inning, I did get in the game. That was when Phil Garner would usually use me, in those situations, to pinch-hit. Mike Matheny came out and I went in. I didn't get a hit. It wound up going extra innings. I went 0 for 3. I think it went thirteen or fourteen innings. We won the

Catcher Jesse Levis played on Yom Kippur in 1996. As he explained his decision to play, "I'm not Sandy Koufax." He went into a slump for the rest of the year.

game. After the game, some reporter came in the clubhouse and knew I was Jewish, somehow put it together, and he said, "You played on Yom Kippur" and he started asking me questions.

I was like, "I'm not Sandy Koufax. I'm not at that level. I'm a Major League player trying to make a living, make a career. I'm not the super-star," which Koufax was, where he could walk in and say, "I can't play today." After the game, Bud Selig, who was our owner in Milwaukee at that time, who is now the commissioner, I guess he gave Garner some grief about it because on ESPN that night, they had a little clip and said, "Jesse Levis, who did play in this game, is Jewish and he went 0 for 3." I was taken aback. I was like, "That's so horrible that they did that." I guess

Selig heard it, and he told Garner and the next morning, Garner called me and apologized for putting me in the game.

It was nice that he did that anyway, apologized. God punished me anyway. I didn't get a hit the rest of the year. We had, I think, maybe another week to go and I was 0 for 10 the rest of the year. He got me.

Let's go back to spring training of '95, where I was out of options with the Indians and they either had to keep me or kind of expose me to the waiver wire and hopefully trade me, which I was kind of looking forward to. Actually, they had an extended roster at the end of spring training, where they were allowed to carry twenty-eight men versus twenty-five because of the strike situation and the three-week abbreviated spring training; so, anyway, I made the team as one of the three extra men — me, David Bell and I think it was Jeromy Burnitz, I want to say.

Anyway, I started the year, and they had three catchers. It was Sandy Alomar, Tony Pena, and myself. I barely was playing. I had twelve at-bats in like a month. Then, May 15, they had to cut the roster down to twenty-five, and I was one of those five guys and they exposed me to the waiver and I wound up clearing. It was a frustrating time in my career. I went to Buffalo, which was their Triple-A affiliate. At that time, they took me off the roster, and I said, "There's no way I'll ever be back in Cleveland. I'll either be with another team or somewhere else in baseball, whatever."

At that time, my wife and I were planning our wedding date; so, she asked me, "Do you think October 29 would be a good date?" I was like, "If Cleveland gets to the World Series and stuff, I'm not going to be up there again; so, just make the date and I'll be there." As it turned out, I played the whole season at Buffalo and did really well. September comes around and they call me up to the big leagues, Cleveland does again, and we make it through the first round, the second round, and we're in the World Series. The date was October 29 and I was an alternate on the Indians' postseason roster; meaning, if someone goes down, they can activate me.

As it turned out, Sandy Alomar was hanging on by a thread. His knee was really blowing up, and it was Tony Pena and me. It was us three and every day, Sandy, I'd see him limping in the training room and I'm thinking, I'm going to get activated. I really wanted it. I mean, this was a great thrill to be a part of a playoff team and it was all the way up to the middle of the World Series. My wife came to Game Two, and then she was calling all our guests and telling them, "We're on standby. We don't know if Jesse's going to be back or not" because Mike Hargrove said, "Hey, you're going to have to stay. If Sandy goes down, you're going to be activated," so I was really torn both ways. We wound up playing Game Six October 28 in Atlanta and we lost. Tom Glavine threw a one-hitter and beat us 1-nothing, and I flew home the next morning, the day of our wedding, and made it to our wedding. My wife was very nervous the whole time.

My wife and I met when we were twelve years old. She was at my Bar Mitzvah. We were friends first. She was two grades ahead of me, but she skipped a grade when she was younger. We have three kids. We have a daughter, Lily, and we have twin boys, Jared and Joseph. When our daughter was born, that was the greatest thing that I ever did. I remember saying that to myself, "This is the greatest thing that can ever happen to me." Then two boys to boot.

I guess my first year, about halfway through, it was a little awkward, he [then-Milwaukee Brewers owner and now Baseball Commissioner Bud Selig] sends a note to my locker, like, "Jesse, I'd like to see you tomorrow in my office," which was in the stadium. I was like, "Oh, my God, he's going to get rid of me. I don't know what I did, but he's not happy with something." He calls me up there, and we're sitting and talking and he says, "I did not know you were a Jew." I was there probably a couple months. He didn't know. Somebody, I guess, told him. It's not like I walked around saying, "Hey, I'm Jewish."

Anyway, he calls me in, and I think it's like close to Rosh Hashanah. It might be like four months into the season. We were sitting and talking and he was telling me how he found out I was a Jewish baseball player and he was excited to have a Jew on his team. I don't think he'd had one in quite some time, if ever. He wound up inviting me for Rosh Hashanah dinner at his house, but I couldn't make it. I thought it was very nice that he invited me, and every time I saw him after that, he was always nice to me. He would come through spring trainings and always go out of his way to say "Hello" and I really appreciated that.

In 1998, I had a shoulder injury, a right rotator cuff tear. It happened during a game. Throughout my career, I had a lot of shoulder weakness, my right shoulder, but I always overcame it. I compensated. I did a lot of work with it, rehabbing and strengthening. I guess that was the warning sign. One game in Milwaukee in '98, early, I guess it was May of '98, we were playing against the Astros and they were a running team. Mike Hampton was pitching and I started, left-on-left, because I was catching Jeff Juden. I became his personal catcher — which was probably the worst move of my career, that Phil Garner made me his personal catcher.

Anyway, Juden didn't hold runners very well and they had run maybe three, four times successfully that game and it was getting to me. Finally, Mike Hampton gets on base and he takes off and steals second, and I'm really flaming and really fired up and I make a throw with pretty poor mechanics, trying to throw it harder than I can throw a ball. I felt a burning sensation down my right arm and I knew something was wrong, but I stayed in the game because I wasn't a regular player where I could come out whenever I got nicked up, so I felt like I had to be out there.

The next inning, I went back out. Jeff Bagwell gets on, the first runner. He takes off, steals second. I have good mechanics. I go to make the throw, and my shoulder pops out of its socket. It's called sublux, where it pops in and out. It was painful, and it was throbbing, but my mentality was pretty insane. This was my thought process behind the plate at the time, "It popped back in. Maybe I can get through it." Then my arm really started hurting, and I kind of walked off. After that, it was a battle through the surgery, the rehab.

I had surgery in July of '98. I tried to rehab it first and come back, and that didn't work. He [Dr. James Andrews] did the surgery. I was released the day after the season was over. The Brewers just released me and didn't give me an opportunity to really come back. That was kind of frustrating because I really kind of gave everything I had for them, and they didn't really give me an opportunity to come back with them. I elected to sign with the Tampa Bay Devil Rays, and I was rehabbing and my rehab was going really well. I signed with the Devil Rays and went to spring training, and I hurt my back rehabbing my shoulder, so it was another setback and I wound up getting back on the field in about May of '99. I went to Triple-A for the Devil Rays. I had an out in my contract in July, where if they didn't call me to the Major Leagues with the Devil Rays, I could say, "All right, I'm going to elect my free agency and go wherever needs a catcher," so I elected to do that.

Cleveland picked me back up, and I finished the season. They brought me right to the big leagues and I finished the season in '99 with the Indians, which was a nice thing. I didn't do very well. I probably wasn't ready, to be honest, looking back. You know, you think you're ready up here [he points to his head], but my shoulder wasn't ready. I was swinging the bat really well in the minor leagues, but I wasn't throwing as well. You're a little tentative after a major surgery like I had. The following year, I went to Triple-A with the Indians and that's where I really started to come back, in 2000.

I never actually heard stuff, but one manager in Cleveland, he saw my brother and I eating matzah ball soup one day in a Jewish deli, and he made some comments that weren't very nice. I never heard anything bad, like "Get this Jew out of here." That would have been awful.

Shawn Green was one [fellow Jewish player]. I didn't know at first, until one Rosh Hashanah we were playing in '96, and he said, "Happy New Year" to both me and Al Clark, who was the umpire at that time. I didn't know Al Clark was a Jew. I was like, "Wow, this is probably the first time in history that three Jews have been at the plate in a Major League park in a Major League game." [There have been other times, but not too many.] Then he came up the second time, and I wished him "Happy New Year" and I said, "This is probably the second time in history."

I was a good defender, like I said, probably an average to slightly above defensive catcher. I rarely made an errant throw. I was doing it since I was six, seven, eight, so I hope I became a good receiver. I really concentrated and I appreciated every day I got in the Major Leagues. It was a great career. It just went too fast.

There was a catching instructor that I had, he's the bench coach now with the Florida Marlins, named Gary Tuck. He was outstanding. I mean, he took me over and really showed me how to take charge of a game, how there's so much more than just catching and throwing, how it's calling a game and living and dying with your pitcher and being able to get the most out of each pitcher on every given day and really taking charge of a game. He really showed me that, and I think that really elevated my game past Double-A and into the Major Leagues. He did it with several other catchers that are a lot more noted than I am, Jorge Posada and Joe Girardi, Kelly Stinnett. I mean, these guys had nice careers and became better catchers because of him. Joe, every time in '96 that I would come to hit, he would want to carry on a conversation with me, where I was trying to bear down. I'm facing David Cone and Mariano Rivera in relief and he's trying to talk to me and I'm trying to really concentrate. It was just so annoying. He was such a jabber-jaw.

In my early Major League career, '92 through '96 with Cleveland, I was faced with a lot of obstacles in players like Sandy Alomar and veteran backups, Tony Pena, Junior Ortiz, and it was really hard to establish myself there. Once I moved on to probably a second-division club, whereas Cleveland was probably a first-division club, going to the World Series and play-offs every year for the next five, six years, I had a lot of confidence, like saying, "Wow, I think I can play in this league," when I saw myself around a lot of no-name guys in Milwaukee at the time I got there, saying, "Wow, I really can play."

I had a very good minor league career. I had good numbers and I was a good player and I had confidence, and Phil Garner used me. I think that's when I really thought that I belonged in the Major Leagues, once I got traded from Cleveland to the Brewers and really established myself as a backup to almost a platoon guy.

I got my first hit off was Mike Boddicker and my first home run off Kurt Knudsen, with the Tigers. The biggest pitcher I hit a home run off was David Cone, with the Yankees, in Milwaukee in '97. My biggest thrill was probably the first Major League hit. I mean, that was a big thrill, the first Major League hit, the first major league home run, in Detroit, old Tigers Stadium. Being on the field when we won the American League Championship with the Indians in '95 was a huge thrill. I was in the dugout with the team, celebrating with the champagne and the whole works. That was a really a big thrill. So was throwing out Ricky Henderson for my first caught-stealing in the Major Leagues.

I just knew that it [being Jewish and being in the Major Leagues] was not a common thing. I knew that there weren't many Jews that played in the major leagues. Just to be a Major Leaguer is a great thrill. There's not many kids that grow up and get to be a Major League player, but being Jewish and a big leaguer, I knew that it was very special.

I had my last spring training with the Mets in 2004 and I hurt my shoulder again. I really felt like I could still play. I was swinging the bat well. I could catch. I was a veteran. I had experience. I thought I might be able to help a team. I was in a backup capacity. Then, I hurt my shoulder — the same shoulder. You know, from my surgery in '98 to 2004, I was fine. I was throwing great and I was playing well, but I hurt it again in spring training of '04. I saw the doctor, Dr. Andrews, and he said, "Jesse, if you have another injury to this arm, you might lose use of your arm permanently." That's all I needed to hear. That's when I knew I needed to move on. [Since retiring, Levis has held several baseball jobs. In the spring of 2011, he became a scout for the Philadelphia Phillies.]

I always thought about being on TV, like news. I thought about maybe being a newscaster, sports. I thought about that in elementary school and a little bit in junior high, but I always knew I would be a big leaguer. It's strange to look back and say that, but I was writing my book, "I know I'm going to be a Major Leaguer," and it worked out.

ADAM GREENBERG
Chicago Cubs, 2005
(1981–)

Adam Greenberg's boyhood dream of making it to the Major Leagues turned into a nightmare when he was beaned in his first (and, as of the spring of 2011, only) big league at-bat with the Chicago Cubs in 2005. Since then, Greenberg has struggled with health problems — the beaning left him with a bout of positional vertigo — but has persevered in his attempt to make it back to the Major Leagues. When this interview was conducted in November 2010, he had just completed his third stint with the Bridgeport Bluefish of the independent Atlantic League.

I go to spring training, go to big league spring training, in 2005. I only had twelve at-bats, 6-for-12, or 5-for-10, or whatever it was. It was the greatest experience of my life. I had been to games, Major League games, during spring training, but never had my own locker and stuff. Every time there was an early morning session with Maddux or Prior or Wood or whoever was pitching, I was always going out. They were asking me to go out and hit at eight o'clock. Nobody wants to do that, none of the big guys. But for me it's an opportunity. I ended up getting sent down from camp, first cut, knowing that was going to happen, but planning on going to Triple-A. Well, last day of spring training, I got sent down and boom, I go to Double-A. So I go from finishing the season at Triple-A, Fall League, big league camp, going back to Double-A. So, just kinda bouncing around.

So started the season, and that year, I actually started slow. I struggled. I struggled pretty good. And then just kept working with the hitting coach and figured some things back out, and then started doing real well to the point where the Cubs were really struggling, and my agent called and the manager told us we were going to stay behind while the team went off to Jacksonville. We were in Sevierville, Tennessee. So Matt Murton and I stayed behind, and my agent tells me, "Root against the Cubs greater than you ever have in your life because you're either going to go to Triple-A or you're going to go back to Double-A." Well, that's we thought, that's what I thought, but he told me Matt's probably going to the big leagues. So a little letdown if he's going to go, and I'm going to go down to Triple-A or whatever. Sure enough, Cubs get swept in the doubleheader by the Braves, Francoeur hits a home run late in the game, so a young kid and we're excited, and that's when we get the call from my manager. We're watching on *Baseball Tonight* and Matt and I are TV, and it's surreal, it's a dream come true. So that's what happened, and I didn't sleep that night, and it was off to Miami to the big league team playing the Marlins.

Getting to the big leagues was the greatest single day that I've ever experienced, just kinda being there and going in and getting your jersey and looking around at everyone. Sitting in and Dusty's [then-Cubs' manager Dusty Baker] talking to me. And they're in dire straits. They've lost eight games in a row, all their heads were down, bad, bad feeling, and I just came in smiling ear to ear, like couldn't be happier to be here. And having been in spring training big league camp with the guys, it wasn't like, "Who's this rookie kid coming in here?" I was received very well, and it was warm, it was heartfelt, it was awesome.

So Dusty told me I wasn't going to play that day — be ready — Dontrelle Willis was pitching, so chill out, enjoy yourself. And then the next night Scott Olson, a lefty pitcher that I had faced a bunch in the Minor Leagues, never had a problem with him, didn't see myself in the line-up, so, all right, I'll be ready. Then the ninth inning rolled around, and there was a righty and a lefty warming in the pen, and myself and Ronny Cedeno were basically the pinch-hitting candidates. But Aramis Ramirez got hurt that day and I wasn't going in to play, just pinch-hitting and be done, so when the righty and lefty were warming up, we were deciding, If a righty comes in, I'm in, if a lefty comes in, you're in. We're not making the decisions, of course, but a lefty comes in, and Dick Pole, the bench coach, says, "Greenie, get a bat, you're hitting." So, OK, figure that out. I didn't care. Throughout my career, I basically had a pretty good ratio righty to lefty. So I got out there and I was ready. I was ready for the opportunity.

Todd Hollandsworth led off and grounded out, I think, and one out, I was up. I was in between: am I taking, am I swinging? And I remember

Called up by the Chicago Cubs in 2005, outfielder Adam Greenberg saw his dream turn into a nightmare after he was hit in the head with the only pitch he has faced as a Major Leaguer (Jewish Major Leaguers).

back to pinch-hitting in a big league game in spring training, and I faced Tom Gordon. And Gordon threw me a fastball, 94 miles an hour, right down the middle. And I was in leadoff mode, take mode, that's what I do. Sure enough, he throws it right down the middle, and I'm like, All right, I've got this guy. Curveball, curveball, curveball, and I was done. Struck out, three or four more pitches or whatever it was, and I was like, I just learned my lesson, thank you. Thank you, Tom, for teaching me a lesson. So I turned that switch on and I was like, All right, I'm swinging. Sure enough, first pitch comes, and I didn't have a chance to swing. I didn't have a chance to swing, and it cracked me. That was scary, a tough experience, certainly, and it started this other life for me.

I was conscious the whole time. I couldn't control my eyes. They rolled into the back of my head, but I was aware of everything that was going on, basically just trying to tell myself to stay alive and stay with it, all that I knew. I actually didn't go to the hospital that night. To the dismay of my agent, I went back to the hotel. I was OK. My whole family was there, except for my older sister who couldn't make it. She had some big exam or something that she had to do. My whole family was there — my mother, father, two brothers and one of my sisters — so after the game they were around that night, kinda making sure I was all right.

I was kinda dazed, but when I went to the field the next morning, that's when I really started feeling the effects. The light was just awful. I couldn't deal with light. My stomach was really sick, and got dressed for the game, and my eyes were shifting. It was just a scary type of feeling. I got dressed, like I'm gonna be playing. And I go out, and I'm seemingly OK, but then I kept having to go into the locker room and just laying down. I felt really awkward, didn't know what to do. It was a really weird feeling. I've never done that, you know, especially not in the big leagues where there's cameras and everything. I'm just like, I can't be out here anymore. I went in and fell asleep a couple different times during the game.

That cycle just started progressing and getting worse, to the point where I was going in the airport and I basically fell, I fell. It was scary. Nobody could really tell me what was really wrong. They were like, "Oh, it's a concussion or whatever," but something in my head told me it wasn't just a concussion. I knew there was something wrong. So it took a while, and then I got kinda diagnosed over the phone by a doctor about a week later. He told me vertigo, positional vertigo. Looked into it, went to this doctor, went to this doctor, went to about seven, or eight, or nine doctors throughout the country. It was really frustrating.

All the while, I was going to the games for seven days. And the Cubs were on a seven-game wining streak when I was there. From an eight-game losing streak to a seven-game winning streak. But Jim Hendry [the Cubs' general manager] called me in the office and basically said, "Sorry what happened, but we're going to send you down. Go get yourself healthy." Which is fine. I can't do anything here, but, you know, I know, it's unfortunate. So that was frustrating, sad, whatever, just unfortunate. So I went back down to Arizona, couldn't rehab or do anything. So it was just sitting stationary, not moving, you know, for days on end.

Finally, I get to a doctor at the Mayo Clinic who teaches me this thing called the Epley maneuver, and it positions you to realign these crystals that you have in your ears to control your equilibrium, blah, blah, blah, the whole nine. And got to the point where they said, "If you're forty-eight hours symptom-free, you can play." So I sat in a chair for 48 hours and didn't have symptoms because I didn't move. Cause I'm thinking, the quicker I show that I'm healthy the quicker I can get back to the big leagues. Boy, was I wrong.

So I come back. The first game I play, I get optioned down to Double-A, which was frustrating because I didn't get a rehab game as a big leaguer. More than anything, that's just money. I played that game, and then the next morning I woke up and all the symptoms came back. And so, just kinda battled through that and had some problems with my manager, and just it was a really hard, trying time. It was the worst experience — went from the best to the worst experience I've ever had. Got totally depressed, down in the dumps, and decided at the tail-end of the season, I couldn't play anymore. I couldn't put myself through that anymore. I basically shut it down for the season, got back relatively healthy, still had symptoms for about a year and a half.

But once I was healthy, got invited to big league camp in '06, but got taken off the roster during the off-season. Got there, didn't really get any at-bats, was kind of a leftover. I was like used-up trash. Frustrating. Went down to Triple-A, and ended up down in Double-A. My manager told me, "I don't know what's going on, but if you go 4-for-4 today, I'm gonna have to sit you tomorrow. You're not an everyday guy." Without me doing anything, and without me playing really, I became not a prospect. I became another guy.

When I was thirteen, I made the AAU baseball team — it was the first AAU baseball team in Connecticut history. I made that team, and that was the experience that changed everything for me. I loved to play all the sports and I grew up watching Major League Baseball and everything. I always wanted to be a Major League Baseball player, but playing all three sports it was hard to pick which one was my favorite because every season that was my favorite sport. We had a tournament in Iowa, the national championship. I was thirteen years old and we actually came out of nowhere and won the whole thing. We won the national championship, I made the all-tournament team, and the experience that I had playing ball — baseball — was something that I wanted to carry on the rest of my life. I made that choice then that I was going to put more time and effort and focus into baseball. But I didn't give up on the other two sports. I lettered in all three from my freshman year on. Four-year varsity in all three sports.

I grew up a Yankee fan. When I was growing up, they weren't like they are today. It was just sheer love for the game, love for the team. But my favorite player growing up was Don Mattingly. Consistent all the time and a professional. Knowing now, that's a pretty good role model. I just loved watching him play, and anytime we went to Yankee Stadium we'd always, when he'd come up, try to go to the right-field wall. Never got a home run or anything, but he was my role model growing up.

When I was young, Little League and everything, I always put in a lot of effort and heart and everything, and I always had success. From the time that I was really young, it's not a story that one day I just all of a sudden turned a switch and, Oh yeah, I was great. I had natural ability, but I worked as hard or harder than anybody. So the success was always there, so in my mind that [becoming a professional baseball player] was going to happen. It may sound crazy, but when I was 13 on that team, that's now with the whole state, and then you're playing against people throughout the country, that's when I realized, I can play with these guys, too. So after that, it was reality, it's realistic that this could happen. Made my high school team, started as a freshman, played center field every day for the rest of my four years. Actually made all-state my freshman year, sophomore, junior and senior, so that just kinda kept reiterating, to me, that at least for me, I was going to do it. There was obviously people that you're too small, you don't have a good arm, you don't have this, so you always hear those things. But the type of person I am, that drives and motivates me.

I went to Sunday school, temple, right on through when I was young. We went to Friday night services when I was younger, then schedules kinda got a little bit crazier. You get games here and there, and my parents were having more and more kids — I was one of five — so it started getting more and more difficult. So we would do some stuff at the house — Friday nights — and then I started doing the Wednesday–Sunday morning Hebrew school till I had my Bar Mitzvah at thirteen. And that was really it for me. I didn't do the continuing education. More than anything, it was schedules—it was really difficult for me. My passion in life was sports. I always had the feeling of being in a minority and having a good sense of who I was and where I came from. That was more important to me than anything, than going to temple.

Then when I went to college at the University of North Carolina, I was the only Jew on the team that people had ever seen. So it was like, What does a Jew look like? The team itself was centralized in North Carolina and the southern states. There might be a lot of Jewish kids at the school, the university, but certainly not the baseball team. So that was fun, and I always enjoyed it. Being a little different, and people asked questions about this and that, so that was fun for me. Taking off in the fall for Yom Kippur and my coach is like, OK, having no idea really what it's about. Educating people on certain things that our religion is about. Not so many misconceptions; it was just more questions, curiosity. And I certainly enjoy that because it challenges me to, if I don't know, I better start knowing.

Once I signed professionally, that's kinda when it really started coming out because that was on a much bigger scale. I signed with the Chicago Cubs [the Cubs drafted Greenberg in the ninth round in the 2002 draft], and Chicago has a pretty affluent Jewish community. I started getting a lot of fan mail and Jewish followers, and the greatest part for me is that I still maintain a lot of those relationships now. One happens to be a business venture that I made with a relationship that started out with a guy looking for an autograph [in spring training]. He's just a guy, a Jewish man, he calls himself a schlepper, long straggly beard, he was there with his son. I signed some autographs, and he started talking to me. He's a chiropractor and way back then, you meet so many in passing, but when somebody says, "Hey, I'm a member of the tribe," or whatever, or something to do with Judaism, because there's not that many, it instantly gives you that connection. He helped me dramatically after my incident in 2005, he actually helped me get on a nutritional regimen and helped fix some things that were wrong. It recently turned into an actual company that we started.

I had a vision training doctor in Chicago as well, same kind of situation, a Jewish guy in Chicago, an ophthalmologist, has a patented vision training program, and wanted to meet me, wanted to help me out after I reached the big leagues and then hit .209 the following season. He knew that he could help me. I was in the Royals system, and they were doing some work with the Royals and they made it a point to bring me in, and that has turned into another friendship. He came to my wedding, and the friendship turned into another potential business relationship. There's been a lot of stuff like that, and then the regular routine fan mail that comes in, some speaking engagements that I've done at JCCs, stuff like that.

In terms of community stuff, when I was in Jacksonville, I went to the JCC and I spoke. I did it a couple places. Jacksonville was very prominent, a lot of the other cities was more individual-type stuff. It's similar to like Latin guys, anybody who's Latin knows each other, in the black community, you never met, but you're brothers. Everywhere that I went, no matter what city it was, there would be one or two—or a bunch—depending on the city.

Some opposing fans [yelled some anti–Semitic things], and when it happened the first time, it stirred something so angry inside me, I literally wanted to jump into the stands and punch the guy. Obviously, you refrain. It literally goes in one ear, takes a second and then out. All it did for me was show how hard it must have been for players in the past — whether it be the Jewish ballplayers or the black ballplayers or whatever because it was constant, it was non-stop, it was in the media, it was at the games, it was on the streets, it was everywhere. I can only imagine what they had to go through, so for me to have a tiny little inkling it makes me have a greater respect to create the situation and environment that we have today.

The home runs happen to be few and far between. My game has always been get on base, so I generally have a .380-plus on-base percentage. That's my game. I bunt a lot, I do drive the ball, doubles, triples—and the home runs happen to come. Sometimes the home runs get in the way for me where I start feeling a little bit too good, but the most I ever hit in a year was eight, so I'm certainly not a home-run hitter. And then steal and create, create offense, create runs, that's my game.

I didn't hear from Dusty Baker or speak to him until 2008. I was released by the Royals after spring training, and he actually received a letter from a hometown fan, and had let him know that I was released. So Dusty went out of his way, found my phone number, and gave me a call — and it was probably the most genuine, heartfelt thing that I've ever received in my life because I had a nice relationship with Dusty, but never anything personal. So for him two years later to go out of his way and find my number and call me and reach out to me the way he did, that really shows the character that he has, and why so many players and coaches and the baseball community respect him so much. He's somebody that I look up to and respect, unconditionally.

A week before spring training, it's now 2009, I got a call from the Cincinnati Reds [Dusty Baker was now the manager of the Reds], and they invite me to spring training. Go down to spring training with the Reds, great, hit it off with everyone. We had some races, and what-not, I was the fastest guy in camp, I was this, I was that. Dusty said, "You look great. This is awesome."

David Bell was the Double-A manager, so Buddy's son, and I had a nice heart-to-heart with David. I kinda just asked him, I said, "Hey, this thing is coming down to the wire, just let me know what's it looking like. I don't care where I go, I just want to know that I'm going to make a team." So one day David comes in, and I had gone from Triple-A down to Double-A with him early, so I'm like, All right, I know that. But David comes in and goes, "Hey dude, just listen, in all these meetings, your name just keeps popping up, they love you. I'm not going to tell you you're not gonna be with me, but it doesn't look like it. They're talking about bringing you to Triple-A." Oh my god, life is great. It's amazing.

So I go in the next day, literally the next day, and I see my name on the Triple-A roster. You don't do that. You don't go down and then back up. Doesn't happen. The Triple-A manager starts talking to me, things are good, I'm starting to play well with them, and then they come over to me and they say, "What's your bat order, can we get you your flight or are you gonna drive, you know, you're on the team." Holy Cow, you know, just days before, this is great. Come in the last day — the last day, I'm going to the big leagues, my first of the year. Go to the game — I am crushing BP. Dusty goes, "Son, keep this up and I'm gonna bring you back up here. You just do you thing, whatever." I'm going, "OK, life is really good."

So game ends, go back home, come back in the next morning. As I'm getting ready to get dressed for the last game of camp, they go, "Hey, they want to see you upstairs before you get dressed." Now, I'm going, "You don't go upstairs before you get dressed just because you're getting promoted." So my heart kinda sinks cause I don't understand why, I don't know what's going on. Get up there and they release a guy in like two seconds in front of me. He's my roommate. Two seconds, he's gone. I get in there, they sit down and they close the door. They didn't close the door for him. They close the door for me.

There's four guys in there, and nobody knew what to say. So the first guy starts off, the farm director, goes, "All I want to say is you have far surpassed any of our expectations. You're this, you're that, you can do anything. You're a big league ballplayer. OK. We have a major problem on our hands." And they started going through the scenario. "This guy accepted an assignment, this guy cleared waivers, this guy's this, this guy's that, our guys in Double-A are young, they're all prospects, we don't have room there, our extended spring training looks like this, you're not even gonna get at-bats here." And the next guy goes, "We want you to be a coach." The farm director goes, "We want that, but you can still play and you're going to get to the big leagues. So right now, it's just not going to fit with us. We're going to follow you, we're going to watch you and everything, but we don't have room." And they were really like heartbroken. And I'm going, "OK, that's all fine and good, and your heartbreaking makes me feel good. But if I'm that good and you want me that bad, you're gonna keep me." So I kinda teared up a little bit, left and then I went home. I packed up my stuff, I walked across the street to the apartment. And I was just like sitting there, going, "What the? What just happened?" I'm going to Triple-A and then to the big leagues to what do I do now? So I call back the Bluefish [the Bridgeport Bluefish of the independent Atlantic League] and tell them what's going on and tell them I need a job.

I haven't spoken to him [Florida Marlins pitcher Valerio de los Santos, who hit Greenberg with the pitch] since the following day. I just saw him for a second. He was driving out of the stadium and he stopped his car and we spoke for minute or two. I hadn't seen or heard from him until the *Outside the Lines* piece [an ESPN story on Greenberg], where I saw what he had said, and after that I never heard from him or saw him or crossed paths. I don't have any resentment toward him or anybody. It was something that happened, and I was kinda glad to see that he made it back. I don't remember who it was with, Colorado, I think, in '08. [Greenberg's Bridgeport Bluefish played de los Santos' Long Island Ducks in 2011, and the two spoke before the game. Greenberg later singled off de los Santos.]

It's not about where, it's about when. I don't want to put myself out there unless I'm 100 percent ready and convinced. Like I said, getting into the weight room the last few weeks and really feeling like the strength is coming back gives me a reason to start getting excited. The more I speak about it, and I tell people, "You know, I'm not going to give up," kinda hold myself to that. I could easily give up. Easily. Have all the reasons to. I just got married. I have some business and some stuff going. Financially, it's been hard doing all this, not making anything during the season, not covered under any insurance. There's lots of things that go on that make it where quitting is the easy, smart choice, I guess. But I'm not there yet.

Once I start getting out there, and working out and playing, doing stuff, I get that itch back, like we talked about with Favre and Willie Mays, these guys, they don't want to say, just that easily, goodbye. I'm only twenty-nine years old, and I keep saying it every year. I'm only twenty-seven, I'm only twenty-eight, I'm only twenty-nine, so an age is a number. It's what you can physically be able to do, and I'm still keeping up with myself, my body, my conditioning, so age means nothing. If I can do it, and I have the support from now my wife, which I do, I'm gonna keep going. As long as I love it, I'm gonna keep going. When I stop loving it, and we all go through those times when I don't love it, but when I don't love it anymore and I don't think that I'm a big leaguer, that's when I'll be done.

Appendix:
Jewish Major Leaguers

The following list includes Jewish players in the Major Leagues as of the 2010 season. Players are considered Jewish if either parent is Jewish and they haven't renounced their Jewish identity or they converted to Judaism before or during their playing days. Bold letters indicate players active as of the 2010 season. List and format courtesy of the Jewish Sports Review, www.jewishsportsreview.com.

Player	Position	Years	Teams
Cal Abrams	OF	1949–56	Brooklyn, Cincinnati, Pittsburgh, Baltimore, Chicago–AL
Lloyd Allen	P	1969–75	California, Texas, Chicago–AL
Ruben Amaro, Jr.	OF	1991–98	California, Philadelphia, Cleveland, Philadelphia
Morrie Arnovich	OF	1936–41, 1946	Philadelphia–NL, Cincinnati, New York–NL
Jake Atz	IF	1902–09	Washington, Chicago–AL
Brad Ausmus	C	1993–present	San Diego, Detroit, Houston, Detroit, Houston, Los Angeles–NL
Jesse Baker (Michael Silverman)	SS	1919	Washington
Brian Bark	P	1995	Boston
Ross Baumgarten	P	1978–82	Chicago–AL, Pittsburgh
Jose Bautista	P	1988–97	Baltimore, Chicago–NL, San Francisco, Detroit, St. Louis
Joe Bennett (Rosenblum)	3B	1923	Philadelphia–NL
Moe Berg	C	1923, 1926–39	Brooklyn, Chicago–AL, Cleveland, Wash, Boston–AL
Nathan Berkenstock	OF	1871	Philadelphia–NL
Bob Berman	C	1918	Washington
Cy Block	3B/2B	1942, 1945–46	Chicago–NL

207

Player	Position	Years	Teams
Ron Blomberg	DH/1B/OF	1969, 1971–76	New York–AL, Chicago–AL
Sammy Bohne (Cohen)	2B/SS/3B	1916, 1921–26	St. Louis–NL, Cincinnati Brooklyn
Henry Bostick (Lifschitz)	3B	1915	Philadelphia–AL
Lou Boudreau	SS/3B/2B/C	1938–52	Cleveland, Boston
Ryan Braun	3B/OF	2007–	Milwaukee
Craig Breslow	P	1998–2006, 2008–	San Diego, Boston, Cleveland, Minnesota, Oakland
Lou Brower	SS	1931	Detroit
Conrad Cardinal	P	1963	Houston
Frank Charles	C	2000	Houston
Harry Chozen	C	1937	Cincinnati
Tony Cogan	P	2001	Kansas City
Alta Cohen	OF	1931–33	Brooklyn, Philadelphia–NL
Andy Cohen	2B	1926–29	New York–NL
Hy Cohen	P	1955	Chicago–NL
Syd Cohen	P	1934, 1936–37	Washington
Richard Conger	P	1940–43	Detroit, Pittsburgh, Philadelphia–NL
Phil Cooney (Cohen)	3B	1905	New York–AL
Ed Corey (Cohen)	P	1918	Chicago–AL
Bill Cristall	P	1901	Cleveland
Harry Danning	C	1933–42	New York–NL
Ike Danning	C	1928	St. Louis
Bob Davis	P	1958–62	Kansas City
Ike Davis	1B	2010	New York–NL
Harry Eisenstat	P	1935–42	Brooklyn, Detroit, Cleveland
Mike Epstein	1B	1966–74	Baltimore, Washington, Oakland, California
Reuben Ewing (Cohen)	SS	1921	St. Louis–NL
Al Federoff	2B	1951–52	Detroit
Eddie Feinberg	SS/2B/OF	1938–39	Philadelphia–NL
Harry Feldman	P	1941–46	New York–NL
Scott Feldman	P	2005–present	Texas
Samuel Fishburn	1B/2B	1919	St. Louis
Leo Fishel	P	1899	New York–NL
Matt Ford	P	2003	Milwaukee

Player	Position	Years	Teams
Happy Foreman	P	1924, 1926	Chicago–AL, Boston–AL
Micah Franklin	OF	1997	St. Louis
Murray Franklin	SS/2B	1941–42	Detroit
Sam Fuld	OF	2007, 2009–2010	Chicago–NL
Milt Galatzer	OF	1933–36, 1939	Cleveland, Cincinnati
Mark Gilbert	OF	1985	Chicago–AL
Joe Ginsberg	C	1948, 1950–54, 1956–62	Detroit, Cleveland, Baltimore, Chicago–AL, Boston–AL, New York–NL
Keith Glauber	P	1998	Cincinnati
Jonah Goldman	SS/3B	1928, 1930–31	Cleveland
Izzy Goldstein	P	1932	Detroit
Jake Goodman	1B	1878, 1882	Milwaukee–NL, Pittsburgh-AA
Sid Gordon	OF/3B	1941–43, 1946–55	New York–NL, Boston–NL, Milwaukee–NL, Pittsburgh
John Grabow	P	2003–	Pittsburgh, Chicago–NL
Herb Gorman	OF	1952	St. Louis–NL
Fred Graf	3B	1913	St. Louis–NL
Shawn Green	OF/1B	1993–2009	Toronto, Los Angeles, Arizona, New York–NL
Adam Greenberg	OF	2005	Chicago–NL
Hank Greenberg	1B/OF	1930, 1933–41, 1945–47	Detroit, Pittsburgh
Eric Helfand	C	1993–95	Oakland
Steve Hertz	3B	1964	Houston
Jason Hirsh	P	2006–08	Texas, Colorado
Ken Holtzman	P	1965–79	Chicago–NL, Oakland, Baltimore, New York–AL
Brian Horwitz	OF	2008	San Francisco
Bill Hurst	P	1996	Florida
Skip Jutze	C	1972–77	St. Louis, Houston, Seattle
Harry Kane (Cohen)	P	1902–03, 1905–06	St. Louis, Detroit, Philadelphia
Gabe Kapler	OF	1998–2006, 2008–2010	Detroit, Texas, Colorado, Boston, Milwaukee, Tampa Bay
Ryan Kalish	OF	2010	Boston
Herb Karpel	P	1946	New York–AL
Bob Katz	P	1944	Cincinnati
Ian Kinsler	2B	2006–	Texas
Alan Koch	P	1963–64	Detroit, Washington
Brian Kowitz	OF	1995	Atlanta
Sandy Koufax	P	1955–66	Brooklyn, Los Angeles–NL

Player	Position	Years	Teams
Barry Latman	P	1957–67	Chicago–AL, Cleveland, Los Angeles–AL, California, Houston
Jim Levey	SS	1930–33	St. Louis–AL
Alan Levine	P	1996, 1998–2005	Chicago–AL, Texas, Anaheim, Kansas City, Tampa Bay, Detroit
Jesse Levis	C	1992–99	Cleveland, Tampa Bay, Milwaukee, Cleveland
Mike Lieberthal	C	1994–2007	Philadelphia, Los Angeles–NL
Lou Limmer	1B	1951, 1954	Philadelphia–AL
Andrew Lorraine	P	1994–95, 1997–2000, 2002	Philadelphia, Oakland, Seattle, Chicago–NL, Cleveland, Milwaukee
Elliott Maddox	OF/INF	1970–80	Detroit, Washington, Texas, New York–AL, Baltimore, New York–NL
Cy Malis	P	1934	Philadelphia–NL
Moxie Manuel	P	1905, 1908	Washington, Chicago–AL
Duke Markell (Harry Makowsky)	P	1951	St. Louis–AL
Jason Marquis	P	2000–	Atlanta, St Louis, Chicago–NL, Colorado, Washington
Ed Mayer	P	1957–58	Chicago–NL
Erskine Mayer	P	1912–19	Philadelphia–NL, Chicago–AL
Sam Mayer	OF/P	1915	Washington
Ed Mensor	P	1912–1914	Pittsburgh
Mike Milchin	P	1996	Minnesota, Baltimore, Los Angeles–NL
Norm Miller	OF	1965–74	Houston, Atlanta
Buddy Myer	2B/SS/ 3B	1925–41	Washington, Boston–AL
Sam Nahem	P	1938, 1941–42, 1948	Brooklyn, St. Louis–NL, Philadelphia–NL
David Newhan	2B, 3B	1999–2008	San Diego, Philadelphia, Baltimore
Jeff Newman	C	1976–84	Oakland, Boston
Barney Pelty	P	1903–12	St. Louis–AL, Washington
Jacob Pike	OF	1877	Hartford–NL
Lipman Pike	OF/2B	1871–78, 1881, 1887	Troy-NA, Balt-NA, Hartford-NA, St. Louis-NA, St. Louis–NL, Cincinnati–NL, Providence–NL, Worcester–NL, New York-AA
Jake Pitler	2B	1917–18	Pittsburgh
Aaron Poreda	P	2009–	Chicago–NL, San Diego
Steve Ratzer	P	1980–81	Montreal

Player	Position	Years	Teams
Jimmie Reese (James Herman Soloman)	2B	1930–32	New York–AL, St. Louis
Al Richter	SS	1951, 1953	Boston–AL
Dave Roberts	P	1969–81	San Diego, Houston, Detroit, Chicago–NL, San Francisco, Pittsburgh, Seattle, New York–NL
Saul Rogovin	P	1949–53, 1955–57	Detroit, Chicago–AL, Baltimore, Philadelphia–NL
Al Rosen	3B	1947–56	Cleveland
Goody Rosen	OF	1937–39, 1944–46	Brooklyn, New York–NL
Harry Rosenberg	OF	1930	New York–NL
Lou Rosenberg	2B	1923	Chicago–AL
Steve Rosenberg	P	1988–91	Chicago–AL, San Diego
Max Rosenfeld	OF	1931–33	Brooklyn
Sy Rosenthal	OF	1925–26	Boston–AL
Wayne Rosenthal	P	1991–92	Texas
Marv Rotblatt	P	1948, 1950–51	Chicago–AL
Mickey Rutner	3B	1947	Philadelphia–AL
Ryan Sadowski	P	2009	San Francisco
Mike Saipe	P	1998	Colorado
Roger Samuels	P	1988–89	San Francisco, Pittsburgh
Ike Samuls	3B/SS	1895	St. Louis–NL
Moe Savransky	P	1954	Cincinnati
Al Schacht	P	1919–1921	Washington
Sid Schacht	P	1950–51	St. Louis–AL, Boston–NL
Hal Schacker	P	1945	Boston–NL
Heinie Scheer	2B/3B	1922–23	Philadelphia–AL
Richie Scheinblum	OF	1965, 1967–74	Cleveland, Washington, Kansas City, Cincinnati, California, St. Louis–NL
Mike Schemer	1B	1945–46	New York–NL
Scott Schoeneweis	P	1999–	Anaheim, Chicago–AL, Toronto, Cincinnati, NY–NL, Arizona, Boston
Art Shamsky	OF/1B	1965–72	Cincinnati, New York–NL, Chicago–NL, Oakland
Dick Sharon	OF	1973–75	Detroit, San Diego
Larry Sherry	P	1958–68	Los Angeles–NL, Detroit, Houston, California
Norm Sherry	C	1959–63	Los Angeles–NL, New York–NL
Harry Shuman	P	1942–44	Pittsburgh, Philadelphia–NL
Al Silvera	OF	1955–56	Cincinnati

Player	Position	Years	Teams
Fred Sington	OF	1934–39	Washington, Brooklyn
Moses Solomon	OF	1923	New York–NL
Bill Starr	C	1935–36	Washington
Jeff Stember	P	1980	San Francisco
Adam Stern	OF	2005–07	Boston, Baltimore
Steve Stone	P	1971–81	San Francisco, Chicago–AL, Chicago–NL, Baltimore
Bud Swartz	P	1947	St. Louis–AL
Don Taussig	OF	1958, 1961–62	San Francisco, St. Louis–NL, Houston
Bob Tufts	P	1981–82	San Francisco, Kansas City
Eddie Turchin	3B/SS	1943	Cleveland
Danny Valencia	3B	2010	Minnesota
Steve Wapnick	P	1990–91	Detroit, Chicago–AL
Justin Wayne	P	2002–2004	Florida
Lefty Weinert	P	1919–1924, 1927–1928, 1931	Philadelphia–NL, Chicago–NL, New York–AL
Phil Weintraub	1B/OF	1933–35, 1937–38, 1944–45	New York–NL, Cincinnati, Philadelphia–NL
Josh Whitesell	1B	2008–09	Arizona
Ed Wineapple	P	1929	Washington
Steve Yeager	C	1972–86	Los Angeles–NL, Seattle
Larry Yellen	P	1963–64	Houston
Kevin Youkilis	3B/1B	2004–	Boston
Guy Zinn	OF	1911–12, 1914–15	New York–AL, Boston–NL, Baltimore–FL
Edward Zosky	SS/3B	1991–92, 1995, 1999	Toronto, Florida, Milwaukee

Index

213